By W. R. CROCKER

The Japanese Population Problem
Nigeria: A Critique of Colonial Administration
On Governing Colonies
Self-Government for the Colonies

NEHRU

A CONTEMPORARY'S ESTIMATE

BY

WALTER CROCKER

With a Foreword
by
Arnold Toynbee
C.H.

New York
OXFORD UNIVERSITY PRESS
1966

PRINTED IN GREAT BRITAIN

To the Memory of
MY FATHER AND MOTHER
Pioneers, and the Children and Grandchildren
of Pioneers, of South Australia

Many books have been written about Jawaharlal Nehru already. Probably many more are on their way, and yet others will follow in the years to come. Much of this voluminous literature will, no doubt, be ephemeral; but I guess that Mr Crocker's book will make a lasting place for itself, and will continue to be read and pondered by serious students of Nehru's personality and achievements—and of his failures and limitations too; for great men and women, like the rest of us, are human; and, in rising above the average level of humanity, they do not escape, any more than we do, the imperfection that is intrinsic to human nature.

There are two ways in which the biographer of a great man can go astray. He can ignore his hero's human weaknesses or he can dispute his subject's claim to be a hero by pointing out his weaknesses and rubbing them in. Idealization and 'de-bunking' resemble each other in being, both alike, unrealistic and misleading simplifications of the truth. As Mr Crocker points out, the truth about human nature is more subtle and complex, and Nehru's character was an unusually complex one. One of the great merits of this book is that it gives a picture of its subject that is true to life; and it does this without any touch of condescension or cold-bloodedness. In his sharpest criticisms of some of Nehru's acts (and on Goa, for instance, Mr Crocker's judgement is severe), Mr Crocker presents the image of a man who is always great, even when he is falling tragically below his own high standards.

To write a biography of any human being is difficult; but the task is particularly difficult when the subject has played a leading part in public life. Is the writer to concentrate on his subject's life or on his times? And, if he is to deal with both, how is he to relate them to each other? Nehru is one of those eminent public figures that would have been both great and vastly interesting if they had remained in a private station. Yet, since Nehru made a big mark on the history of the times in which he lived, his personal life has to be placed in the setting of the contemporary history of India and, indeed, of the whole World; for, in Nehru's generation, the World was growing together, for good or evil, into a unity, and Nehru was a pioneer in taking nothing less than the World itself as the field for his public activity. Mr Crocker has been markedly successful in coping with this problem that besets all biographers whose subjects are statesmen. He has special qualifications for the job. He himself has had a varied and distinguished experience of public affairs, including the experience of dealing with Nehru officially, and he is also interested in human character for its own sake. In his own words,

'It was my job to watch Nehru day by day. Had my job in Delhi been anything else, I would still have watched him, out of interest—almost helpless interest. He was interesting because of his political importance, but still more interesting because of himself.'

This synoptic vision of Nehru the statesman and Nehru the human being, and this first-hand acquaintance with Nehru in both aspects, are two features of Mr Crocker's book that are going to give it an enduring value. Fifty years from now, later biographers and historians will probably have more written documents accessible to them than Mr Crocker has had in 1965. But the most illuminating of all documents is first-hand knowledge. Mr Crocker has lived with his subject and has felt, in himself, the feelings that Nehru produced in the hearts of his contemporaries. A contemporary's impressions are priceless, and they are irreplaceable. A posthumous academic study of the archives can be a supplement to them, but not a substitute for them.

'Most people', Mr Crocker writes, 'found Nehru captivating. I certainly did. When in his presence, I usually found it necessary to keep jolting myself back into detachment.'

If I may speak, in parenthesis, for myself, I can report that I did not have to try to practise detachment towards Nehru in my own far less frequent meetings with him, since I had no official business to transact with him; so I could let my captivation by him have a free rein, and I found it carrying me to the length of loving him. It is unusual to love someone with whom one's acquaintance has been slight; yet 'love' is not too big a word for my feelings for Nehru. I felt towards him something of what one usually feels only towards one's closest friends and towards the members of one's inner family circle. I have met other great men and women and have felt, towards them, the admiration, combined with awe, that one felt, of course, in Nehru's presence too. But Nehru has been unique among them in arousing this warmth of feeling in me.

I also shared with Mr Crocker a feeling that comes out in many places in this book. I took delight in Nehru as a beautiful living creature—one of the noble works of God's creation. He delighted me by his youthfulness of spirit and body—a youthfulness that he retained till after he had turned seventy. He delighted me by his spontaneity, by his utter freedom from pompousness, and by his complete immunity to the corrupting influence of power (a point on which Mr Crocker rightly lays stress). When I saw him for the last time and found him now bowed down by the burden of the China crisis, I felt a grief which was something more than sorrow on his personal account. It was sorrow over a human being's unescapable fall, in the end, to 'Time's wreckful siege of battering days'. Nehru had withstood this siege so triumphantly for so long that one had come to feel that here was one human being of whom Time was not going to get the better; and Nehru's long triumph over Time seemed like a triumph for all humanity. So, when Nehru, too, succumbed at last, this brought home to one the poignancy of human life, even at its highest potency. Does this sound excessive? Excessive or not, it was what I truly felt. Like Mr Crocker, I was 'captivated'.

What is extraordinary about the strength of the feeling that Nehru could arouse—and did arouse in me, for example—is that this lovable man 'seems to have developed something like a horror of intimacy', and 'this aloofness is one reason, why, unlike Gandhi, he evoked respect rather than love in those working with him.' I am sure that this judgement of Mr Crocker's hits the truth, and I think the apparent paradox is explained by the words 'in those working with him'. Mr Crocker points out, as one of Nehru's defects from his official colleagues' and subordinates' point of view, that he lavished on strangers, including people of no political importance, precious time and energy and kindness on which his fellow-workers in public affairs felt, not unreasonably, that they had a prior claim. I am conscious that I have been one of the beneficiaries of this characteristic of Nehru's—a characteristic that was so amiable for comparative strangers like me, but was, for this very reason, rather exasperating for people who were closer to him. In this, Nehru illustrates something that is perhaps common to all powerful personalities. Their radiation produces different effects at different ranges. At a medium range it may be beneficent, while at a closer range it may be almost searing.

However, at close range, too, Nehru could win love and keep it. He won and kept Sheikh Abdullah's love, for instance, though Nehru's last official transaction with this old friend and colleague had been to hold him in prison for eleven years. Yet, when Nehru's body was being cremated, 'before the fire had died down, Sheikh Abdullah leapt on the platform and, weeping unrestrainedly, threw flowers on to the flames'. Mr Crocker records that, while Nehru was holding Sheikh Abdullah in prison, he took an active interest in the well-being of the Sheikh's family, including the education of his son, and had the young man to his house. I think this could have happened only in India; but, besides being something generically Indian, it was also something characteristically Nehruesque.

It is impossible to do full justice to Mr Crocker's book without quoting it *in extenso*, which, in a Foreword, would be an unpardonable misdemeanour, so I must simply refer the reader to passages in which the writer deals with other facets of Nehru's character—for instance, his combination of cleverness with goodness (confuting the ruthless rhyme), and, above all, his courage—the virtue that he most admired and that he superbly practised. Mr Crocker also puts Nehru in his setting in time and space, as being, besides the unique personality that he was, the historical product of 3,000 years of Brahman lineage and of a century and a half of British radical and rationalist philosophy. He puts him, too, in relation to some of his outstanding Indian contemporaries: for example, Rajagopalachari and Krishna Menon. Mr Crocker's sketch of Krishna Menon is particularly interesting. It is drawn from the life, and it differs considerably from the conventional picture of this controversial figure. These are just a few more points among the many that make this book a notable one.

April 24, 1965

CONTENTS

INTRODUCTION

To sum up any man's life is rough justice at the best. The effort, the achievements (real or meretricious), the failures, the suffering, the secret soul behind the face, and the long long years themselves, can seldom be contained in a few thousand words.

To sum up in a few thousand words a life like Nehru's, nearly twice as long as Napoleon's, and nearly as full, risks being an impertinence. Nehru was the first Prime Minister of India, and during most of the eighteen years he was Head of Government he wielded an authority usually reserved to dictators. If his political ideas were fairly uncomplicated, Nehru the man was not.

For some years I had thought of writing his life, and to this end devoted my leisure hours. But I gave it up. For one thing two biographies appeared while I was still at work, and though they stopped at a point relatively early in his Prime Ministership they were good books. For another, I came to feel that things we need to know, such as about Kashmir, or what really happened in Sino-Indian relations, or in his relations with certain individuals, or what Nehru really had in mind at this or that point, will not be revealed until the letters, diaries, memoirs, or other papers of certain persons, as well as the official papers, have been made public; which will be some time well in the future. By that time the world will have forgotten and will care as little as it does now for matters which once inflamed public passions, such as the Ems Telegram, or Jameson's Raid, or the Ulster Rebellion in 1914, or how and to whom Lloyd George sold peerages after World War I. As for Nehru himself, he seemed frank, and in some respects was frank; but much remains concealed. He was reserved by nature; the years of high political responsibility intensified the reserve.

Final judgement, as always, is for the historians. It is possible that future revelations will heighten, or will lower, Nehru's stature. But it is not probable. It is unlikely that the picture we have of him by 1964 will need much change.

Whatever the verdict of History on Nehru may be, either as leader or as man, he will remain one of those rare personages who form an inseparable part of their age. There will therefore be many more books on him, and room for more than one view of him.

Over two periods between 1952 and 1962 it was my job to watch Nehru day by day. Had my job in Delhi been anything else I would still have watched him, out of interest, almost helpless interest. He was interesting because of his political importance but still more interesting because of himself. Mostly I admired him; occasionally he was disappointing; but always he fascinated me. As I watched him longer than his biographers, and saw him come full circle from the highest to the lowest point in his reputation, I am setting down these personal impressions, as recollected in August 1964, while they are still fresh in my mind. The historians in the future will know more of the documents but not Nehru himself nor the men who figure in the documents.

In setting them down my concern has been not to please anyone, and still less to hurt anyone, but to tell the truth as far as I could know it. Nehru, like India itself, is big enough for the warts not to be left out of the picture.

The views expressed are my own alone. They have no connection with the views of either the British or the Australian Governments in whose employment I was serving during my years in India.

I am grateful to Mrs Indira Gandhi for the photograph of her father.

Chapter 1

WATCHING NEHRU

I first saw Nehru in 1945. At the time I was serving in the British Army, and the end of the War happened to find me in India for a while before demobilization. Nehru had not long been out of prison and was making a triumphal tour in Bengal. Crowds gathered to see him at the railway station in my Area; huge and enthusiastic crowds. I noticed at the station where I was waiting for him that his evident satisfaction with the crowd's welcome did not prevent him from impatiently pushing—some of my brother officers said slapping—people who got too near him. Neither as a Britisher, nor as a soldier concerned with law and order in Bengal at that moment, was I predisposed towards Nehru, one of the arch agitators and trouble-makers, as we thought him. We were ignorant of his story, and ignorant of mistakes made on the British side, but Lord Wavell, the Viceroy, had recently reproved him publicly for some of his speeches, and the reproof seemed to us to be well merited. Nehru's speeches had been inflammatory and had again and again thrown doubt on the good faith of the British Government—Attlee's Government—about its willingness to give India independence though at that very time discussions were taking place for arranging independence. The nationalist agitation, moreover, in its mass parades, its mass chanting of slogans, its badges and symbols, and its frenzy and raving, reminded us uncomfortably of the Nazis to stop whom we civilians had become soldiers.

I left India in August 1946 just after the great killings, as the Calcutta massacres of Muslims by Hindus and Hindus by Muslims of that August, came to be called. The carnage, already horrifying, would have been unspeakable had British Army units not taken over control. I was glad to go, as this was the third mob uprising, and the most bestial, I had witnessed in Calcutta, the others being in November 1945 and in February 1946. Of India I had seen only Bengal, and only for about a year; but what I had seen I did not like and I soon put India out of my mind. I neither expected nor wanted to see it again.

But, by one of the accidents of life, less than six years later I found myself back in India, in 1952, as head of Australia's Diplomatic Mission. I stayed in India for three years. I found these three years so interesting that I gladly accepted the chance to return four years later in the same capacity. On this second occasion I stayed for three and half years.

During the six and half years I was serving as High Commissioner Nehru was the focus of my daily working life. Inevitably, I saw a good deal of him.

He lived in the house formerly occupied by the British Commander-in-Chief, a big two-storeyed house set in a garden of several acres. Unlike many Indians—there are conspicuous exceptions, such as M. Krishnan—Nehru had an interest in Nature; he was fond of gardens and flowers; his garden was one of the best in Delhi. But for all his flowers and his pandas and other pet animals there was little of a private house about the Prime Minister's Residence. The greater part of the ground floor was taken up with offices where men worked in shifts throughout the day and night. This was part of the Prime Minister's own secretariat; the other part was in the External Affairs Ministry. (When Parliament was in session he spent much time in his office in Parliament Building.) The daily stream of visitors began with the assemblage in his garden at 8.30 most mornings, when anyone with a grievance, or a suggestion, or just a wish to look at him, could come. Few were the weeks when special deputations of the people were not coming to his house. Often they took up quarters on the footpaths adjoining or opposite to it. Families running into scores, men, women and children, would camp months on end opposite his gate, cooking, bathing, and sleeping there. He showed irritation with them at times—they were a health hazard at the least—but his pity and his sense of duty, no less than his politician's instinct to be seen with the people, were such that the police were forbidden to drive them away or to harass them. They came for many different reasons—to protest against some injustice, such as a poet carrying out a hunger strike for eight days in front of Nehru's gate to protest against the closing down of the Hindustani Theatre, because of drought, floods, or hunger, and above all as refugees from Pakistan or from some troubled area inside India itself.

I had many occasions to see Nehru in a different role, that of the formal and ceremonious Prime Minister, such as at Delhi airport for the official welcome, or farewell, to the Queen of England, President Eisenhower, Khrushchev, the Crown Prince and Princess of Japan,

Chou En-lai, Nasser, U Nu, a variety of Commonwealth Prime Ministers such as St Laurent and Diefenbaker of Canada, Mohamed Ali and several other Prime Ministers from Pakistan, Menzies of Australia, Nkrumah of Ghana, and Kotelawala and Mrs Bandaranayike of Ceylon. No Head of Government could be more distinguished, more at ease, yet more welcoming, than he was on these occasions. His felicity, combined, as it was, with energy and gravity, made him, without any effort on his part, the cynosure. This was true too of the various banquets and garden parties at the President's Palace, and of the great national celebrations in New Delhi, such as the Independence Day ceremony held each August in the Red Fort, or at the Republic Day Parade held each January when a procession two to three hours long passed down Lutyen's superb creation, the Central Vista, or Raj Path as it is now called.

On these occasions Nehru never ceased to be in full possession of his very quick wits. For instance, when the Queen of England was a guest at the 1961 Republic Day Parade, there was a good deal of parading done on their own account by Indian politicians. Amongst these a group arrived a little late and, no places being reserved or left for them on the seats, they were asked by the attendants to sit on the ground, where in fact some hundreds of their fellow citizens were already sitting. This affronted their dignity and they went protesting to Nehru, who was sitting near the Queen. Nehru quietly got his daughter and the Speaker to leave the Queen's entourage and to lead the M.P.s away and to sit on the ground with them. . . . I recall a reception eight years earlier at Constitution House when some M.P.s fell like famished boys on the tea, cakes, and bananas, and, in that Indian way born of centuries of having sweeper outcastes ready at hand to pick up any mess one cares to make, threw banana peel on the floor. Nehru, seeing this, pointedly got up, came along with a plate, and, without saying a word, shamed them by picking up the mess himself. . . . At the reception given to Sir John Hunt and his Mount Everest climbers in 1954, Nehru, with the preparedness and drive habitual to him, arrived early to look over the arrangements, including the placing of the chairs. Finding a horde of photographers taking up positions which would have blocked the view of the spectators he drove them off peremptorily, and as though he would strike them; they scattered before his wrath. . . . At the last Delhi Flower Show I attended in 1962, I saw him again in an unceremonious temper with photographers when they were crowding around him in suffocating numbers and blocking his view of the flowers. They too scattered before his wrath. . . . It was always refreshing to see Nehru falling on this plague of modern public life. His outbursts of temper could be calculated but mostly they were spontaneous. They were not deterred by any public setting, as those who once saw him dealing with a talk-ative 'society' woman at a music recital in Delhi are not likely to forget. Another outburst which will not be forgotten by those present occurred at the launching of the Community Development campaign at Alipore in 1952. The purpose was to stimulate the villagers into modernization and development through self-help and village demo-cracy, but, in the way so familiar in India, it was turned into a social occasion, with much parading, exhibitionism, and other vanities. It was uncomfortably hot, too. Nehru looked impatient when he arrived, the lower lip protruding in a way which always bode trouble, and cast his eyes threateningly around the gathering and the preparations. The proceedings then began with a speech from the President, broadcast from his palace in Delhi. It went on and on, irreproachable platitude following irreproachable platitude, and Nehru got more and more restive. As soon as the speech stopped he jumped up angrily, denounced speech making, vetoed any more speeches (several orators were waiting to say their pieces), and then led them off to dig a drain. . . . I once saw him stop a Minister of Agriculture in full flight, tell him to sit down, and then make a speech on the theme of the inadequacy of the white collar man in farming matters. These things made him feared rather than loved. . . . Each year this disciple of industrialization took his part in the ceremonial assemblage of dignitaries devoted to spinning cotton in celebration of Gandhi's birthday. His expression betokened, I thought, mixed feelings.

An example of the quickness of his control of a situation was pro-vided when the Pakistan Prime Minister of the day, Mohamed Ali, came to Delhi on an official visit. As Mohamed Ali walked from his plane the vast crowd broke through the police cordon, surged forward, scattered the line of formally dressed Ambassadors (the unfortunate Japanese Ambassador was trampled underfoot and when at length rescued had to be carried off the field), and threatened to crush the two Prime Ministers. Nehru shouted at and harangued the crowd, he re-activated the discouraged police, and, to give an example, grabbed a policeman's truncheon and laid about him. Order was restored; the crowd retreated.

Then there were the occasions when Nehru was a mourner. While I was at Delhi old and close political associates died, such as Pandit Pant, also Nehru's son-in-law, Feroze Gandhi (who had no connection with Mahatma Gandhi: Feroze was a Parsee), and various others with whom Nehru had close political or personal ties. He was not too proud to weep on occasion; notably when Maulana Azad died. An agnostic, he had no consolations from notions of a future life or of seeing the dead again. For him death was the end. I once had to stand near him for a quarter of an hour or so at the funeral of an Ambassador of Nepal. Nehru's solicitude for the family concerned on these occasions was delicate and without any shirking.

Naturally, I heard him make many speeches; scores and scores of speeches, both in and out of Parliament. The range of his speeches, most of which were unprepared, and most of them without a note, must be without parallel—on political matters in a huge variety, and also on technology, science, art, morals, history, welfare, and a host of good causes. I have known Nehru to make three speeches on entirely different subjects in the one day. He had an astonishing facility for speaking for half an hour or so in English and then, without a note, repeating it in Hindustani, the translation, according to my Indian friends, being word perfect. For years he was averaging, so I have been told by one of his secretaries, about twenty-five speeches a month outside of Parliament. Speaking *ex tempore*, conversationally (as was his way), so often, and on so many themes, he was bound to repeat himself at times and bound to leave some ragged edges; and occasion-ally what he said was indifferent stuff. But his speeches were a part of his political action and are to be judged as such and not as exercises in oratory, let alone in the profundities. He was seeking to get a view across to a particular audience, or to evoke reactions, or even to spread adult education among the illiterate masses, and even on such things as hygiene or manners. At times he would provide a little un-intentional comedy, as in his speech at Amritsar in April 1961 unveiling the memorial at Jallianwalla Bagh (the scene of General Dyer's shoot-ings in 1919), when, seized with enthusiasm for the achievements of the Russian astronauts announced at that time, he spoke at length about the wonders of space flight and weightlessness and the promise of man's mastery over Nature. His audience consisted mostly of illiterate peasants whose thoughts were mostly on their bullock plough and the next meal. His speeches at times were musing aloud. And in his old age, speaking too much and too long, his speeches occasionally became a jumble of clichés, anti-climaxes and non sequiturs; not unlike the speeches of Ramsay MacDonald at the end of his career. But only an unusually well-furnished mind, and unusually concentrated, could carry off Nehru's quantity and quality of public speaking throughout the half century prior to his decline.

I heard him on many dramatic occasions in Parliament. For instance the debate in 1953 over extending the old British Preventive Detention Bill when there was an exchange between him and S. P. Mookerjee, the latter being a still more effective speaker than Nehru and, after Nehru, the most forceful personality in Parliament. (Mookerjee died in Kashmir not long afterwards, in controversial conditions.) Or Nehru's announcement to a crowded and silent House that Sheikh Abdullah, the Prime Minister of Kashmir, had been arrested. With the Sheikh Nehru had previously worked closely and he used to extol him as a personal friend as well as a loyal collaborator with India. Or in 1960, after the Dalai Lama's flight to India and the subsequent revelations, especially in 1961, of the border tensions with China, the country which for years had been lauded as the ever faithful Asian brother; when angry disillusioned debates flared up on India's relations with her and with Tibet, including bitter passages with his old Gandhian and Congress colleague, Kripalani. Or the affair of the resignation of General Thimayya, the Army Chief of Staff, following on a dispute with Krishna Menon; and on several other dramatic occasions when Nehru spoke up passionately for Krishna Menon to a critical House. Nehru's mastery of the House, and of its psychology, were as outstanding as his Rupert-like courage. After watching him during these years one could have no doubt that Nehru was without a match, let alone a master, in the Indian Parliament. He had perhaps only half a dozen equals in the other Parliaments I have had occasion to observe—the House of Commons, the Australian House of Representatives, the Netherlands Parliament, and the Canadian House of Commons. Further, Nehru, by persistent conscious effort, had schooled the Indian Parliament into the best models of business-like procedures and dignity, including respect for the Chair.

Then there was Nehru in holiday mood—going up in a glider (aged 71 the last time I saw him doing that), going on a trial flight in the first jet plane which came to Delhi, playing in a cricket match, enjoying Indian classical music and classical dancing, and showing off his pets or his flowers. These occasions became less frequent in the last few years; but it is an incomplete and misleading picture of Nehru which does not give some place, though it can never be a major place, to his outbursts of gaiety, as also to his wit.

For example, the smile, half-gentle, half-wry, with which he greeted me after an incident which occurred at a time when there had been some excitement in the Indian press over the White Australia policy, and especially over a speech made by the Australian Prime Minister in South Africa which Indian newspapers denounced as a seal of what they called the Malan–Menzies Axis (i.e. of anti-coloured policy). This was the moment chosen by an Australian sheep breeding expert, who had been appointed to carry out an experimental project under Technical Aid to improve Indian sheep by crossing them with Australian sheep, for getting a little publicity for himself. He gave an interview to an Indian journalist. He had discovered, he told the journalist, that a colour bar existed amongst sheep: the Australian rams didn't care for Indian ewes and wouldn't mate with them.

It was pleasant to see Nehru enjoying the ancient Hindu festivals, especially *Diwali*, the lovely poetic festival of the lights, and *Ram Lila*.

According to old friends—and I knew several who had known him closely for over half a century—Nehru had always preferred his own company, and for long had little taste for social life. Yet no man could be a better host than Nehru, whether at formal dinner parties or, best of all, at small dinners and lunches, especially *en famille*. The same traits were invariable: good breeding, elegance combined with simplicity, and wholesomeness. Alcohol was not served but the food though plain and unspiced—more English than Indian—was always of good quality, well prepared, and with an abundance of the best fruit. Unlike most of the Indian leaders he was not a vegetarian though for a time he had been. One was spared too long a period at table or too much food: three courses and fruit were the rule. Nehru himself was attentive to his guests without being pressing or fussy. He delighted to recommend a choice fruit and then to peel it or to cut it up for a guest. He was nearly always relaxed, or, more likely, he took pains not to show any of the cares agitating him; for there could scarcely have been a time when cares were not. He was always ready for interesting conversation, his own contribution being lively, various, quiet-voiced and unegotistical. He was interested in facts and ideas for their own sake and not in himself. If he told a story involving himself—for instance, about bureaucracy: the first time as Prime Minister he was brought a sealed envelope marked *Confidential* he found on opening it, not, as he expected, some secret of State, but the daily meteorological report— it was tersely worded and was told to illustrate a point, not to glorify himself. (He had no time for the bureaucrat's spirit; he had knowledge of and contempt for the Indian variety.) I have seen him on these occasions with scientists like Lord Florey, the pathologist, Sir Mark Oliphant, the physicist, and others whose investigations and talk he relished; with political figures like Lord Attlee and Bevan, who were obviously congenial, and with those, better left unnamed (especially a fading Conservative Minister who before he faded into an Earldom moved unerringly from cliché to cliché), who were probably not; but Nehru's good manners never failed him. A Prime Minister from a Commonwealth country who, as he himself remarked, was no reading man, was once asked by Nehru in my time whether he would like to be taken to Agra to see the Taj Mahal. 'The Taj Mahal? What's that?', the visitor asked. Nehru explained patiently. On another occasion a Prime Minister from another Commonwealth country missed the point of a story told by Radhakrishnan, then Vice-President of India, which the latter had from Khrushchev himself. (Khrushchev when visiting a collective farm looked in at the school and questioned some of the children to see what they knew. At the end he called over a boy and said to him 'Who wrote *War and Peace*?' 'Not I, Sir, I didn't write it,' the frightened boy pleaded.... Next morning the Principal of the school called and asked if he could see Mr Khrushchev over something urgent. When admitted to Khrushchev's presence he blurted out that he wanted to report that the boy had come to him with a confession: he did write *War and Peace*.) The visiting Prime Minister had not heard of *War and Peace*. Another memorable lunch was one he gave for an American Admiral of great power in the Dulles days, at the suggestion of the American Ambassador. The Admiral for some years, and especially when on his Pacific or South East Asian travels, used to make public statements along the most menacing lines of brinkmanship and massive retaliation and so was one of Nehru's *bêtes noires*. The American Ambassador felt that if he could get the two men together they might think better of one another. Hence the lunch. The Admiral came and brought his wife with him, a lady who turned out to be no student of India or of current affairs. On being introduced to Nehru's son-in-law, Feroze Gandhi, who was not Gandhian in type, she thought she was meeting the Mahatma himself, and gushed over him accordingly before the Ambassador could head her off. The Mahatma had been assassinated some years before.

Nehru's first visit to the United States had left an impression on him which endured; especially the week-end at the Government Guest House, presided over for the occasion by a Cabinet Minister, where the other State Guest was a female cosmetics magnate; or, again, the banquet of Business Leaders in New York when Mr ——, the famous banker, is said to have opened his speech of welcome with: 'Mr Neeroo, there are fifty billion dollars sitting around this table...." Nehru by then had learnt with surprise, but apparently not with appreciation, that the ticker tape showered down on him during his procession along Fifth Avenue was done, as a regular routine by a private commercial enterprise hired for the occasion; one or other *Welcomes, Inc.*

President Johnson came to India—said to be his first visit overseas—not long after becoming Vice-President but his activities with bullock carts, babies, and camel drivers represented a different sense of humour from Nehru's.

Nehru's visit to President Kennedy in 1961 apparently modified some of his earlier reactions.

Finally, there was Nehru with the Indian crowd. His relationship with it was unique, not equalled even by Gandhi's. His prestige with the Indian people had something of the magical about it. Here was the source of his power. Here was why over a dozen years or so he could have been a dictator if he had so desired, without guns or propaganda. How this prestige came about, how the Nehru myth had been created, is something for the psychologists to explain. The vast majority of Indians had never set eyes on him; and those who had would in the vast majority of cases have done so for an hour or two at the most. The myth owed nothing to the projection of his personality through the mass media, for few villagers had any acquaintance with the radio or the cinema and none with TV, and four out of five were illiterate. That is to say, the myth owed nothing to the synthetic fabrication of personality by the artifices of 'Public Relations'. It is unlikely that much discrepancy between public reputation and the private truth will ever be unearthed about Nehru, in the way, for example, it has recently been unearthed about Lloyd George—this darling of the Welsh chapels being revealed as redoubtable in adultery, and in keeping injured victims at bay, as in political wiles, though the secret remained intact throughout his life. Nehru did his fair share of looking happy with the crowd, and of loving the little children, and at times he got near to demeaning himself by this Hitler and Stalin type of histrionics. But in general what acting he did was little in comparison with what the average politician in the United States or even in England goes in for. Nor was the truth ever long in coming out that at bottom Nehru was alone. The notion of Nehru's spending halcyon hours relaxing with peasants is comically wide of the mark. It would be too much to say that while he loved India he did not love Indians; but he undoubtedly disliked certain Indian traits. Yet wherever he travelled in India he could count on crowds running into half a million or more flocking to him. Men and women often spent a day or two to get to the place where he would be speaking, or even merely passing by. Nor did his oratory account for this magnetism. He was a good rather than a stirring speaker. His speaking, delivered in a clear and well modulated but also in rather a light voice, was rarely uninteresting and often it was persuasive, but in his last decade it was more didactic than rousing. Moreover, he had to speak in Urdu (or Hindustani) rather than in Hindi, or in English; many in his audience, especially in South India, therefore could not undertstand a word of what he was saying.

His incomparable prestige was based on other things. It was based in part upon the fact that the people believed that he had been chosen by Gandhi as his political heir; in part upon the charm and aliveness of his mere presence; in part upon his devotion to the national interest as he saw it, so self-evident and so marking him off from the run of

Indian politicians; the rich man who renounced his wealth and who for years lived something of the hard life of the Indian people, even to travelling Third Class; in part upon the fact that the Indian is traditionally a hero-worshipper (the classic British writers on India have recounted from their experiences many significant examples, including the deification of dead Rajas and Maharajas) and not a few of the Indian villagers had been apt to see him as the great new Maharaja; and, finally, in part, and not least of all, upon the fact that Nehru survived. All his potential rivals and all his equals (except Rajagopalachari) died off in his active life time. Had Bose or had Sardar Patel lived as long as Nehru the story might have been different.

Towards the end, however, great as Nehru's prestige remained, his worshippers or admirers were the countrymen rather than the townsmen. This was one of the ironies of Nehru's position, for he was entirely the townsman and disliked, if he did not loathe, the life of the Indian villager, just as, being a declared agnostic, he disliked the villagers' religion and social rules. Further, even the villagers, though they might gather in their hundreds of thousands to hear him or to salute him, more and more voted against Nehru's men or disregarded Nehru's urgings. The Nehru myth, in short, though mighty in India up until the end—so mighty that he could not be unseated during the great disillusionment following on the Chinese attacks in the winter of 1962–63—was declining in his latter years, even amongst the country people. Amongst the townsmen, especially amongst the educated classes, it had declined sharply for some time. He had, moreover, positive and active enemies. Owing to the Security Service, not to his own wishes, Nehru never moved without a security guard, and his house was carefully guarded day and night. On the occasions when he dined at my house one of his security guards inspected the kitchen thoroughly and stood by to watch the cooking of the dinner, so that there was no risk of his being poisoned; an armed security man dressed like a servant waited upon him at table; and a squad of men were hidden in the shrubbery surrounding the house.

But the diminution of his prestige, and these risks of assassination—after all Gandhi himself had been assassinated—do not affect the cardinal fact that few if any leaders in any country have attained to such a prestige amongst their own people; or have held on to it for so long. The great bulk of the people of India sensed, and they never lost the sense, that Nehru wanted only to help them and wanted nothing for himself; and that he was a ruler who had pity and kindness.

My last official business with Nehru was over a trifle. Not long before I left India in 1962 he had received a request from a students' group in the University of Adelaide. He consulted me about it, questioning me about the University and asking my opinion on the request. There were delays in carrying out his intentions, due to various crises and to illness. As a result the Shield he donated as a trophy for inter-faculty debating competitions in the Universty reached Australia a few weeks after he died; the last gift made by him to anyone. There was no call whatever on Nehru to bother with the Adelaide students; there are hundreds of Universities in the world as well as a score of crushing problems in India; but I could see that he sensed the Adelaide students' goodwill and that some gesture from him would give them pleasure. I felt, too, as I had been made to feel more than once, that he was concerned about certain fears widespread in Australia regarding Asian neighbours and colour and he would lose no opportunity, even the smallest, for reassuring Australians that Asians could be good neighbours.

Chapter 2

THE SETTING: INDIA AND INDIANS
IN NEHRU'S DAY

Nehru's life, like the life of any other man, has to be set in its proper context of place and time. The place was India; and the time, essentially, was the first half of the twentieth century.

About India one must never forget its scale. In size, in population, and in antiquity, it transcends any country we know in Europe. Its area, extending nearly 2,000 miles from its most southerly cape to its most northerly Himalayan peak, and over 1,500 miles from its eastern to its western extremities, amounts to about 1·3 million square miles. This is bigger than Europe without Russia. Its population is now nearly 500 million. This too is bigger than Europe without Russia, and it is over twice the population of all Africa. Its civilization is so old that it has been more or less the same for the last 3,000 years; and it may well be 5,000 years since the people of the sub-continent ceased to be barbarians, if a vague word can be used for describing a fact which is not vague. India was a going concern when most of Europe was peopled by barbarians. It had invented writing and mathematics before the Greeks. Though now rapidly moving from a society of Status to a society of Contract—it was in India that Maine, the English jurist, worked out his famous generalization—Indian society is still a society in which Status counts for more than money.

A man who has lived in India long enough to know the landscape, the people, and their faiths, will never be quite the same afterwards. He might disapprove of this or that, and he might dislike the heat and the dust and a certain greyness of spirit as well as of matter, but the stamp of this vast and resplendent country is on him for life. The huge mountains in the North, the hills and plateaux of the Deccan, the eternal green of Bengal, Orissa and Madras; the colours of Rajasthan and the deserts; the great rivers; familiar daily sights over most of India, such as the yoke of oxen pulling the plough, the cattle coming home to the villages at sunset, when the air is fragrant with the *gober* burning in the braziers, the women at the wells, the *saree*, in innumerable colours, but always graceful, the moonlit nights, sunrise and sunset, and the movement of the animals and birds (Malcolm MacDonald when British High Commissioner listed 130 different species of birds in his Delhi garden); Indian faces, not a few cruel or crafty, not a few cringing or bullying, but so many with so much beauty; the old white-bearded Sikhs, or the Tamil Brahmins, or Jat or Mahratta peasants; the festivals; and the roads where is concentrated so much of the life and colour and variety of India; so much of what Kipling described on the Grand Trunk Road two generations ago still being there.

In India the differences in men and their languages and their ways of life are as great as the differences between people from one part of Europe to another—from Sweden to France, from Spain to Poland. Being vast, India is various. It is a world of its own, not merely a country. Yet amidst the varieties there is a common impress. It comes mostly from Hinduism.

Hinduism

Since the last World War the idea that there are national characters has been frowned upon by intellectuals and "progressives". The idea in favour is that peoples are more or less the same and that what really differentiates them is the degree of economic development in their countries and the distance they stand, in consequence, from what is called a high standard of living, including democracy. Other differences, such as religion, are regarded as adventitious or peripheral. The correlative idea, though recently a little less self-confident, is that gaps in standards of living can easily and quickly be reduced, if not closed, by the application of Know-How, which was first thought of as an American secret but is now conceded to be in the gift of all the industrialized countries. The United Nations was largely a result of this kind of thinking, and in its turn it has spread the thinking further. Yet, curiously, the antipathy to the idea of national characters has been flourishing at a time when nationalism has never been more exaggerated or more irrational, and has never found such opportunities for expression like those provided, and encouraged, in the United Nations.

Individuals, doubtless, do have much in common, if only because all the varieties of *Homo Sapiens* have more similarities than dissimilarities. But cultures differ profoundly. This truth remains though, thanks to modern intercommunications and the machine, local cultures are crumbling away. Thus religion, to mention one factor in national character, is not to be disposed of lightly. If, for example, one has been living out of Europe for ten years or so, *in partibus infidelium*, and then returns and travels over it one is astonished at the impress of Christianity. A majority of Europeans might be atheists; but Europe is still Christendom. And so in other Continents subjected to other religions. The view of the world, and so the springs of action, derive in large measure from the dominant religion. The longer a country has been subjected to it the more will its people be conditioned by it. This remains true even after they have renounced, and might even hate, the traditional religion. Hinduism has been conditioning Indians for several thousand years. Nehru might have disliked 'the tomfoolery of Hinduism' (as I once heard a member of the Nehru family describe it) but much of what he was derived from Hinduism. He is not to be understood before we grasp the fact that India has a civilization of its own and that it is different, often very different, from European civilization.

How much Hinduism is holding its own in India today is disputed by Indians themselves. Some think that in spite of its declining in urban areas Hinduism is as strong as ever. Some believe that it is even in for a revival, as a social force if not as a religion, and they see the rise of political parties like the *Jan Sangh* as a sign of this. In any case only one Indian in five lives in cities; it is easy to overrate the representativeness of city Indians. The four Indians in five living in the villages and country towns are almost, if not quite, as Hindu as they ever were. And in cities, and even amongst the educated classes, certain basic parts of Hinduism, such as the transmigration of souls, the notion of *Karma*, the attitude to cows, Astrology, propitiatory rites, and caste, not to mention marriage, funeral, and other primal occasions, are still very much alive. I have known two Indian scientists, both FRS, who were devotes of Astrology and made no move of importance without first consulting the omens. I have known a medical scientist, later a Vice-Chancellor, who ascertained the omens for good days and bad days and based his day's programme on them. This man refused to have a cobra living near his home killed because he considered it to be the reincarnation of his mother. In 1961 the late Shri Raghu Vira, who had a reputation as an expert on China affairs, created a sensation by announcing in Parliament, with great certitude, that China would explode a nuclear bomb by such and such a date. After the date had passed and it was evident that no explosion had taken place he said that his information had been based on astrological calculations which had turned out to be faulty. At the end of 1963, just before Nehru had his stroke, the astrologers were proclaiming that 1964 would be a year full of danger for Nehru. As a result one of the senior Ministers was doing a series of *pujas* (religious ceremonies) in the Prime Minister's house so as to minimize the malignancy of the stars; presumably without Nehru knowing, for he repeatedly condemned Astrology. It is doubtful if the Communist movement will make much progress in India until it makes allowances for Hinduism and comes to terms with it. Some of the Communist leaders are known to be devotees of Astrology, and some go in for the fast, that typical Hindu method of protest.

Hinduism as first seen by the foreign visitor surprises and baffles and occasionally it repels him. There will be, for instance, the erotic carvings and statues in some of the temples, though they are subdued in comparison with much appearing in novels or on the stage or in advertisements in the West today. There are few areas in India where he will not see the *lingam* (phallic symbols), often 15 to 20 feet high. When the British left India the first Indian appointed as Governor to one of the senior provinces, a Cambridge graduate, immediately had erected in Government House grounds a *lingam*, as a sort of chapel. If the foreign visitor goes to Banares he will be able to see the *Kashi Vishwanatha*, the ceremony of pouring water from the sacred rivers on the *lingam*. The foreign visitor will be told, too, of prostitutes attached to some temples; and of *sadhus* (monks and friars) who in their hundreds of thousands have abjured the world, but while some are genuine many are idlers and a number are wicked, kidnapping children, maiming them, tyrannizing over gullible village women, robbing and even murdering. If he goes to Banares he will be struck with the dirt and disease and smells not less than with the beauty. If he goes to Calcutta he can see the Temple of Kali, the Goddess of Destruction. This Goddess idol, nine or ten feet high, has four arms, one of which holds a decapitated head dripping with blood, another a blood-stained scimitar; around her neck hangs a garland of skulls; and out of her monstrous face protrudes a red tongue. Goats are sacrificed to her daily; buffaloes at times; the precincts reek with blood. This is only one manifestation of one form of Hinduism, and in one place. Some Hindus dislike it, just as they dislike other manifestations of popular Hinduism, and it would be as misleading to make too much of this cult as it would be to make too much of certain manifestations in Catholic churches in Latin America as expressing Christianity. But the Kali temple shows at least one aspect of Hinduism, and it reminds us of the difference between Durga and the Virgin Mary as exemplars of life, just as the Shiva *lingams* remind us of the difference between Shiva and Jesus Christ as examplars of life.

To summarize Hinduism, or to explain it to those who have not lived in India, is not easy. It has no organized Church; no Holy Book;

no organized priesthood. This formlessness is paralleled by a variety of sects and, more important, of levels. Polytheism is widespread; pantheism is nearly universal. The levels range from fertility cults, animism, and idolatory, up to theism and philosophy of an exalted kind, like that in the *Vedanta* and the *Bhagavad Gita*, which shape the Hinduism of men like Rajagopalachari[1] and President Radhakrishnan. Their kind of Hinduism has been much affected, both through action and reaction, by ideas and practices brought in by the British, more particularly British missionaries, which resulted in, amongst other things, Brahmo-Samaj, Arya-Samaj, and the Rama Krishna movement.[2] Gandhi called himself a Hindu and although he, like Rajagopalachari, did not go to temples he did derive some of his values from Hinduism; on the other hand he derived some from the Christian Gospels. Then there is the tantric layer, often deep down and remaining only in deposits and therefore bewildering to the outside observer but doubtless a factor in places. It is possible, for example, as Aldous Huxley remarked when he was in India in 1961, that Tagore, for all his Bramo-Samaj background, was not unaffected by tantric deposits. Some of his strange paintings suggest as much.

Some part of Hinduism can best be comprehended by comparing it to the world of the Greeks in and before Homer's time. In that way we can understand at least the place and the nature of polytheistic mythology. In Hinduism the mythology is vast and the gods and goddesses are numerous. Some parts of Hinduism have fossilized religious development at the stage it had reached in that far-off epoch. But here again there is a fecundity which is specifically Indian and which is foreign to the Greeks. It is a case of Homer in the tropics. It is this swarming proliferation, so alien to the Attic spirit, which led a French observer to describe Hindu India as *cette Grèce excessive*.

Here are some of the characteristics of Hinduism which seem to

---

[1] Cf. his books, *Hinduism* or *Our Culture*. The books of President Radhakrishnan, for years a Professor at Oxford, are well known in the West. Some interesting side-lights on Hinduism are given in a recent book, *The Serpent of Paradise*, 1963, by my friend and former colleague, Miguel Serrano, who as Chilean Ambassador in India for ten years spent a good deal of time in *ashrams* and with mystics. H. Zimmer, *Myths and Symbols in Indian Art and Civilisation*, is a useful introduction. It should be explained at this point that in order not to burden the reader footnotes will be used only in special cases. My many debts to other students, and in particular, to Indian friends who have given me information verbally, will thus not be recorded.

[2] Brahmo-Samaj, originating largely from Raja Ram Mohun Roy in the first half of the nineteenth century, is to be compared with Quakerism in England for its outstanding intellectual and moral contribution to India and for the relatively small numbers constituting this elite. The Tagore family belonged to Bramo-Samaj. It was mainly a Bengali movement.

me to have had an effect on Indian mentality and which people of European civilization are apt to overlook but ought to bear in mind:

First, the notion of transmigration of souls. This gives the Hindu a different attitude to time from us. For us time goes along a line; for the Hindu it goes in circles; and the circles repeat themselves endlessly. What does being late matter when you have to live through a cycle of countless lives? What do change and planning matter when nature is an endless cycle of creation, destruction, and re-creation? Human effort can thus do little against destiny except to accept and to suffer it. Punctuality amongst the traditionalist people, for instance the villagers, who have no timepieces in any case, is pointless. There is always time. There is in fact too much of it. Bliss, *Nirvana*, is achieved by breaking out of the endless cycle and being absorbed into the universal spirit, which is virtually nothingness.

The Hindu's attitude to death is thus also different form ours. Death has not the tragic finality for him which it has for us. So is his attitude to free will, and therefore to responsibility, different from ours. Fatalism is a strong part of his make-up.

Next, and related to the foregoing, there is the Hindu idea of the person. People are not individuals in the way they are in Christendom, or even as they were in Greece or Rome. This makes our ideas of moral responsibility meaningless in certain areas of Hindu life. It also makes the idea of 'Human Rights' as alien to traditional Hindu thinking as is the European idea of romatic love, or as is the idea of equality of souls which is inherent in Christianity. Hence Hindu social institutions like caste or *suttee*.

Caste is primordial; at least as a matter of social structure and practice (for a Hindu of the universalist and transcendental outlook of a Radhakrishnan could claim that the core of Hinduism is deeper than any social structure). Foreigners can best get a grasp of what it means by thinking of orthodox Jewish practices—no marriage except to Jews, food taboos, and the various forms of social solidarity. There are over a thousand different castes, while the sub-castes, which are the groupings which matter in daily life, are well over ten thousand. The *nation* could mean little to men when caste meant so much. The caste, which is more, as well as less, than the nation, is a closed society; and it gives each member, even in the lowest castes, a most valuable sense of belonging. The term normally used by Indians of their caste, 'my community', is exact. On the other hand the very closeness produces an attitude of distrust for your fellow humans, not excluding those in your own caste and your own family, if only because they will commonly sponge on you. It is worth adding that the predominance of Brahmins in the leadership of the Communist Party has not been accidental.

33

The Brahman for some thousands of years has seen himself, as indeed other Indians have seen him, as the natural guardian and expositor of the true dogma. If he accepts Marxism he is merely adding to the dogma; and when economic changes have hurt him, or his group, or his locality, it is not surprising that he takes to Marxism.[1]

Then there is the attitude to truth. Truth is not black or white as with us. Truth is apt to be a variety of shades in between black, and white; and these shades change according to psychological and other conditions. Everything is mixed; the categories are not clear-cut, as they are to Europeans. The statues or carvings in Hindu temples illustrate this mentality of blurring. Hence in a Hindu's mind what we see as incompatibles can co-exist or can be fused. There is no call to go into the details which exemplify or explain this phenomenon. It is enough to say here that whatever changes are now taking place in response to modernization, what we regard as lying, or duplicity, has been rather more common amongst Indians, and more commonly accepted as a fact of life, than it is amongst Europeans. The truth at times can be regarded as sheer bad manners, too. Though duplicity is not uncommon amongst us we do salute truthfulness as a standard. The traditional Indian attitude to truth is not without a bearing on Indian official policy on Kashmir or Goa, as well as on the Indian preference for compromise settlements. Those who know India know that European complaints of 'insincerity' or 'deceit' can often be sincerely meaningless to traditional Indians.

Another complicated subject which has to be reckoned with if one is to have an insight into Hinduism is *Yoga*. There are various levels to Yoga, ranging from physical exercises up through meditation on to a growing mastery of body and spirit which can be dangerous spiritually, getting near to the notion that the practitioner has become divine; which is near to the Christian's idea of Original Sin.

Hindu morality, traditionally, is different from Christian morality. While one should not exaggerate the differences, and while there is much in common in our respective ideas of good and bad, there are also some significant differences. The *Mahabharata* Illustrates them. In particular, there are strict moral obligations to your own group or groups, especially to your family and your sub-caste, but the obligations to people outside your group are much less pressing or might be seen as non-existent. The notion of the brotherhood of man is thus alien to traditional Hindu practice. That is why, traditionally at least, you can, with a clear conscience, exploit the misfortunes of people outside your

[1] There are scores of books on caste. Among recent studies those by Adrian Mayer, and by Karve and Damle (e.g. *Group Relations in a Village Community* (Poona 1963) are reliable, and illustrative.

group, such as those starving in times of famine. This seems to be particularly true of the *Baniya* caste. The Jains, an offshoot of Hinduism, are so strict against taking animal life that they wear masques so as not to swallow gnats; but they can also be the most blood-sucking of money-lenders in a country which has several groups of pitiless blood-sucking money-lenders. The Jains, too, it must be added, are also noted for their widespread custom of renouncing the world. The Hindus get near to the Jews as regards the notion of being the Chosen People, a people apart; and they share the moral consequences of the notion. Some observers have listed self-love as one of the consequences; but self-love is common enough amongst all of us. An illustration of the apartness is provided in the recent novel of Raja Rao, *The Serpent and the Rope*. This, a novel of quality, is the Indian version of Kipling's pronouncement that *Never the twain shall meet*. A Europeanized Indian marries a devoted French girl who, in spite of her outstanding moral and mental qualities, and of the birth of a son, Pierre Krishna, and of the Indian's predilection for the white skin, is abandoned for the Indian woman who, though a Rajput, and though sophisticated in Eastern and Western culture, puts flowers on the adulterer's feet and then abases her head on them. In the case of neither Jew nor Hindu can you be converted to their world; you have to be born into it. Yet, like the Jews, the Hindus have a capacity for world-wide views.[1]

Hindu morality has not the same clear-cut distinction between good and evil as Christianity or Islam has. This is another example of the blurring I have mentioned. It sees evil as a part of Nature. The sense of sin, if it exists at all, is of feebler intensity than the Christian's sense of sin.

A people whose religion has as many rules about ritual cleanliness as has Hinduism, combined with a certain indifference to normal cleanliness (or what Europeans regard as cleanliness), are bound to have something of what Europeans see as pharisaical spirit. This comes out in various things. There are, for example, rules, very strong in certain areas and amongst certain groups, against taking animal life. Some animals, such as the cow, the monkey, the peacock and the pigeon, have a quasi-divine status. Yet the same people can treat, or suffer others to treat, animals with much cruelty. Bullock drivers can

[1] Regarding the notion *Never the twain shall meet*, there are many educated Indians who combine East and West in a remarkable way. The present Maharaja of Mysore, for example, is a devout Hindu and learned in Indian Philosophy but he is also a gifted pianist and organist and learned in Western Music. His sister could have been one of the eminent concert pianists of her day had she not been an Indian Princess.

be vilely cruel. This mixing of, or what to us is inconsistency about, moral standards can, and at times does, taper off into chicanery. The traditional institution of *gurus* and swamis who devote their lives to teaching spiritual truth is a good one; and there are good *gurus* and *swamis*. There are, too, however, a large number of mountebanks who exploit the spiritual troubles of people. India has many Gudjieffs. Some of those with a European clientéle are dubious, to say the least. There is a steady stream of Europeans, usually highly solvent financially, to India in search of peace of mind; the sort of people attracted to a Gudjieff. Mr Somerset Maugham's quest of some years ago is still spoken of wonderingly by Westernized Indians. This stream, like the reverse movement of Indian *swamis* to California or Ottawa or London or San Francisco or Amsterdam (I have seen them doing well in all these places) is a sign not of the spiritual health of India so much as of the spiritual sickness of industrialized America and Europe, and of Indians' readiness astutely to supply the market. (J. Krishnamurti, it should be added, has nothing in common with these *swamis*. This Brahman and relapsed Theosophist and friend of Aldous Huxley may seem a Buddhist or an Anarchist or a Nihilist; in recent years he has been bringing not comfort but a broom to sweep away illusions.) Here again it is shallow to write off this or any other part of Hinduism as hypocrisy. It is a religion in which ritual and myth play dominant roles, at times supplanting rationality.

Given the difference between the European's and the Indian's attitude to moral obligations, to time, to free will, and to truth, the European often finds something elusive about Indians, not excluding their greatest, such as Gandhi or Nehru. Handling Indians can indeed feel like handling a fish: you think you have got a grip of them but they somehow slip through your fingers. It is for this reason that Englishmen in the old days used to ask themselves whether Indians could be trusted, or that they used to prefer dealing with Muslims, a less intricate people than Hindus. The English conceded the general intellectual superiority, normally an outstanding intellectual superiority, of the Hindu over the Muslim, but they tended to feel less alienation from the Muslim morally. Muslim ethics, like the Muslim religion, have some common origins with Christianity.

There is, of course, a relativity about these things. The average Indian when compared with the average Indonesian is directness itself. And Indians who show the outstanding moral stature of J. P. Narayan are not rare. But if we are to understand, and not just to criticize, Indians we have to bear in mind certain characteristics of Hinduism and the fact that these characteristics have left deposits in the minds of the most modern of Indians, including Nehru, and have to some degree or other conditioned them. We need the more to remind ourselves of the fact because educated Indians are apt to speak English so well as to seem to be virtually Europeans, and so, through no fault of theirs, virtually to conceal their Indian essence. Educated Indians can even confuse themselves as to the differences between Hindu and European civilizations because of their facility in the English language.

And whatever shortcomings Europeans might see in the Hindu religion or in Hindu social practices—and a long line of foreign writers, mostly unfriendly, especially the missionaries (who are often unreliable on non-Christian religions), and not always intelligent, from the Abbé Dubois (who was intelligent) up through the American Miss Mayo (who was too unfriendly) have described these shortcomings in detail—the fact remains that the Hindu religion goes on satisfying most Indians, including most of the best Indians. Christianity has made very few converts except amongst the outcastes and the pagan tribes.

Further, and this is as primordial as caste, the religious spirit counts for more in India than perhaps in any country in the world. Whether the religions be regarded as good or bad or primitive, the spirit of religion dominates the Indian air. A missionary friend of mine in the Cambridge Brotherhood, who lived and travelled like the Indian poor, said that his clerical gown, to his embarrassment, always evoked great respect, such as in the overcrowded trains and buses, for to the poor he too was 'a holy man'. And some of the habits induced by the Hindu religion, such as meditation and the study to be quiet, and non-attachment, have great value in promoting harmony and serenity. Moreover, while the acceptance of Nature, including things we see as evil, may lead to a defective social conscience, even to lowering the value of the individual, and on occasion to condoning cheating and exploitation, it also leads to reduced tensions and to a remarkable capacity for survival.

Finally, there is not only much social and psychological wisdom in Hinduism, well illustrated in everyday life by the more common achievement of peace of mind than amongst Europeans, but there is also ethical value as is attested in such Hindu scriptures as the *Bhagavad Gita* and the *Upanishads* or in Gandhi's *Dharma*, or in the benevolence common in much of Indian life. When we see some of the daily evils around us in India, such as the cruelty to animals or the maiming of beggar children, we need to remember the other side. We should remember, too, the native sobriety. Hinduism on the whole provided a balanced view of life.

A notable value in Hinduism is the spirit of co-existence, and with it the habit of tolerance and compromise which has become second nature in a country embracing millions of people of different languages, cultures, religions, sects, and indeed races. It should not be forgotten that in addition to Hindus and Sikhs and Jains there are Christians, Buddhists, Parsis, Muslims, and animists.[1] One of the great merits of the caste system was that it enabled different groups of people to follow strictly different rules of life and yet to live in proximity without conflict. The caste system was a closed system but the Hindu mind was less closed than the Christian or the Muslim mind; Hinduism never urged, or countenanced, the killing of people because they were not Hindus.

It is necessary to stress the merits as well as the complexity of Hindu civilization in order to avoid seeing only those aspects which repel Europeans. On the other hand it is equally necessary to take account of the aspects which are out of harmony with European values and not to fall into the vogue current in some quarters a few decades ago when all things Indian, including Indian religion and Indian art, got a little over-valued. There is good Indian art, and some especially good; but there are few branches which surpass, if they approach the stature of, their European counterparts—in music, in painting, in sculpture and perhaps in literature—or which equal the Chinese in painting. The aesthetic excess has already been mentioned. With it goes what to us is a strange lack of, even a distaste for, symmetry. Europeans living in India will have noticed how often Indians do not hang, or keep, a picture straight. It is not common to see cottages with a little garden or flowers; nor is decoration to a home as common as in Europe or in much of Asia. This fact is not to be disposed of by the plea of poverty. Africans or Malays, also poor, are more disposed to try for prettiness and decoration. (The Indian visual arts today are so imitative of modern art in Europe and America as to have little that is specifically Indian about them.) Moreover, there are relatively few Indians who have the feeling for the beauty of Nature which is fairly common amongst Europeans. There is no sign in Gandhi's voluminous writings that he had any feeling for it. Naipaul found Indians to have 'non-seeing eyes' and he thought this diminished their sense of wonder. Certainly creativeness has not been a characteristic of Indian civilization as it has been of European civilization. And if the utmost freedom was permitted in philosophical speculation or in spiritual life,

[1] The 1961 Census gave 360 million Hindus, 8 million Sikhs, 2 million Jains, 47 million Muslims (probably an understatement), 11 million Christians, and 3¼ million Buddhists. These last would nearly all be outcastes who have recently become, or claimed to have become, Buddhist converts, like their leader Ambedkar.

no freedom was permitted in social practices; for these were rigid. In short, Hindu civilization is an enormous swarming elaboration of the human spirit at one stage of its development. Whether the development did or did not reach an advanced stage, there is no doubt that the intelligence involved was of a high order including things no longer liked, such as the subtlety in the subjection of women or of the outcastes. Never, too, did a civilization possess such a capacity to soften and absorb other civilizations as the Hindu civilization did. Much of the old aloofness of the English in India was probably, though unconsciously, due to the will to resist absorption. A British Governor who believed in transmigration of souls once told me that he thought it was impossible to live amongst Indians for thirty years without taking on this belief and certain other Indian beliefs.

Foreign Rule

Religion is the first conditioning factor in the Indian character. The second is the long experience of foreign rule.

The Muslims had ruled India for nearly a thousand years, though not all of India and not without ups and downs. British rule was incomparably shorter as well as incomparably milder. It came in gradually from the eighteenth century, not by settled design, indeed its extension was often resisted by London, but as part of the process of filling up the gaps left by the collapse of the Mogul Empire, and in the interests of the law and order required for trading. The British *raj* as we in our day knew it lasted only for about a century and a half; in some parts for less than this. And it achieved its main purpose— to bring law and order in place of anarchy. Any doubts on this score are soon dissipated by the historical records. There is ample documentation, from the *Remonstrantie* of the Dutch trader Pelsaert in the early seventeenth century[1] and onwards, on what life was like, and the pitiless exploitation, before British rule was established. Indian plunderers and freebooters, joined by a scum of piratical European adventurers, some of whom rose to control small armies though they could not read and write, were scourging the land throughout the eighteenth century.

In order to survive the foreign rule, cruel and predatory as it often was, especially that prevailing before the British came, and exercised by foreigners less civilized than themselves, Indians developed certain traits, such as indirectness, dependence, and, in some groups or areas, wiliness.

[1] The English translation of the *Remonstrantie* of Pelsaert, who lived in Agra for about seven years, can be found in Moreland and Geyl, *Jahangir's India*, Cambridge, 1925.

39

The Indian Character

Whether due, and to what extent, to the Hindu religion, or to the social structure, or to the centuries of subjugation by foreigners, or to predatory rulers of their own, or to the climate, or to the soil and the quality of food produced from the soil, the Indian character has, like other national characters, certain distinctive traits. Some of them need to be noted because of their bearing, positively or negatively, on Nehru or on Indians in Nehru's day. But before noting them it must be emphasized again that India, being vast, has vast variations, ranging from the skin-and-bone physique of men on the Orissa plains to that of the Sikhs, the most burly race in the world; and from the deviousness of the urban Bengali to the directness of the Jat peasant, or from the meanness of the Rajasthan or Gujerat Baniya to the generosity of the Punjabi.

The first quality to strike most foreigners, apparently, is dirt. India is not a tidy country; Indians do not tend to be clean in the way Japanese or Thais or the Dutch tend to be clean. Asian and African visitors remark on the dirt as much as Europeans do. Often enough it is only a matter of a few weeks before new houses, or new furnishings in a house, become disfigured with finger marks (the practice of anointing the body and hair with oil makes for such disfigurement); and what is broken is left unrepaired. One word summarizes most Indian dwellings, villages and towns—dilapidation. Hence the common appearance of being run-down—buildings, trains, buses. There are few countries where hospitals get into the state which is common in India. Is there any other country where medical students would tolerate the condition of the kitchens in Medical School hostels in India? African villagers would not tolerate the unhygienic state of the average North Indian town. Here is a main reason why ordinary people in Fiji or the West Indies do not like Indians coming into or living near their neighbourhood—hygiene. They see Indians as slum-makers. This is unfair to many individuals, particularly to Maharshatrians and South Indians, who tend to be cleanly. It also overlooks the traits of elegance in Indian living. Vulgarity is much less common in India than in Europe, America, or Australia.

Another quality which soon strikes the foreigner is ineffectiveness. It is the more noticeable as Indians are generally intelligent and quick-witted. We in the West might over-value efficiency, but Indians, for all their cleverness, strike the foreigner as having more bent for talk than for action. Their habit of lolling might be connected with this. At all events, up to the present their intellectual quality has not been equalled by a capacity for organizing or for executing. Too often a good statement, rather than action, is accepted as a good solution.

Indian pilots tend to be skilful; the groundwork in Indian air services tends to be defective because of carelessness. Examples abound—from the conditions in the docks—from Calcutta docks a bulldozer and an 18-ton transformer were stolen in my time and from Bombay docks a 100-ton parcel of steel rods—to Government Ministries, down to agricultural experimental stations. A characteristic example was the sequel to the world conference on Family Planning held in India in 1959. A great effort was then made in the way of publicity, speechifying, social occasions, and Resolutions. The foreign delegates were delighted and felt confident that India would now pioneer measures for coming to grips with the population problem. Within six months of the Conference the organization, as well as the drive, had melted away. Not a single action resulted from it. One of the ladies who was most active at the time, the wife of an important official and herself a medical graduate, soon dropped out of the movement altogether. There is of course a relativity about these things, too. Some Indians have great executive capacity, and most Indians have more executive capacity than most people from South East Asian countries. Nor should it be forgotten that Russian executive capacity was rated so low forty and fifty years ago that knowing people laughed at the notion of Russia ever being industrialized: ballet dancers, novelists, even mathematicians, yes; but Russians as engineers and organizers, never! The higher levels of the Civil Service in India are good and could presage a spread of the habits of action.

Another quality with which the foreigner soon becomes acquainted is what he regards as trickery. I got to know several Indians who had worked in a confidential capacity for Gandhi, rather like secretaries. They had habitually been making, and keeping for themselves, apparently surreptitiously, copies of letters written to or from Gandhi. I know of several other national leaders whose confidential assistants did the same thing. This habit of exploiting, and at times betraying, confidences can be carried to curious lengths. The aptitude for simulation and dissimulation fairly widespread in India has evoked some heart-felt testimonials over the centuries; but, it must be emphasized again, it is not necessarily insincerity or deceit. To cite a contemporary instance, there are now about thirty different research institutes (e.g. Physics, Housing, Leather, and so on) scattered over India. It is not too much to say that half of them are unproductive; more than one is just about bogus. At the National Physics Laboratory, which is not bogus, when I went to Delhi in 1952 there was much ado about a solar cooker which, it was claimed, had been invented at the Institute and was being produced and distributed in great numbers. It was going to save India's cow dung for the soil instead of its being used as the staple cooking fuel, and it was going to usher in a beneficial revolution for all the hot countries. I was presented with one to send to Canberra so that the Australian Government could see what Independent India was capable of achieving. Over the years, however, I could never find an Indian village which had heard of a solar cooker. Ten years later a national newspaper published the following explanatory item:

'Research is a slow and delicate process. It can only suffer by some people's anxiety to anticipate it in search for big news. At a time when the National Physics Laboratory had not produced a single ceramic condenser (i.e. solar cooker) the Director announced that it had produced a million. His motive was the noblest—to get publicity for the Laboratory . . .'[1]

From this kind of nobility on to duplicity and not keeping your word, and then on to plain corruption, is not a long step. Corruption is common in America, and it is common in several European and most South American countries. Is it worse in India? We need make no moralizing comparisons, but the truth is that it is widespread. Often a doctor's sickness certificate for an absentee employee or for a visa applicant is worth nothing; life-saving drugs are adulterated; the food sold is adulterated, sometimes dangerously adulterated; the milk is white but it is watered; the textile is proclaimed to be, and looks like, silk, but it is cotton; the charity is needed but the charity-appeal is a racket. The most worthy causes, for instance blind children, blood banks, or comforts for soldiers on the Chinese border, can too often be turned into rackets. One develops a wariness over the years but so clever are the tricksters that one can go on being inveigled into some false charity or other. Indians are apt to distrust one another, even brothers or castle colleagues, rather more than we distrust one another. Some observers, including Indians, feel that corruption goes so deep in India,[2] and that, owing to economic development in the way and by the mehods pushed in Nehru's time, it has so affected political life, that it can now never be cleared up short of a Communist dictatorship. Some foreigners argue that corruption is widespread because money-mindedness, notwithstanding the veneration for those who renounce the world, is an Indian characteristic. A judgement of this kind is worth little if it is not qualified

[1] *Organizer* August 1962. This Director, a FRS, and an expert on Persian poetry as well as on Chemistry, was a devotee of astrology.

[2] Cf. Vivian Bose report on Dalmai–Jain group; also the Mundra affair; the Santhaman Report, and the Das Report in 1964. There is much less corruption in the South.

by such considerations as the poverty of India or the degree of money-mindedness amongst Europeans and Americans.

Foreigners also complain that asking for things is common, even at high social and political levels, and speak of the 'beggar mentality' in India. Some of them write about its playing a considerable role in India's attitude to Aid. They say that this is why the Food and Agriculture Ministry has for some years been running on the basis that it receive millions of tons of grain each year from America, and the Finance Ministry on the basis that it receive millions of dollars in Aid.

Some of these critics go on to complain that Indians, moreover, feel little or no gratitude; that if you give a *sadhu* or a beggar alms a common response is 'That's not much' or 'Can't I have more?'. The official Indian attitude to foreign aid has certainly not always been felicitous. And there are Indian quarters where the feeling prevails that the world owes India a living.[1] But according to my observations the attitude to aid has not been exceptional; and Indians have as much gratitude as the human average, which is not high. One of the Indian proverbs says that no gods forgive ingratitude. Some Indians have been the severest critics of themselves, saying that there is not enough honesty or shame, and that there is too much self-righteousness, too much censoriousness, too much backbiting, and too much vindictiveness. One of the big efforts, and for a time one of the big effects, of Gandhi was to give Indians more moral fibre. Nehru, who was much concerned with the matter, also had a similar effect for some time.

Indian men are, or traditionally were, spoilt at all levels and in all castes because the traditional Indian social institutions worked towards the subjugation of women—child marriage (the father of the present King of Nepal was only 14 when he begat him), the dowry system, polygamy, purdah, no divorce for women, treatment of widows, suttee, and exclusion from property rights. There is more to be said for some of these institutions than appears on the surface; in any case they are now being changed; but the point is that the male was greatly favoured at the expense of the female, brothers being waited on by sisters, as well as husbands by wives. This, like the way of life in the joint family households, was bound to have an effect on the Indian character.[2]

For me a quality which I found not uncommon and disliked much was the snobbery about power; at its worst, licking the boots of those above you and making those below you lick your boots. This hateful quality is not confined to Indians, of course, being common enough in

[1] The speeches by the Indian Ambassador in Germany in 1959–60 are an example.
[2] Cf. Nirad Chandhuri, *Autobiography of an Unknown Indian.*

Europe or America, but it is unpleasantly common amongst politicians, bureaucrats, and journalists. One of the changes in India in the last fifteen years has been the rise in the importance, and therefore in the self-confidence, of journalists. They themselves, as well as the new political figures, now know that they can influence votes. Simultaneously, the quality of journalism has gone down. There are still good journalists but there are few Shiva Raos or Pothan Josephs or Frank Moraes or Subba Raus left today.

To finish with the less ingratiating traits in the Indian character, the foreigner is apt to complain of a talkative self-assurance; especially the foreigner from certain Asian countries. He finds Indians too little in doubt about the rightness of their own cause or claims, be it Kashmir, or NEFA, or aid, or just getting promotion for themselves or for members of their family. But here again there are many exceptions. At the average Afro-Asian meeting the Indians usually stand out for their sobriety.

There must be no illusion that the traits sketched in the foregoing paragraphs sum up India, or indeed that anything so vast and old and various as India can be reduced to a few pages. I have singled out these traits so as to clear away notions that India is about the same as Europe or America, merely lacking their economic development.

There are traits in the national character, on the other hand, which are ingratiating. As they are positive virtues they can be stated briefly.

Thus there is the great quality of loyalty. This may be limited to one's group but it is common enough in any relationship, for instance between officer and man, or employer and employee, where respect has been engendered. As for members of one's own group, what Indians suffer for members of their family or sub-caste is exemplary; and though the loyalty can become nepotism and favouritism—for instance putting your fellow Kashmiri Brahmans or your fellow UP men first, or if you steal government funds or subvert justice in the interests of a cousin that is not wrong—it is a valuable quality. So long as the Indian family system endures there will be little need for social insurance and its resulting bureaucracy.[1]

Then there is the intellectual quality of Indians. This is outstanding, especially amongst South Indians and Bengalis; and as there is a strain of seriousness in the Indian temperament minds are put to use. Potential FRS and Nobel Prize men exist by the scores in India. There is surely no group in the world with more intellectual capacity than the

---

[1] The first President of India renounced part of his salary but in accordance with Indian attitudes to family life brought children and grand-children and other relatives to live with him in the Palace; it was said to the number of about forty for some time.

South Indian Brahman. Further, many of them are capable, in spite of nationalistic aberrations, of considering the other side. There is an adultness about the good Indian writers and scholars. A few years ago one of the weeklies in India published a series of about twenty articles on prominent living Indian writers, some of them writing in the vernacular: the quality of most of the writers' remarks was as impressive as their faces. The capacity for self-criticism is shown abundantly in the *Readers' Letters* to the newspapers. (These *Readers' Letters* also show the command to which Indians attain over the English language.) A related quality is tolerance. Apart from bouts of nationalistic or mob excitement, Indians tend to be sane as well as tolerant. Mention has been made of the characteristic in Indian life of mixing up attitudes in a way unfamiliar to Europeans, of the co-existence of what to us are incompatibles. This explains why there is a good deal of violence in Indian life but at the same time a strong feeling against violence; even against bad temper. For all the disorder of these days I have seldom seen Indians outside of a mob fighting or quarrelling in public.

Indians are sensitive above the average; there is little of the clod about them.

They have a respect for, and often some attainment of, spirituality. A friend of mine, a South American poet, who spent some years studying Indians, considered them a comparatively unsensual people.

And they have a capacity for suffering, for enduring, for putting up with things, which is unsurpassed in my experience.

Finally, they have a capacity for affection.

Perceptive Englishmen never hesitated. In spite of the poverty—unimaginable to the working class in the West, a world of hunger, disease, skin and bones, rags, hovels, with millions owning nothing but their name—and in spite of whatever shortcomings they might feel in the national character, perceptive Englishmen found much to admire and to love, especially the intelligence and, amongst many, a beauty of soul. What foreigner having lived for some years in India would not return there if he could? or does not feel in most other countries something like bathos? Indian civilization is one of the great archetypal experiences of the human race.

The Nationalist Movement

This then is the people amongst whom Nehru was born and spent his life. We cannot, I repeat, understand him without reference to the matrix from which he sprang, or to the kind of people he was ruling. Nehru has been judged too often as if he had sprung from New York or Edinburgh or Sydney, or was ruling Americans or Scots or Australians.

45

Nehru was born at a time when India was going through the nationalist ferment. By and large there was no nationalism in India a century earlier, and not much until about the time he was born, because Indians did not much feel that they were one people. Hinduism gave them some sense of unity, but not enough to triumph over regional and linguistic and caste loyalties and prejudices. After all, Europeans had a bond of equal force in their common religion, Christianity, but that did not prevent nationalist differences from flaring up into ferocious hatreds and sanguinary wars. Moreover, In India Hinduism was not the only religion. Islam numbered its adherents by the millions and had been in India for severl hundred years; the Parsees were in India for about 12 centuries; the Christians were there still longer, as Christianity came to India early (according to legend, before it came to England or France); and there were millions of tribal pagans. India never existed as a single unity, not even at the height of the Muslim Empire. It was Britain which made it one. India is a creation of the British.

The origins of Indian nationalism are not yet incontrovertibly established though there is ample evidence to suggest that it arose, step by step, as the British spread their education. This is how it arose also in Africa, and throughout the French, Dutch and Belgian Empires. The Indian Mutiny—Mutiny is the correct description, not 'War of Independence' as some Indian nationalist historians are now claiming— was mostly in the North and was mostly taken over by the Muslim ruling class. It was only one, though the biggest, of a series of mutinies in the first half of the nineteenth century. All the same, it is one of the watersheds, partly because of the manner of suppressing it and partly because of a distrust for Indians which it left in the British rulers through certain cases of treachery and cruelty. Trevelyan's *Cawnpore* is an illustrative document of the period.

The effects would have been worse had it not been for the Viceroy, Clemency Canning, whose nickname, given in odium at the time, is a measure of the honour due to him. Further, not only did the process of governing improve after the Mutiny, and corruption or money-making by British officers disappear, but within two decades the British were engaged on a huge programme of economic development. An illustration of what was done is given in Tandon's *Punjabi Century 1847–1947*—irrigation canals and drainage opening up millions of acres of land, roads, bridges, railways, posts, telegraphs, schools, and law and order. (Other testimony will be found in Edwardes' *A Year on the Punjabi Frontier in 1848–49* and Percival Spears' *Twilight of the Moghuls*.)

The British *raj*, as will be seen when historical truth takes the place of current subjectivity about the British Empire or about colonies, was in practice a vast programme for what is now called Technical Assistance. It brought to India as a whole, and not only to the Punjab, superior technology, schools, universities, irrigation, railways, roads, bridges, telegraphs, public health measures, disciplined police and army, regular, honest and efficient administration, respect for truth and honesty, a system of even-handed justice, social reforms like the prohibition of widow burning, or the suppression of Thuggee, and, finally, the idea of, and the machinery for, a unified India. Not being an Englishman I am free to add that the English are a gifted and superior people, and that their best qualities were well represented in this effort in India.

Personal relations, though not as cordial as in the days of Colonel Meadows Taylor or General Sleeman, were generally correct and often good. Many of the British were passionately interested in India, carrying on the long tradition of Indological scholarship, as did Alexander Cunningham, John Marshall, or William Jones, or ordinary Civilian and Army Officers like Tod, Elphinstone, Malcolm, Taylor and Sleeman. The British, it must be remembered, were living in a climate, and amidst diseases, which afflicted most of them most of the time. No one knew what caused malaria or cholera or the dysenteries or typhoid. There were no antibiotics; no frigidaires; no air conditioning. They were separated from their children, whom they saw every fourth year at the most. A large proportion of them died in their thirties and forties, as British graveyards in India testify. Further, the main bar to personal relations came from the Indian side, not the British. The rulers had to keep a certain distance because of any tendencies to exploit a personal courtesy or kindness—that familiar making of 'a little request'—but the main bar came from such facts as that Indian ladies above the outcaste groups were still in purdah in North and Central India and were illiterate and were married as children, and that the food taboos prevented Indians from eating with others than their own caste.

That is not to say that the British could not have done better. The strutting pomp and vanities surrounding the Vice-Regal Court, for instance, went on right until Linlithgow's time in the 'Forties. If the Viceroy's daughter shopped, a red carpet was laid down for her; and if she went riding in the Central Vista anachronistic precautions were taken for her safety or status. There was no doubt some race prejudice, too, among some of the British. On the whole, however, most of the British behaved well, though stupid wives and some of the *classe subalterne*, and especially the Eurasians, have something to answer for. The snag was not bad manners, still less injustice or exploitation, but something different. William Archer, the dramatic critic and the pioneer of Ibsen, happened to spend much of the year 1912 in India. (This happened to be the year Nehru returned home from England.) His brother was an officer in the Indian Army. Archer, a level-headed and observing man, found little rudeness amongst the officer class, and no injustice, but he was struck with the *foreignness* of the British *raj* in India—'all orders in a foreign accent'. This emphasized the crude fact of racial domination.[1] This foreignness, not wickedness, was in fact the unanswerable charge against the British *raj*. As the British officials were only a handful—how small a handful we are apt to forget (when Nehru returned to India in 1912 there were only 1,500 British executive officials and 75,000 British soldiers in the whole of what is now India and Pakistan)—their tendency to protective aloofness would have been the greater. Foreignness and myopia were the flaws. That is why the British underrated and misunderstood Nehru. They saw him as 'one of our chaps who has gone astray'. That is why they overrated the Princes. There was also occasionally some littleness, as in the arrests, for instance of Mrs Pandit's husband, a gentle harmless scholar, in 1942, as well as errors in policy.

Nehru, who was prone to extravagant language at times, once described British rule as 'unbelievably evil'. British rule in India, on the contrary, was both efficient and beneficent; it is one of the few bright pages in history—the pages of which are mostly dark to black. The rule of a people of one race and culture over a people of another race and culture, ten times their numbers and at the opposite end of the world, and throwing up able men by the thousands, could only be temporary. Indian nationalism arose not out of the evils of British rule but out of a steadily growing and understandable resentment for foreign masters; the resentment spreading as English education produced more and more Indians capable of practising the English techniques of Government. And, it must be added, the spearhead of resentment became racial; and at times that involved colour. This racial or colour element became more and more powerful though other factors, such as being repelled by European meat-eating or not washing enough or in accordance with Indian ideas, also counted.

It is difficult to make clear to those who do not know India from within how obsessive is the preoccupation with colour. The only other group which can compare with Indians in this respect are the American negroes. Not all Indians have it. South Indians for instance have much less of it than North Indians. Brahmans have less of it than

---

[1] William Archer, *India and the Future*. The manuscript was handed to the publisher the day War broke out in 1914; the book was therefore not published until 1917. It seems to have been little noticed or known.

other castes; South Indian Brahmans have little or none of it. Like most people who have spent a good deal of time with Indians I have had experience of it, and in some astonishing forms, including from Chiefs of Staff, heads of great Departments, Vice-Chancellors of Universities, Ambassadors, all people educated, and with good friendships, amongst Britishers. The sensitiveness can sometimes become unbalanced; what is taken to be a slight can be imaginary, such as when an Indian Ambassador could not get a room at a motel and jumped to the conclusion that it was due to a secret colour bar, not to what was the truth, namely that the motel was full; or when an Indian University Lecturer from Australia who wanted to call on me in Delhi and when asked by the receptionist (an Indian) to wait a while as I had another visitor in my room, jumped to the conclusion that he was being slighted and made an excited complaint about a colour bar. In September 1962 *The Observer* published an article on the Common Market by 'A Senior Indian Diplomat' which he entitled 'A Club for Europeans'. A significant title. The European Club, preserved by the British for themselves so that they could escape from the workaday world for an hour or two and be in England again, became a black myth for not a few Indians and was blown up into extravagant proportions. (It was, of course, inexpedient to maintain an absolute ban on Indian membership of these Clubs, certainly after the 'Twenties; but that is another matter.)

The Indian student in England, often an impecunious man, sent and kept there at great personal sacrifice by his family, living in poor lodgings and on unpalatable foreign food and under the damp grey skies of England, felt wretched in any case. He usually put down his troubles to treatment meted out to him because he was coloured; and Indian students' clubs fanned this feeling. Indian students nearly all became strongly nationalist, though until they had left India they had rarely thought of themselves as Indian, only as a member of this or that sub-caste in this or that linguistic group. Krishna Menon gave two decades of his life to propaganda and other work amongst Indian students in England.[1]

Anyone who knows India knows not only what a commanding role caste plays, but also that caste is connected with racial and even colour factors. Today there are nationalists who try to explain away *varna*, but I have heard Nehru himself link caste with original racial and colour factors. Moreover, the man who knows India knows too that the interest of Indians in a fair complexion is undeniable and not seldom

[1] Migration from India also had the effect of wearing down caste and regional feelings and of making the migrants feel Indian instead. This happened amongst the Indians in Fiji, Mauritius, and the West Indies.

is infatuated. The matrimonial advertisements, which are common in a country where marriages are normally arranged, illustrate it. Here are some taken from *The Hindustan Times* in one day in 1953:

> A suitable match for a Bisa Agarwal white-complexioned, tall, and beautiful girl of 20, appearing for BA this year. . . .
>
> Wanted—white-complexioned matches for Brahman boys of UP. . . .
>
> Very fair tall educated girl for Agarwal boy. . . .
>
> Match for a brilliant permanent Class 1 Officer in Central Govt. (Punjabi Brahman, 28, pay Rs. 900/-). Only tall fair-complexioned girls need apply. . . .
>
> Wanted—suitable match for the daughter of a very respectable and rich business man, white-complexioned. . . .

Ten years later *The Statesman* reported that the Magistrate of Howrah sentenced Manik Hazrah, his mother, and his two brothers, to a fine of Rs 100 each for assaulting Maya Hazra, wife of the first accused. The last was married to Manik Hazrah a year previously. She came to live with her husband in his family home two months after the marriage. The mother-in-law then began ill-treating her because she was dark. All three sons soon joined in. Then one night all four fell on the wretched girl, beating her, tore off her ornaments, and locked her outside to pass the night there, without food. The next morning the husband dragged her on to the road and told her to be gone.

Did Nehru think of such incidents, of which he would have known not a few, when, passionate as usual over *apartheid* in South Africa, he took an angry part at the Prime Ministers' Conference in London which led to South Africa's leaving the Commonwealth? Indian caste was the prototype of *apartheid*, as Gandhi knew and said.

It is at least partly because of this infatuation with fair skins that Indians see slights over colour where none is intended; and that they hate the whites in Africa, since the latter lump them with Africans. Though little known to Indians in India, the Africans do not in general like Indians. Indians for their part do not in general like Africans. The average Indian father would not be happy at the prospect of his children marrying Africans.[1]

In extreme cases Indians can dislike their own average Indian colour. (I say 'average' Indian colour as skin colour in India varies all the way from white to black.) A westernised and light-skinned

---

[1] According to *An African Student in China*, Pall Mall Press, 1963, the Chinese have similar feelings.

Chief Minister of a Province in pre-Independence days once said to a British Governor of my acquaintance, 'The truth is we don't like the colour of our skins'. I could cite comparable remarks from my experience. Nirad Chaudhuri, the Bengali author of the *Autobiography of an Unknown Indian*, a book not liked in India but one of undoubted merit, has some revealing passages on the point.

These facts about Indian colour sensitiveness do not, of course, explain away rudeness or prejudice or insensitiveness on the part of some British. We Europeans must take our share of the blame and should therefore make allowances for the Indian side.

Indian nationalism, in short, had the usual and not irrational resentments felt towards foreign rule, but it sometimes had, in addition, an element which gave it a special, and occasionally an irrational, quality, born of an acute sensitiveness about colour. This sensitiveness is now lessening but at the time of the Nationalist struggle, and in Nehru's younger days, it was a significant factor, and it made it doubly difficult for the British to deal with Indian nationalism. Chinese nationalism was different. There was no sense of regret in it; on the contrary the Chinese felt themselves to be superior, so much so that social relations with them were relatively easy. The truth, the great basic truth, is that Indians though differing profoundly in traditional culture from Europeans are related to Europeans in race. Much of the sensitiveness arises from this racial cousinry and the feeling that it is slighted.

Yet Indian Nationalism, even at its highest height against the British, remained a minority movement. In essence it was a movement amongst Westernized Indians, educated in the English language and in English thinking, and usually in England. They turned English weapons against the English. As regards the vast majority of Indian people there was no ill-will towards the British. Years after the British renounced sovereignty, villagers could be encountered who would ask, 'When are the British coming back?' Probably not more than ten to fifteen percent of the Indian people were against the British, though the majority would have been indifferent rather than actively in favour of the British *raj*, or indeed of any régime. The tumultuous and friendly reception given to the Queen when she visited India in 1961 was due in part to the Indian love of *tamasha* (e.g. ceremonial spectacle), and to the Queen's own grace, but also in part to a respect for the British which was always widespread and was still alive. The hostile ten to fifteen per cent included the educated and the forward-looking but it was because the proportion of the actively anti-British was so small that the nationalist leaders had to resort to stirring up discontent, largely by fabricating myths or worse, in order to get mass support.

It was this kind of compaigning, which, in spite of Gandhi's policy of non-violence, stirred up excitement and then hatred and was bound to generate violence. And it brought an entirely new force on to the Indian stage, namely the mass. In order to sabotage the British Government the nationalist agitators ended up by sabotaging government itself. It was they who called in the mob, that terrible monster of modern India; who made it passable for students—students in North India become at times a part of the mob—not to pay railway fares and to commit arson. The nationalist agitators sowed the wind; India is now beginning to reap the whirlwind. What that dire harvest portends no man can be sure. Mob riots over a Telegu-speaking State in Andhra, over language in Bombay, over almost everything in Bengal, over trifles such as getting on to the dais or into the food kitchen at the Congress meeting in Patna in 1962, are examples of what is now frequent, as are student riots because the examination papers are not easy or because the students are not allowed into cinemas without buying enough tickets or because stall-holders resist their stealing food. Nehru never condoned terrorism, as the fascist-minded Bose did, but he stirred up agitations which led to the hatred which led to disorder and to terrorism.

Although Gandhi's methods of calling in the mob were bound to lead to mob violence and indeed to hatred, and although Gandhi was not without some deception, including self-deception, and not without some unattractive qualities, such as harshness to his sons, it still remains true that what saved Indian nationalism from becoming murderous was Gandhi. His outlook, whatever his lapses, was based upon non-violence and upon love, not hate. He had schooled himself into this lesson in twenty years of effort in South Africa. Gandhi made mistakes, including the grave mistake of the *Quit India* movement of 1942; he never quite freed himself from a rather endearing snobbery about social class (on the surface, probably); at times he resorted to something close to the trickery for which his caste, Gujerati Baniya, was reputed; and some of his ideas now look like puritanical fads or anti-Science obscurantism. But Gandhi had a powerful originating mind, enormous political flair, and a capacity for action which is usually found in only the great captains. He had, too, in a high degree, courage, self-criticism, and humour. The world of nationalism is a world of self-pity, scapegoat-ism, lies, and innuendos; Gandhi would have little of that world. He seemed to me in Calcutta in 1945 (and I was not predisposed to like him) a very impressive human being. Twenty years later, with more facts and less passion at my disposal, he seems to have had the power which belongs to the saints.[1]

[1] The books of the American Quaker, Richard B. Gregg, who lived in Gandhi's entourage for some years, and of Rev J. Doke, who worked with

Gandhi was unique but he was not the only remarkable Indian thrown up by, or during, the movement for Independence. There were several scores of remarkable men, including Nehru, Rajagopalachari and Tagore. To this extent it is not true to say that Nehru had no competition.

Nehru's Part

Nationalist agitation dominated India politically and culturally during the first half of this century; and it reached its zenith in two decades between the two World Wars, thanks to the genius of Gandhi and to the mistakes of certain Englishmen. To destroy the British *raj* became the beacon-light of Nehru's existence. He was the implacable extremist, stopping short only of the terrorism common in Bengal and the Punjab. All of Nehru's dedication was brought to the cause; but much unreasonableness too. Some of his speeches of those days make wild reading now. Thus he castigated the *Government of India Act of 1935* (which is the basis of the present Indian Constitution) as 'a new Charter of slavery to strengthen the bonds of imperialist domination and to intensify the exploitation of our masses'.[1] In 1937 he opposed a coalition of Congress with the Muslim League on the ground that there were only two parties in India—Congress and the British. Jinnah, we are told, was hurt; which is scarcely surprising. Some Indian historians indeed date the inevitability of Pakistan from this stand. Examples of Nehru's exaggeration or extremism can be multiplied without much research. On one occasion he was beaten in a *lathi* charge by the police, and it is far from sure that his foolhardiness did not invite it.

It has often been asked how was it that Nehru, whose father had carried to far lengths his admiration for the English gentleman and to bringing up his son on that model, and who himself lived so much more as an Englishman than as an Indian, could have become so passionately, so whole-heartedly, an enemy of the British *raj*. In India one used to be told of various episodes which had wounded his feelings, such as finding himself excluded from some place or other in a Hill Station not long after he returned from England, or, to mention another case cited, a similar episode at Allahabad. Whether such episodes occurred or not, there is no need to have recourse to them to account for Nehru's conversion to Nationalist agitation. I never asked him about them as I felt that if they had happened he would have regarded them as

Gandhi in his South African days, are worth particular mention amongst the many revealing books on Gandhi, though there is no substitute for Gandhi's own books.

[1] Quoted Rafiq Zakaria, ed. *A Study of Nehru*, 1959, p. 32 (63 articles by various writers, mostly Indian).

irrelevant. It is certain that a man of his proud sensitive nature, a Brahman, and with the education and social background of the English upper classes in an epoch when class meant a great deal—few of the English officials in India could claim all three of Harrow, Trinity College, Cambridge, and the Inner Temple, or would have had Nehru's private means—would not accept an inferior status in his own country. Sooner or later the fact of foreign rule, and the fateful tragic racial fact, would assert itself, and the assertion could have only one consequence on a man like Nehru.

It is probable that an equally potent factor with Nehru would be regret, and in some cases probably shame, for certain things Indian— for the illiterate *purdah* women, for the child marriage, for the polygamy, for the subordination of women and outcastes, for the astrology, for the cow worship, for the poverty the delapidation and the illiteracy, and for the cringing. He was as much moved to change Indians and to get them to stand up erect as to get the British out of India. The more he admired the British—and there is no doubt about his admiration— the more he hated Indians' subjugation to them. Nehru was passionately determined to show that Indians could be as good as the British.

Reason, as well as passion, was on the side of Nehru when he threw in his lot with the Nationalists; for it was impossible to go on pretending that only Englishmen, and not Indians, were fit to govern India. Nor were mistakes, including some grave mistakes, lacking on the British side. Think, for example, of British miscalculations about the power or the rootedness of the Princes—even when one allows that rule in most Princely States was better than in the rest of India. On the other hand it was unreasonable of Nehru to pretend that the English wanted to rule for ever, or to rule without Indians sharing in the work of government. There were many Indians, including members of the Nehru family, holding senior executive positions in the British *raj*.

So, by 1915, three years after returning from England, Nehru started public work. He started with the peasants. Before long he took the significant step of giving up wearing European clothes. Gandhi (whom Nehru had met for the first time in 1916) was a guest in the Nehru family home in 1918, but Nehru remained a moderate, almost a social worker, until the Jallianwalla Bagh shootings in Amritsar in 1919; that fateful day when General Dyer ordered a fusillade on a public assembly which had met in defiance of a ban, killing about 400 and wounding over 1,000.[1] It was then that he resolved to give his life to

[1] Cf. Sir John Smyth's letters in the *Times Lit. Suppl.* February 20th and April 26th, 1964. There are several books and brochures on Jallianwala Bagh, which is a watershed.

fighting the British and to ending 'the slavery and disgrace of the Indian people'. The fire was now in his belly. In 1928 he became General Secretary of Congress. By 1929 he had become so much a national figure that he was elected President of Congress, Gandhi backing him against the older and more experienced Patel. At the Lahore session of the Congress it was he who got carried the 'Declaration of war against the British', though this was the period of Irwin's Viceroyalty and of Ramsay MacDonald's Prime Ministership.

Nehru's record for intransigence has to be stressed because there is grave question whether his way of getting independence for India was the only way, or indeed a good way. Equally patriotic and equally clever Indians, such as Sapru, thought not.

After all, the Labour Party in England was committed to the principle of independence for India as the goal; and the Conservative Party had the same goal though it was rather further off. Baldwin, that over-criticized and misunderstood Prime Minister, was ready to hasten all possible steps towards Self-Government; and the memoirs of Lord Percy make it clear that influential groups in the Conservative Party felt as Baldwin did.[1] As it happened, I was living in, or based on, England in those days and though having no interest in India I, like the men around me, took it for granted that, leaving aside a handful of men like Churchill and Beaverbrook, the only point at issue for Englishmen in general regarding India's independence was *when*—not whether—it could be given. Such hesitation as existed about *when* arose from the risks to unity and to law and order; risks since shown to be not imaginary.

But Nehru refused to believe this. He was convinced that the English would not go without being pushed out; and, apparently, too, he was convinced that Hindu–Muslim communalism was a mere bogey, not a reality, or that where it existed it was the result of British plotting or design. Happenings like Crewe's disavowal in 1912 of Hardinge's adumbration of self-government for India, or the Rowlatt Bills in the 'Twenties, which did much to prevent the nationalist movement from being taken over by men like Sapru, and the lack of statesmanship in men like Reading or Simon who failed to be more than clever lawyers, and the violent attacks on the *Government of India Act of 1935* led by Churchill, and later, after the outbreak of war, the rejection of Rajagopalachari's courageous offer at Poona, over Gandhi's head, of armed co-operation in the War in return for a political settlement, these are amongst the tragic costly deviations on the British side which might be pleaded on Nehru's behalf. Nor did enough of the Viceroys have the quality of Irwin and Wavell. All the

[1] Lord Percy of Newcastle, *Some Memories.*

same, the verdict of the historians will almost certainly be that Indian nationalists would have done just as well for their cause, and at the cost of much less destruction, if they had accepted, step by step, every concession offered by or wrung from the British. The follies on the British side were equalled by the follies on the Indian nationalist side, such as Congress forcing the Provincial Ministries to resign, or the *Quit India* movement, in 1942, or the bringing in of the mob. And as it was, the Indians got their independence cheap; as the costs paid by Algeria or Indo-China remind us. The bloodshed and the destruction took place after the British had quit; the slaughter of Indians was perpetrated not by the British but by Indians.

Nationalism, like Revolution, is a respectable word today; but the reality itself is ugly. It is justifiable when it stands for self-government; too often it stands for ignoring or for flouting the rights of others; a primitive tribal thing, and prone to murderous hate. Nehru himself did not wholly escape the taint. There was no self-pity in Nehru the man, just as there was none in Gandhi; but the Indian nationalist movement was full of self-pity. The ceremonies performed for the odd handful of men killed in riots and dubbed 'the martyrs' illustrated this; as did the habit current for some years of blaming every evil in Indian life on the British, even to such things as the poverty, the over-population, the usurious moneylenders, and the Bengal famine.[1]

It is now seventeen years since the British left. Few Indians today would claim that the poverty, the over-population, or even the money-lenders, are less than in British times. The truth is that conditions in India today are in some respects worse than they were twenty or thirty years ago. They are worse not because the British have gone, or because the Congress Governments had failings, but because the basic problems are cumulative and almost intractable. We will see shortly how Nehru as Prime Minister of the Republic of India fared in dealing with realities, hard brute realities, and not just the fictions of the nationalist agitator. We will also see how the nationalism which he and Gandhi and those associated with them fanned in order to hasten the British out of India became too strong for them and got beyond their control. Gandhi himself was assassinated by a Hindu nationalist. Nehru in the last years of his Prime Ministership was cornered and maimed by Indian nationalism.

Indian nationalism won and so England withdrew from India. There was no just, indeed there was no practical, alternative to

---

[1] An example will be found in Ram Gopal, *British Rule in India: an Assessment*, which though published as late as 1963 repeated the charges common in the 'twenties and 'thirties and could be collected in a few hours from the newspapers of those days.

England's going. But the loss of India was a tremendous blow; how tremendous is still little understood. Apart from the loss of power—for instance the former use of Indian Army units in so many countries— there has been the loss of outlets of a peculiarly constructive and enlarging kind for the best of British youth. Jobs in advertising agencies, or in TV, or in 'property development', are a poor substitute for a career in the ICS or the old army. Worse, there has been a loss of outlook for the whole nation, a narrowing of views and a lowering of the sights. The opposition of men like Churchill to Indian independence, whatever their errors, was connected with a divination of this loss. They belonged to an era, and an outlook, when England was able, and dared, to be great.

Chapter 3

NEHRU'S PERSONAL BACKGROUND

Jawaharlal Nehru was born in 1889. His father was Motilal Nehru, one of the leading Indian barristers of the day, and his mother, who was Motilal's second wife, was Swarup Rani.

The Nehrus are Kashmiri Brahmans in origin. The title of Pandit (Doctor) applied to Nehru—against his proclaimed wishes—comes from this origin. It used to be applied to Kashmiri Brahmans, and to some others, automatically, whether they were learned in Sanskrit or not. Nehru himself did not know Sanskrit.

The Kashmiri Brahmins were coming down to the plains of India from their mountain valley in the seventeenth, eighteenth and nineteenth centuries, rather as the Scots were coming down to England in the same years. They came for the same reason—poverty at home and better chances in the South for men with brains and stamina. Kashmiri Brahmans were thus found in many of the Principalities in North and Central India, occupying positions of trust, as well as in the service of the Mogul Emperors. Like the Scots of those days, they acquired a reputation for being ambitious self-seekers, and for favouring their own kith and kin unduly.

Early in the eighteenth century a Kashmiri Brahman called Raj Kaul, highly reputed as a Sanskrit and Persian scholar, gained the notice of the Emperor Farrukhsiar and came to Delhi, the Mogul capital. 'A *jagir* with a house situated on the banks of the canal was granted to Raj Kaul, and, from the fact of this residence, "Nehru" (from *Nahar*, a canal), came to be attached to his name. Kaul had been the family name; this changed to Kaul-Nehru; and, in later years, Kaul dropped out and we became simply Nehru.'[1] The family experienced vicissitudes of fortune in times of trouble. Our Nehru's great-grandfather, Lakshmi Narayan Nehru, became the first Vakil of the Sarkar Company at the shadow court of the Emperor; and our

[1] Nehru: *An Autobiography*, p. 1. *Jagir* was a sort of fief.

58

Nehru's grandfather, Ganga Dhar Nehru, was *Kotwal* of Delhi until the Mutiny in 1857. The Mutiny put an end to the Nehru family's connection with Delhi for nearly a century—until Jawaharlal Nehru returned in 1946 as the first Prime Minister of India.

After the Mutiny the family had moved to Agra, 120 miles south of Delhi.

Nehru's father, Motilal, was born in Agra, in 1861, three months after the death of his father. The family seems to have been poor at this stage—the highest caste in India is not necessarily, or indeed commonly, rich—and the burden of the family fell on Motilal's two older brothers—Bhansa Dhar Nehru, who soon afterwards entered the Judicial Department of the British Government, and, because of being posted from place to place, was largely cut off from the rest of the family; and Nandlal Nehru. It was the latter who brought up Motilal. Nandlal entered the service of Khetri, a small Rajput principality, or rather feudatory, in the hills of north Rajasthan. He served there for ten years and, at a young age, rose to be Diwan (i.e. Chief Minister). He then left to study and practise Law at Agra, a new profession resulting from the British bringing in their legal and judicial systems. When the High Court moved from Agra to Allahabad Nandlal moved with it, taking Motilal with him. And so it was that Allahabad became the Nehru home town. Nandlal rose to be one of the leaders of the Bar there.

Motilal, whose education included a good grounding in Persian, Arabic and Urdu, and later in English, studied Law in Kanpur (Cawnpore) and then worked with his guardian brother in Allahabad. Nandlal, however, died suddenly, and, like the father, before his time. Motilal was thus left to make his own way in the world.

He did this triumphantly. Some time after the death of his first wife in child-birth he married Swarup Rani. Their first child died. Jawaharlal—the name means *Red Jewel*—was the second child. An only son of a prosperous father bereaved twice before, and for the first eleven years of his life the only child, he was treasured highly. (Mrs. Pandit was born in 1900, and the third child, Mrs Raja Hutheesingh, in 1909.) Many, including Nehru himself, say that he was spoilt. This is probable; but if so the spoiling excluded any softness.

The family background in general meant in addition to the lavish affection which is common in Indian homes, a big house with ample space and garden and flowers and fruits and horses, which is not common. Contrary to what is often said, Nehru's background was not aristocratic. He himself always spoke of it as middle class; in English terms of that day it would have been upper middle class. His personal standards were aristocratic though he gave his life to destroying one set of conditions, and to creating another set, which could result only in the end of aristocracy. *Anand Bhavan*, Abode of Happiness, seems to have been not an inaccurate name for the Nehru house. It was usually full, in the easy-going hospitable Indian way, with relatives, other Kashmiri Brahmans of distinction, including Sir Tej Bahadur Sapru, and a varied group of Hindus, Muslims and Europeans. Allahabad, an old Mogul city with Hindu origins, still has charm. In Nehru's boyhood it was civilized and urbane as well as tranquil, free of either mobs or factories. Motilal, its head, was by all accounts a man of considerable intellectual force, strong character, handsome presence, vitality and a winning personality, though not of so fine a clay as his son. He was a free thinker, modern and western in outlook, contemptuous of religion in general and of Hinduism in particular, worldly, and a free spender who enjoyed all the fruits of his prosperity. Also, he was given to bouts of temper, which frightened the son, much as the son's bouts of temper frightened people a generation or so later. Jawaharlal always admired his father. The mother was the traditional Hindu lady, with little or no formal education but with the stamp of her Brahman caste on her. Caste in India meant breeding for quality. And no doubt she would have seen to it that the *Tulsi*, the plant sacred to the Hindus, was in the house, that *pujas* were performed, and that Jawaharlal heard about Sangam, Gaya, Muttra, Puri and the other sacred places.

Nehru speaks of a lonely childhood. Whether in this environment it was or was not as lonely as he thought, it is certain that Nehru by nature was lonely, and must always have been lonely. He would probably have been lonely if he had had a brother a year older and another a year younger than himself.

Motilal being the enthusiastic Westernizer which he was in those days, pro-English enthusiasm being not uncommon in India then, the Nehrus lived in the English, not the Indian, style, as regards food, speech and dress; and the Nehru children were educated by English tutors or governesses. Jawaharlal's tutor, called Brooks, was an Anglo-Irishman with some French blood, and seems to have influenced him considerably, notably by giving him a taste for Science, also a taste for Theosophy, and perhaps a taste for anti-imperialism. (Brooks for reasons which have never been established committed suicide later.)[1] At the age of 13 Nehru was initiated into the Theosophical Society, Mrs Besant herself performing the rites. (A few years later, and a thousand miles to the south, in Madras, another Indian destined to

---

[1] I was told suicide by persons who knew the Nehru family in Allahabad, but others say he was drowned accidentally. Cf. Pothan Joseph in *Swarajiya*, April 4, 1964, p. 10.

become well-known in the new Republic of India, Krishna Menon, was inducted into one of the Orders of Theosophy, *The Star of the East*, and put on the habit of the Order. In the case of neither man did the conversion endure.)

Another element in Nehru's upbringing was the 'Islamic flavour'. Nehru speaks of the effect of Munshi Mubarak Ali. But the flavour derives from more than one man. In his childhood and youth Nehru would have seen as much of Urdu-speaking Muslims of education as of Hindus; perhaps more. The governing class in his Province was predominantly Muslim. Urdu, not Hindi, was the maternal language. Yet in temperament Nehru had always been Hindu, not Muslim; while in conscious attitude he tried to be just Indian and to regard being a Hindu or a Muslim first as irrelevant, and then, under the pressure of facts, and so more realistically, as subordinate to being Indian.

In 1905, Nehru, then 15, was taken to England by his father and put in Harrow School. Much has been made by some commentators of the Harrow background but the truth is that Nehru was an outsider there and knew it. His age as well as his race was against him; boys have no peers for conformism. For the first time in his life he felt that he was Indian. Possibly, deep down, unbeknown even to himself, the seeds of his nationalism were planted at Harrow. Two years later, in 1907, he went up to Trinity College, Cambridge, where he read for the Natural Science Tripos, taking it in the Second Class. He seems to have enjoyed Cambridge, and was sensible enough to do what was possible in those days, not to concentrate on mere examinations. He coxed his College boat. After Cambridge he went on to the Inner Temple where he spent two years, also happy, in preparing for the Bar.

After he was called to the Bar, in 1912, he returned to India. He had been away continuously for seven years, at a very impressionable time of life. England had an influence on him, both positive and negative, both for attraction and for repulsion, which never ceased.

Back in India he worked in his father's chambers at Allahabad. When he cared to apply himself he did well enough; but, to his father's disappointment, his heart was never in the Law. The legal background of himself and of the class from which he came, however, has importance. The great majority of the fomenters and leaders of anti-English nationalism were products of that new thing introduced by the British *raj*—the English legal system, including the profitable profession of lawyers. And they showed a brilliant aptitude for using the English law in their cause and for turning it against the English rulers. In 1916, at the age of 26, which was an age well beyond the normal marrying age in those days, he married Kamala Kaul. It was a typical caste marriage, she being of Kashmiri Brahman stock and belonging to Nehru's clan. It was also an arranged marriage. She was 17 at the time. Indira was born in the following year. A son was born in 1927 but died almost immediately. (It was not known until later that Nehru belonged to the Rhesus negative blood group.)

In addition to the difference between them in age and in experience of the world, Kamala had little formal education. The importance of formal education, especially in the case of people marrying within high castes, where racial quality and social solidarity are primordial, has been exaggerated in our days of the neo-literate. The real difficulty in marrying a man like Nehru would arise from the fact that he was already married, and that his first marriage absorbed him entirely. He was married to a cause. The cause was overriding, and it left little or no place for family life or comfort. 'I was', he wrote of himself, 'a most unsatisfactory person to marry.'[1] Sometimes Nehru and Kamala quarrelled; sometimes she was a little frightened. It is characteristic of the frankness and self-criticism which Nehru, for all his reserve and finesse, was capable of, that he should say this. We can add that so fastidious a man would not have failed in delicacy or generosity, and that if his interests were not centred on Kamala they were also not centred on any other woman, or on himself.

Six years after his return to India, and in his twenty-ninth year, he launched himself on his political career. In 1918 he became the secretary of the Home Rule League in Allahabad. This was the moderate movement founded by Mrs Annie Besant which looked to India's remaining a part of the British Empire. In 1919 he started, with money supplied by his father, a newspaper, significantly named *The Independent*; and in 1920 he attended the special session of the Congress at Calcutta held after the Jallianwala Bagh shootings. Henceforth it was Gandhi, not Mrs Besant, whom Nehru followed. In the following year, at the age of 32, he served his first prison sentence.

During the quarter century between then and 1946, when he became Head of the Government of India, Nehru was in the forefront of the Independence movement. He held high office in the Congress during most of this time, and in 1929, and again in 1936 and 1937 (and also, after Independence, in 1946 and 1951–54), he held the highest office, that of President.

He spent over nine years in jail—not continuously but the various terms add up to that figure. It is a measure of his conviction and his purpose that he succeeded in turning his father, Motilal, into an extremist and into renouncing wealth and comfort and the prized English clothes and European associations and into going to prison

[1] *Discovery of India*, pp. 25–30.

for the cause. The imprisonment was humane and civilized; but prison is always prison; as Nehru could scarcely have forgotten when his Government kept Sheikh Abdullah of Kashmir in prison for eleven years—and eleven years continuously.

The young Nehru also joined battle with his fellow Indians. His contact with the Indian masses was so effective that only Gandhi could draw crowds as big as he drew. His effectiveness, united to manifest dedication, made him at a young age one of the topmost leaders. Gandhi encouraged him and supported him. He loved this rich young man who had forsaken all for the poor of India. Yet Nehru had no sympathy for Gandhi's religion, or for any religiousness at all. He never disguised this; more than once he attacked religion bitterly. To the end there was much in Gandhi which remained a puzzle to Nehru. When I asked him about Gandhi and his relations with him, Nehru said that Gandhi had such goodness and such an appeal that one felt that one had to strive to be worthy of it and to do one's best; one still felt this when one differed from him; Gandhi's authority was somehow not lowered by what one felt was a mistaken judgement, for which reason entirely different people felt constrained to bow to his purpose and standards. It is clear that for Nehru Gandhi was not as the scribes but had some authenticity above the merely political. 'The light of our lives', as he said of Gandhi when he announced his assassination. What Nehru felt, and the kind of man Nehru was, came out in the short speech which he broadcast in a broken choking voice that night; with something of the greatness as well as something of the poignancy of Lincoln's speech at Gettysburg.

Nehru had conflicts with other leaders, such as Rajagopalachari, Rajendra Prasad (first President of India), and Patel, over Socialism; with Subas Chandra Bose over the Fascist approach; and with Jinnah over the status of the Muslims. Nehru's contests were always over ideas, never over any personal interests of his own, though he waged them without quarter and provoked a good deal of personal enmity.

Nehru had a vision of India in which getting the British out of it was merely the preliminary stage. What he was concerned with was a modernized India, with an industrialised economy and an egalitarian society. Nationalist leader though he was he hated many of the things which most Hindus hold dear—cow worship, subordinate status for women, temples, sadhus, astrology, and caste. He remained remarkably consistent in these aims, as his *Bunch of Old Letters* shows.

From time to time, he withdrew from political life. That is why Lord Lothian could tell Sir Thomas Jones confidentially in 1936 that

E

'Nehru has probably given up action for philosophic meditation for the rest of his life'.[1]

In addition to his political troubles Nehru also had his fair share of family troubles. His father died in 1931, to his unaffected grief. His wife's health had already caused much anxiety. He spent nearly the whole of 1926 and 1927 in Europe so that she could get treatment for tuberculosis, a fateful malady in the days before antibiotics had been discovered. He used such of the time as he could when in Europe for pursuing his interest in international relations—always a lively interest —and in socialism. He saw such men as Romain Rolland, the French novelist and an authority on Beethoven, who had close relations with Gandhi, and Ernst Toller, the German Communist, later disposed of by the Nazis. He joined up with the *League against Imperialism* and attended its conference at Brussels; and, at the invitation of the Soviet Government, he went to Moscow to attend the tenth anniversary celebrations of the Russian Revolution. He then saw Lenin's corpse, and, in an odd Nehruesque burst of humourless enthusiasm, he wrote of it as having 'a strange beauty . . . even his eye-brows looked peaceful and unclouded'.[2] Eight years later, in 1935, his wife became ill again. She left for Europe by sea. Nehru shortly afterwards joined her, travelling by air, an unusual and daring way of travelling in those days (he had always been an enthusiast for flying; he had tried to persuade his father to let him learn to fly while he was at Cambridge). She died, in Switzerland, in February 1936, twenty years after their marriage. His mother died two years later. His daughter, Indira, who had had a slight respiratory ailment, remained in Europe; she returned to India only in 1940, after the Second World War had broken out. Not long after Indira returned she made a marriage which did not give Nehru satisfaction. Before this the marriage of his younger sister had, according to that lady's unguarded memoirs, given him no satisfaction either.

In 1936 Nehru published his *Autobiography*, dedicated to 'Kamala, who is no more'. It had an immediate success, making Nehru as famous outside of India as he already was inside it. Over twenty printings of it have been sold since then.

Nehru was in Europe again in 1938. That summer, in company with Krishna Menon, he visited Barcelona on the invitation of the Spanish Republican Government then fighting a losing war against Franco. He spent five days there and was with the Republican forces.[3] From Spain

[1] Jones: *A Diary with Letters* p. 177.
[2] Rafiq Zakaria, op. cit. 17.
[3] References will be found in *A Bunch of Old Letters*, p. 300 *et sq.* I was concerned with an anti-Franco group in Catalonia at the time; an Indian

he went to Sudetenland to see for himself what the Nazi claims were worth. By the time the second World War broke out Nehru's interest in fighting against Nazism and Fascism was second only to his interest in getting independence for India. He hoped that the British leaders would offer a political settlement which would make it possible for the Indian Nationalists to join England in fighting Nazism. Linlithgow was wooden enough to declare war without a gesture to them; and Churchill was hostile. Yet, Gandhi having rejected Cripps' Mission in 1942 and having launched the *Quit India* Movement, miscalculating that Japan would defeat England in Asia, Nehru toed the Gandhi line, though after much inner struggle. Rajagopalachari did not. This is one of the least admirable episodes in the life of Gandhi, and one of considerable significance as regards Nehru. He argued and pleaded with Gandhi; he was revolted by the Nationalists who welcomed Axis victories as a stroke against England. Defeating the Axis he saw as a priority just below getting Indian Independence. But in the end, apparently out of loyalty, he bowed to Gandhi. He found himself in prison once more, serving his longest continuous sentence, three years.

Prison life had come hard to a man of Nehru's active nature. During his earlier imprisonments his nerves had been affected. But, being Nehru, he disciplined himself by a régime of physical exercise, mental control, and hard study. Syed Mahmud, an old friend and associate of Nehru and his family, has told me how Nehru shepherded his fellow prisoners, nursed them, cooked for them, taught them to fend for themselves, and kept their spirits up.[1]

It is to his years in prison that we owe his three main books, *Autobiography*, *Glimpses of World History* (1939), and *Discovery of India* (1946). He had already written *India and the World*, *The Unity of India*, *Soviet Russia*, and *Eighteen Months in India*, some of them written partly in prison. In addition, he wrote many letters, examples of which can be seen in *A Bunch of Old Letters* (1958).

Nehru's writings illustrate a cerebral life, and a power of self-discipline, altogether out of the ordinary. Words by the million bubbled up out of his fullness of mind and spirit. Had he never been Prime Minister of India he would have been famous as the author of the *Autobiography* and the autobiographical parts of *The Discovery of India*.

The *Autobiography*, at least with some excisions here and there, is

friend doing medical work for one of the International Brigades and *au fait* with the visit tells me that it was at the request of Nehru that Gandhi wrote to Negrin.

[1] Some account of Syed Mahmud during his student days in England will be found in W. S. Blunt's *Diaries*.

likely to be read for generations. It is a mixed, unevenly written, and occasionally irritating, book; but it is honest and alive and has dimension. Like Nehru himself. It provokes the same variety of reactions in the reader which personal contact with Nehru was apt to provoke; but in both cases favourable reactions usually predominate. There are, for instance, the characteristic touches of truism and anti-climax, strange in a man who could both think and, at his best, write so well; for he wrote (and spoke) better English than most of us born to the language. There are, moreover, the lapses from objectivity, even from common sense. At times, too, there is more liveliness than depth. Nehru's writing lacks the hammer power habitual to Gandhi's or to Rajagopalachari's writing. There is the occasional pointless censoriousness over trifles; not much humour; and a characteristic mingling of personal frankness with personal elusiveness. What the book is especially coloured by is its motivation, namely to get the British out of India, which was the consuming purpose of Nehru's purposeful life. This leads him to set forth history which is distored and occasionally false. Did he really believe that it was the British who, on the principle of Divide and Rule, started, or fomented, Hindu against Muslim and Muslim against Hindu? Or that India was either united or independent before the British came? Or that the British did more harm than good? At times he gets near to hate. And always he is the revolutionary, the extremist, and therefore against the gradualism which the British were offering, and which some Indians were favouring, and against a negotiated settlement.

He is haunted, too, by shame of Indians as well as by love for them. He must have seen something of that India which is revealed in the Courts—for nothing reveals a country, be it India or Russia or America or France, more truthfully than the cases which come up in the Courts—the India of violence, of perjury, of bottomless intrigue. In particular, he is haunted, and shamed, by the poverty of India rather than haunted by compassion for the poor. Here is a difference from Gandhi: The *Autobiography*, in fact, owes as much to Harrow, Cambridge, and the Inner Temple as to India—to the outlook he imbibed in England and Europe as well as to his reactions against England and Europe. A torn troubled spirit.

It paints a portrait, warts and all, of an unusual man and, in the main, of an attractive man, often an unusually attractive man. Three hundred years earlier John Milton was given at Cambridge the soubriquet *the Lady* because of his purity of life and motive. If we can use this old-fashioned word, *purity*, in our advanced times, something of the same quality is apparent in Nehru—never sensual and never unclean. Nehru in his *Autobiography*, as in his life, displays wholesomeness and truthfulness, including the hard truthfulness about himself, as far as he, a man capable of self-criticism, saw it. In addition he displays generally detachment, generally sanity, generally fairplay, and always loyalty, resilience, courage, and dedication to his cause. Wealth, comfort, wordly prospects, family life, were all scarificed to his cause. And furious though his nationalism could become it was usually humanized by, and often subordinate to, internationalism. What he was mostly aiming at was to give Indians both more backbone and less poverty. He wanted to see them walking with their heads up—just as the young men at Harrow and Cambridge did half a century ago. (Those young men lived in a world which knew servants and which did not know an education system dominated by examinations and state scholarships or a social system which absorbed over a third of the national income in taxes.) Moreover, he is divided in himself; as divided about the English as he is about the Indians. The real storms for him were, as he said, the storms that raged within him. This self-contradictoriness can be an awkward quality to the possessor, and was awkward to Nehru the political leader; but it is the quality of the full man: the man who knows that there is more than one side. It is the quality which made him appreciate, even when impatient with, the non-political and internationalist Tagore. Nehru shows, too, the untenability of the proposition that *Never the twain shall meet*; he shows in himself that the best in East and West can be synthesized.

The *Discovery of India* carries the story of Nehru's life a decade further, and contains a good deal of Nehru's reflections on life in general and on India in particular. Its tone is more nationalistic: perhaps a reflection of the long prison sentence. He was also at pains to show that the world is bigger than Europe—a lesson much needed then by Europeans. He had expounded this lesson in *Glimpses of World History*, which is Asia-centred and to some extent a reaction against Europe. Some of its facts have been questioned but the book has Nehru's inimitable quality. It also shows Nehru as the teacher, the Brahman. It is in form a series of letters and lessons to his daughter.

The *Autobiography* was published twenty-eight years ago and *The Discovery of India* eighteen years ago. The facts of the last eighteen years, during which Nehru changed from the role of agitator to the role of ruler, and India went through such experiences as the grant of Independence, the Partition, the migrations and the massacres of the refugees, Gandhi's assassination, and Nehru's long Prime Minister-ship, have yet to be added. Nehru died before he could add any more.

An account of any man is incomplete if it leaves out his immediate family circle, and more particularly the womenfolk in it. Nehru was a lonely man but he was far from a solitary or an unsocial one; and, in any

Chapter 4

PRIME MINISTER OF INDIA

In 1946 Nehru became Head of Government with the title of Vice-President of the Executive Council. Next year, with the departure of Jinnah and his men, Nehru became Prime Minister of India. That was in August 1947. He was 58 at the time.

It is unusual for agitators to be saddled with the responsibility of running a government at this age, after a lifetime of agitation. It is still more unusual for agitators to survive the responsibility for long. Nehru was Head of Government for eighteen years without interruption, a performance exceeded in very few Parliamentary régimes.

So long an unbroken term would be remarkable if it had taken place in an established State, and of normal size, and with nothing much happening. Nehru's Prime Ministership was in a State containing over 350 million people who grew in this period to nearly 500 million, a revolutionary change in itself; and it carried through a series of revolutionary changes of its own devising. Moreover, this was done under the shadow of war, both inside and outside India. During the ten years I was observing India, on the spot or from the outside, there was scarcely a fortnight without a crisis of some sort to worry the Cabinet.

Nehru did not begin his new career auspiciously. Shortly after he took office one of the more pessimistic predictions of British officials came true: the Indian sub-continent did not hold together. The majority of the Muslims broke away and founded the State of Pakistan. The breakaway involved a transfer of population, largely in the form of a wild stampeding of terrified Hindus into India and of terrified Muslims into Pakistan, totalling between 15 and 20 millions.[1] And it

[1] Cf. Sir Penderel Moon: *Divide and Quit*. The author, *quondam* Fellow of All Souls and a member of the ICS, spent 30 years in India, leaving in 1961. His *Strangers in India*, 1944, is acutely observant and shows where the British raj was lacking. Also see Michael Edwardes: *The Last Years of British India*; dedicated "to the men, women and children murdered in the fields and streets of India who though they did not fight for their country's freedom paid for it with their lives".

involved massacres, of an unknown number but running into hundreds of thousands, on a scale of butchery, on both sides, which were bound to have left Nehru with broken hopes about the inhabitants of the Indian sub-continent and with shaken confidence in his old speeches on the theme of the British-made artificiality of Hindu–Muslim communalism. This breakaway of Pakistan, moreover, did not solve the Muslim problem for India because about 50 million Muslims remained, or were stranded, in India. Some millions of Hindus remained, or were stranded, in Pakistan.

In addition to having to settle millions of refugees, Nehru and the successive Governments he headed had to deal with the creation of the Republic of India (during the first three years of its Independence India was a British Dominion); with integrating over 600 Princely States into the Republic; a feat engineered by Patel which was comparable with Bismarck's integration of Germany or Cavour's integration of Italy; with working out a Constitution, including, in particular, with seeing that the Republic was made a secular, not a Hindu, State; with organizing and carrying out General Elections covering 150 to 210 million voters, in 1952, in 1957, and in 1962; another remarkable feat, as the elections were both efficient and fair; with drawing and re-drawing the boundaries of the States; with working out Plans for economic development; with working out social legislation, often bitterly resisted, dealing with women's rights, children's protection, education, outcastes, and the non-Hindu tribes; with coping with crop failures and famine; with coping with the population explosion; and, finally, with working out and executing a foreign policy.

No man could run a Government for so long, or deal with such a range of problems, without incurring criticism. Indians of the highest standing, including those with long and high office in the Independence movement, such as Rajagopalachari, President Rajendra Prasad, and Kripalani, deplored Nehru's policies increasingly in the last five or six years of his Prime Ministership. The press, for so long so docile, indeed in the first half of his Prime Ministership so sycophantic, had by the end of the 'Fifties become more and more critical.

Internal Affairs

We will now look at his performance, and we will begin with what he did inside India.

His first concern was to see that India did not fall apart. To this end he encouraged a nationalism which would make Indians feel that they were Indians instead of feeling that they were Tamils or Punjabis or Dogras or Assamese or Brahmans or Kshatriyas or this or that caste, as they are apt. He gave special consideration to the Muslims so as to induce them to feel Indian. For the same reason Christians and other minorities could always be sure of Nehru's unflinching protection. The 'Secular State', that is to say a non-Hindu and all-Indian State, was fundamental to this concern.

His second concern was to modernize India in the way he had long dreamed of—change the *status of women and Outcastes; Industrialization; Socialism; Planning;* and *Parliamentary Democracy.* India, it must be repeated, was still mainly a status society, having little in common with the money-nexus society.

Nehru, it is said by Indians who have known him well, was a man of *voltes faces:* he could change overnight. This seems to be true as regards particulars and perhaps as regards a few big things, such as the policy of dividing India into States according to their languages, a policy which was thought to be dangerous for Indian unity but which he accepted precipitately in 1953. Yet, and this is the point to be emphasized, a comparison of Nehru's letters and speeches in the 'thirties, while he was still an agitator, with what he said and did as Prime Minister, shows that what is remarkable has been his consistency, above all as regards economic and social policy.

For Nehru nationalism, as has been seen, was largely a preliminary step to the major step, which was to modernize India, and, especially, to bring in socialism. Nehru's socialism had been held with such conviction that he would have been a Communist were it not for the rigid dogmatism on the one part—his favourite taunt to the Communists was that they were old-fashioned and out of date—and the mixture of coercion and violence on the other which go, or which have gone, with the Communist's sort of socialism. For Nehru the end rarely justified the means. A Minister in Nehru's Cabinet once said to me, 'What the Americans'—this was in the days of Dulles when some Americans thought, and one of Dulles' Ambassadors was known to have said, and had no doubt reported to Washington, that Nehru was a crypto-communist—'What the Americans don't see is that Nehru is the last of the Liberals.' How much Nehru was misunderstood about Communism was shown in the idiotic rumours current in some quarters in the early 'fifties that he was secretly supplying arms to the Chinese Communists over the new Indian road into Kashmir. In Nehru's make-up there was a strong strain of what passed for Marxism in the 'twenties and 'thirties, but a still stronger strain of nineteenth century humanistic liberalism which in turn had been influenced by the Christian Socialists. It was this strain in him which made him almost excitedly appreciative of the Encyclical *Pacem in Terris* of Pope John XXIII. What fired Nehru was that men and women could be and should be given opportunities for living better lives and, in particular, should be spared avoidable ills. His political ideas, including his version of Marxism, were nearly all derived from English sources. Also, like so many Indians, he shared with the English the pragmatic, instead of the doctrinal, approach. In particular he was too much of the Western humanist ever to reconcile himself to any Communist requirement of giving up freedom of thought.

On the other hand, just as Nehru was never taken in by the dogmas of Communists so too he had never been taken in by clichés against Communism, such as those which were supreme during the Dulles years and were associated with 'The Free World', 'the free men', 'monoliths', and so on. He, like Pope John, rejected the Communist system but not Communist men. Nor could he ever overlook the fact, which is still overlooked too often in the West, that when poverty is so great that millions of men count themselves fortunate if they get two poor meals a day, the quickest way to achieve economic development is by Communism; that is to say, by totalitarian planning and by totalitarian mobilization of resources. About 100 million men in India are partly if not wholly unemployed, just sitting about in idleness, their massive capital and productive value unutilized. It is also overlooked in the West that in backward societies Communism is the transmitter of certain important Western values: thus it suppresses polygamy and other aspects of the servile status of women, astrology, beggars, illiteracy, and exploiting priest-craft. Given Nehru's feelings on these things, as also his feelings on poverty, and given his appreciation for people like Aruna Asaf Ali, it says much for the strength of his liberal humanism that he had foregone the temptations of taking the Communist's short cut. Further, it is overlooked in the West that indiscipline can reach the point where Communism becomes the counter-Revolution.

In latter years Nehru's time and energy were taken up more and more with just running the apparatus of government, and less and less with initiating new policies or with testing or developing those already adopted. Few Ministers in any Government have the intellectual or nervous energy to master the details or to grasp the full operation of their Ministry. Nehru had this energy; but more and more his old pioneering drive was lost in the routine job of keeping a very large and complicated machine in action, of keeping his Party in control, and of keeping himself in control of his Party. He could not do much more than get from one crisis to another. This politician work made ever heavier demands on his time; and it also had a good deal to do with his supporting, or conniving at, Ministers who were notoriously corrupt and at times got near to gangsterism.

Achievements

An undoubted achievement of the Government headed by Nehru—until his last four years or so he was so much the head as to be *the* Government—was to hold India together. Eighty million Muslims were lost and formed Pakistan; but the rest of India, now running into nearly 500 million people, with fourteen different official languages and many others spoken which have no official status, is a going concern. This is comparable to running Europe as a single political entity; and it remains an achievement to Nehru's credit even though it was the British who created India as a single political entity and even though their creation was not seriously threatened during Nehru's Prime Ministership. Nehru's fight to keep the English language, though he wobbled on the matter in his last weary years, was due to his understanding of the unifying force of English in India over and above the intellectual and international advantages which English gave to India.

His next achievement was to encourage the growth of the parliamentary and cabinet system which the British started in India. He made it work; and he also made the majority of Indian politicians in his time want to make it work. Moreover, he maintained his own leadership by democratic means. Over and over again Nehru demonstrated that he had no equal, let alone superior, in the game of parliamentary politics in India. In his latter years he was living too much on his wits; but what wits they were, and what political wits! However much of myth or magic there might have been in Nehru's prestige with the masses there could be no doubt about the reality of the weapons in his politician's armoury. Thus he usually displayed the acutest sense of timing. It was displayed brilliantly in the debates on the Sino-Indian Border affair in 1959–60; an affair which would have destroyed almost any other Prime Minister in any other country; and again in getting rid of S. K. Patil and Morarji Desai and other Ministers through the so-called Kamaraj Plan in 1963. Thanks to his timing, combined with his fighting courage and his agility of mind, Nehru dominated Parliament even when the majority were critical and, in the last years, in their moods of disillusionment, actively hostile. Further, he had resilience in uncommon measure. Again and again I have seen him so tired and worn that I thought the beginning of the end was in sight; then, a couple of days later, I have run into him and found him looking as though nothing had happened. Even disloyalty of the ominous kind, such as President Prasad's kite-flying speech on the President's powers in 1960, or the same President's opposition, not always above board, to Nehru's social policies, seemed to leave Nehru unshaken. (He defeated Prasad's moves by astute moves of his own, including spells of silence and then referring the memorandum on the President's powers, which he lured Prasad into writing, to a technical group for a report on it. Their report in effect killed the President's pretensions.) So with disloyalty and ingratitude from other quarters. Finally, Nehru countered any Indian tendency to fly to extremes. He was nearly always the moderator and the conciliator, seeking out how to smooth away and not to ruffle the prickles among his colleagues. He had learnt, though not easily, that the first rule in politics is to suffer both fools and self-seekers gladly. And he had learnt another lesson, namely when he must bow to opposition and to retreat.

His third achievement was the modernizing of India—making it a secular State, free to all religions and to atheism; piloting through a variety of social reforms, notably the legal changes on behalf of women's rights as against Hindu orthodoxy; and, as the basis of the great revolution he wanted to bring about, the three Five-Year Plans.

The Plans

The Five-Year Plans aimed at raising the standard of living by modernization in general and by industrialization in particular, and by setting down what Nehru called, with a vagueness typical of his pragmatism but prudent under the circumstances, 'a socialist pattern of society'.

Nehru had long been interested in planning. Before the War he insisted on trying to interest Congress in it. He got little support except from the left-wing group which later formed the spearhead of the Communist movement in India. When he became Prime Minister he gave the Plans the highest priority, and members of the Planning Commission the rank of Cabinet Ministers with himself as the Chairman. A large secretariat was set up.

The Plans run into thousands of pages and were being enlarged continuously. They began in 1951; the Third Five-Year Plan finishes in 1966.

Their main emphasis was on investment for capital formation, and especially for heavy industry and its subsidiaries. They could be carried through only by reducing popular consumption, low as this already was, in order to put savings into hydro-electric schemes, steel plants, factories, and so on. The promised rise in the standard of living was therefore for the future, not for this generation.

As home savings could not be enough for the great size of the Plans, Aid had to be got from the foreigner. The degree of financial dependence on the foreigner was (and remains) another major characteristic of the Plans. This had gone so far that by 1963 even essential imports were dependent on the bounty of the foreigner. Hence Indian efforts to get Aid in cash (preferably) or in goods untied to any specific project. By the end of 1960 India had already received Rs 18,000 million in the shape of loans and Rs 6,000 million in the shape of grants. In the first half of the 'sixties the required figure was estimated to be not less than £12,000 million. The Aid-India Consortium has been raising over $1,000 million a year in recent years. Yet India's unfavourable balance of payments continued to get more and more unfavourable. The fruition of the Plans will in fact depend upon the willingness of the foreigner to go on pouring in Aid. India at times had been using the Cold War, much as she attacked the Cold War as an institution, for getting both sides to give her Aid, though usually she had no need to do this as she could count on both sides playing against each other, the East against the West and the West against the East. The US and other Western Powers committed themselves to a heavy load of Aid as an insurance against Communism in India; risky insurance to say the least, even if Communism has any solid prospects in India; and in any case the foreign aid will probably have slight effect on Communism, one way or the other. They have in effect underwritten India's Planning Programme. Lovers of India hope they will continue to do so; but in such a way as to avoid taking on a bottomless pit. India was well aware of the emotional compulsions behind the West's interest in her Plans, and, at least until the defeat inflicted on her troops by the Chinese in 1962, not a few Indians were secretly rather contemptuous of them—of the West's fear of Communism. Indian leaders cannot be blamed for taking advantage of these compulsions. There was not much inhibition about asking for aid; and, according to some critics, not much gratitude. A frequent note was: Aid should be bigger. Will India be able to retain complete independence under these circumstances? The independence of the foodless or the heavily mortgaged debtor is normally precarious. Or will the future see some saviour of the people, some Indian Sukarno, rising in India to agitate for the repudiation of the huge foreign debt, in the name of breaking the neo-colonial yoke?

Meanwhile inflation has been playing its usual baneful role of social damage; for 'deficit financing', the contemporary euphemism for falling back on the printing press for money, became an accepted part of the Plans in Nehru's time. Prices nearly doubled during the time I was in India. They are still rising. Taxation has gone up even higher. The land-owning classes have been obliterated; peasants cannot own more than about 30 acres of land; even this figure might be reduced, thanks to the land ceiling legislation, which is some of the most ill-considered and merely emotional or merely political legislation of post-Independence India. (The abolition of landlords not only infringed the property rights promised by the Constitution but, combined with the land ceiling legislation, has deprived the Indian village and countryside of the class which, alone living above the animal subsistence level, could aid rural civilization and at the same time could afford to experiment in farming and to improve its techniques.) Further, the professional and middle class, already ground down by taxation and by premature social legislation and trade union restrictiveness as well as by inflation, sink lower in the economic scale. The classes which have benefited most have been the speculators, the urban developers, and, above all, the Baniya and Mawari magnates, perhaps the vilest money-making group on earth. The outcastes in the urban areas have also benefited. Government, if the Parliamentary régime holds, will, it must be remembered, depend upon the votes of the majority cast in secret ballot boxes. The majority are the very needy; besides being ignorant they are not likely to take the forward-looking public-spirited view. Once they discover their power, the discovery being made for them by politicians seeking their votes, the damaging process will be accelerated.

State intervention, too, grew apace under Nehru's Plans. Permits, licences, controls, foreign exchange prohibitions, were always increasing. With them corruption increased too. A good deal of State regulation is no doubt unavoidable under the circumstances of the time; but as regulations and the bureaucracy multiply so too does the freedom of the individual diminish. In the end, with 'the revolution of rising expectations' amongst the urban proletariat well under way, the frail structure of democracy will risk being crushed by a dictatorship or an oligarchy.

As for what the Plans will achieve, they will no doubt achieve— they already are achieving—some industrialisation, and some increase in irrigation. This fact remains though some of the industrialization will be expensive for what it returns, and inefficient as well as jerrybuilt. Industry in India is high-cost; reports have recently been published showing average factory costs at 40 per cent above British and still more above American costs. What the Plans will assuredly achieve is to bring about still bigger cities, and with bigger slums; Calcutta, for instance, conceivably growing from 6 million to 15 million. Planners never seem to think about planning cities. In some places or sectors the Plans might even raise the standard of living a little. And they have had the effect of increasing the power of the Centre over the States and to that extent they have been a factor for cementing India together—assuming, what is not certain, that it is a good thing for India to be a union instead of a federation.

But agriculture, and the whole process of producing food for the millions, showed little advance. Before long there will be no escape from giving them the overriding priority which the Plans in Nehru's time failed to give. The parlous food position in India, including the low, and still falling, yield per acre, was concealed, purposely but dangerously concealed for years by some of the Ministers concerned, through the millions of tons of free or dumped food from the United States; for which reason the long-term effects of PL480 could be bad for India both as regards inflation and as regards the agricultural output. The latter remained about stationary for the last four or five years of Nehru's life. Though an urgent need, and obvious from the time of the Bengal Famine in the 'forties, there was still no proper granary or storage system in Nehru's time. Famine thus followed glut, and the grain speculators and hoarders flourished.

For the Five-Year Plans reflect the urban mind. Nehru, like most Indian politicians, was urban. Outside of their towns the politicians are like fish out of water. This is why agriculture, though given thousands of pages, millions of words, and various huge schemes, such as *Community Development* or the *Grow More Food Campaign*, was not given enough effective action; and why thought and money could be spent instead on plans for a People's Car, India-made jet planes, and so on. Since 80 per cent of Indians live in villages and depend, directly or indirectly, on agriculture, the case for basing the whole planning effort on the villages, and for building up from that base, instead of on heavy industry and the like, was overwhelming. This is what Gandhi would have done. But of no country is it so true as of India that the nearer one gets to the Capital the further one gets from the realities. The majority of villagers after more than a decade of the Plans, and of the publicity for them, knew little about them. And it is certain that over most of India the low standard of living in the villages has not risen, over much of India it has fallen, in the last ten years.[1] Socialist governments, notoriously, run into difficulties over food production; as Communist China did in recent years, and as Soviet Russia has been doing even 40 odd years after the Revolution.

Mechanization, moreover, will not lessen unemployment. It is

---

[1] The Mahalanobis Committee report on Distribution of Income was symptomatic of the malaise in the Planning. The Committee, consisting of 3 senior Civil Servants and 5 Economists under the Chairmanship of the Central Statistical Institute, was appointed in 1960 with the motive to produce data showing an increase in wealth. It took three and half years to produce a few uncoordinated trifles, and some figures which disproved any appreciable rise in income throughout the nation but proved that the middle groups were worse off, as also the agricultural workers. Some of the worst sycophants and talkers connected with the Plans were on the Committee.

bound to increase it, at least for a generation or so. Already there are probably more than 20 million fully unemployed, and perhaps as many as another 80 million partially unemployed, in India.

Finally, can Indians with their genius for verbal fluency as contrasted with executive ability, and with their penchant for dilatory lolling, organize or carry through huge economic changes under an easy-going Parliamentary system at this stage in their development? Have they trained up enough Managers—in the way the British, trained up enough Indian administrators for the needs of their time? Is there enough of the executive's temperament or art yet?

As for the Nehru Plans considered specifically, and apart from the general strategy, they run into hundreds of different projects, ranging from small technical schools to big hydro-electric schemes, but they have tended to be too imprecise in priorities or aims; too lacking in a groundwork of solid intellectual and then solid technical preparation; too much slanted towards big schemes as well as too much slanted towards industrialization and non-agricultural development; too much intruding of politicians' interests (a road or bridge or school in this constituency, a railway in that, harbour works here, this or that factory there); too much defectiveness in execution so that there has been a shortfall as regards many, perhaps most, targets, and virtual failure as regards some like the huge Damodar Valley Scheme; and too much propaganda of the extravagant kind while at the same time too many of the country people were either ignorant of the Plans or felt no personal involvement in them. Amongst other things it should have been explained to the people why controls were unavoidable—as some undoubtedly are—and why consumer goods must be sacrificed in the interests of future well-being.

It is hard to escape the fear that the main achievement of Nehru's economic and social policy will turn out to be social disruption; and that this will break out into violence, thanks on the one hand to the legacy of violence from the days of Nationalist agitation, and, on the other, to the vast mass of detribalised neo-literates being turned out in the post-Independence schools. For in the haste to modernize, Universities and University students have been multiplied, with the result that there is an inflation in educational standards, which have become as diluted as the money. Moreover, there are not enough jobs for the graduates. The same is true of the schools and the school matriculates. India has thus acquired some of the essential ingredients of the classical prescription for Communism.

It is certain that Nehru had no wish to pave the way for Communism. But it is equally certain that he, like many Indians in authority at the time, shared the illusions which flourished in the West from the time

of President Truman's famous *Point Four* speech in the late 'forties
about the relative ease of developing undeveloped or under-developed
economies, and about the potential role of foreign aid in this trans-
formation. It was not seen that the gap in economic productivity is a
gap in total or general historical development, and that a gap of
centuries cannot be bridged in a few years, however beguiling the
phrases about 'the take off', 'know-how', landlords, or reactionaries.
A great part of foreign aid in most recipient countries has so far been a
waste; and inevitably.

Two defences could be pleaded on behalf of Nehru's Plans.

The first defence would be the poverty of India. This is so great
that something must be attempted to alleviate it.[1] If the European
visitor looks over Calcutta and the poverty there he will feel that
Europe's problems of poverty or shortages are so trifling in comparison that they no longer rate as problems. For all but a fraction of
Indians the food is vegetarian, and for a very large proportion it
consists of the cheap coarse grains. The sanitation and comfort we
take for granted for our poorest is for only a minority in India. And
with an absence of sufficiency goes a level of health below par. Accord-
to recent FAO publications the annual *per caput* income of the United
States is 2,164 dollars, of the United Kingdom 960, of Japan 250, of
India only 60; the daily consumption of animal protein is 66 grams
in the United States, 51 in the United Kingdom, 15 in Japan, and 6 in
India. Statistics of this sort must be taken with a grain of salt,[2] but
other indications of the poverty could be multiplied. In Calcutta, for
instance, according to a semi-official survey made in 1961, 17 per cent
of the population have no living accommodation of any kind; they live
on the street pavements; 30 per cent live three families to a room,
33 per cent live one family to one room, only 4 per cent live one family
to three rooms; or, to take lavatory facilities, 15 per cent have none at
all, 4 per cent have one lavatory to 100 families, only 9 per cent have
one lavatory per family; 70 per cent share one lavatory for 10 to 100

[1] Cf. reactions to the poverty from Western literary visitors, e.g. John
Wain in *Encounter*, 1961, or V. S. Naipaul, the Trinidad novelist, in *An Area
of Darkness*. He comes from a family which is U.P. Brahman by origin. Not
long after I arrived in Delhi I once had occasion to go unexpectedly to the Chancery
about midnight. I discovered that the gardener, who had no other dwelling,
was sleeping in the library and with him were two still poorer relations or
friends one of whom, having no blanket, was wrapped up in the big Australian
flag which we flew in the day-time.
[2] When statistics are cited in this book they are meant to show trends not
to state facts precisely. Even in the most highly organized countries statistics
on Income, the National Product, Price Movements, Foreign Trade, etc., are
subject to wide margins of error. Cf. Oskar Morgenstern *On the Accuracy of
Economic Observations*, Princeton, 1964.

families. Poverty in India is so great that millions are reduced to an animal level.

The second defence which could be pleaded on Nehru's behalf is the population problem. This is the first problem in India, and the gravest by far. Since I went to India early in 1952 the population has increased by about 100 million. These are figures of doom. The population problem, like some other real and concrete problems, was lost sight of for three decades during the euphoric agitation against the British *raj*. The urgency of the need for increasing food production cannot be much longer evaded; still less can the urgency of the need for slowing down the rate of population growth. The Birth Rate is high, but the new and explosive factor is the fall in the Death Rate. As a result the life expectancy has risen from 26 years in 1940 to 41 years now. Although there are few religious or social inhibitions against family planning, the efforts, organized by the Government itself, to spread it have so far won few adherents. Indifference is the cause. The indifference is due in part to lack of education, but only in part. Indians amount to a seventh of the human race. Their numbers are swollen each year by 12–15 million. About 20 per cent of the population in most villages is already surplus—no work for them to do as well as too little food for them. At current rates of growth the population will have grown to about 1,000 millions by the end of the century. Apart from the wastage of human life and spirit involved in this pullulation, it makes the Plans, whatever their merits or demerits, futile. The increase of wealth cannot catch up with the increase of mouths. The statistics collected by the Central Statistical Institute leave little doubt that population has grown faster than the net economic growth achieved by the Plans. The disparity may be as great as 2·5 per cent for population growth to 1·6 per cent for net economic growth. Indeed there will soon be a problem not only to feed the millions but to get enough water for them. Much of the wild life in India will disappear under the rising tide of human beings. And the immense social disarray caused by the population explosion, and exacerbated by well-meaning economic and social legislation of the Nehru years, predisposes to the short-cut of dictatorship.

Can effective alleviation of these two root material problems of India, Poverty and Over-population, which Nehru wished to give, be given, without totalitarian methods?

I am omitting any discussion of the case for industrializing Indian from the point of view of defence needs in a world of Power Politics for I think Nehru was not much concerned with them when launching the Plans. It is probable that in latter years they did come to count. These needs indeed will confront India with terrible dilemmas, especially if the new nuclear weapons proliferate and the world does not acquire a stable balance of power.

What was wrong with Nehru's Plans is that on the one hand they were not big enough, not drastic enough, to produce a significant rise in the standard of living or a real dynamic of change; but, on the other, they were big and drastic enough to bring in disarrangement, and, in particular, to eat into India's greatest wealth: the traditional spirit of contentment of the Indian people, the capacity to put up with life, the capacity to suffer, even hunger itself. So far the Plans, together with Congress Party political promises over the years, have made Indians unwilling to accept hunger as they did over the past centuries; but they have not produced the wherewithal to alleviate hunger. The Marxist and the liberal strains in Nehru remained muddled and were not worked out into a functioning synthesis.

How much did Nehru go astray over the Plans through his alienation from traditional India and more particularly through his love of machines? He loved machines as the expression of man's mastering of Nature. He was too observant not to be aware of certain dangers going with mechanization. I have heard him say that the machine way of life is likely to turn men more and more into robots; the vision of a world of steel and concrete and glass and the hygienic but bored millions carrying on their automated lives did not escape him. He was in two minds about TV for India. And latterly he did some speaking up for decentralization. I have also heard him on some of the inevitable effects of government by parliaments elected by majority vote, about which he also had no illusions. Yet his enthusiasm for, getting close at times to a mystic adoration of, the machine remained. Hence his dithyrambic praise of the first Indian jet planes as 'gazelles of the sky', or of hydroelectric plants and factories as 'the temples of our age'; or his enthusiasm for the architect Le Corbusier, who was the senior planner of the new Indian city of Chandigarh, that emblematic creature of modern noise and tension and ferro-concrete to whom a fitting memorial stands in the High Court Building until the discontented Judges refuse to use it any more. The Plans, the result of Nehru's values and drive, were to a large degree wrongly conceived—too imitative of America on the one hand and of Russia on the other; not sufficiently indigenously Indian.

Gandhi knew that instead of machines enabling men to master Nature they are more likely to master men; what the motor car is now doing is a reminder for us; and he knew that Nehru took too little account of this. He once wrote to him:

'Though I was beginning to detect some differences in viewpoint between you and me, I had no notion whatever of the terrible extent of these differences. I see quite clearly that you must carry on an open warfare against me and my views. The differences between you and me appear to be so vast and so radical that there seems to be no meeting ground. I suggest a dignified way of unfurling your flag.'[1]

Gandhi had his fads, he could carry subtlety to the point to trickiness, and he accepted hospitality from Mawari plutocrats like the Birlas. But Gandhi knew that there are worse evils than poverty.

Nehru was right in wanting to plan; and the case for some industrialization, as also for some socialism, was strong. But he cannot be acquitted of at least some superficiality; and this, as not infrequently happens in political decisions, led to pseudo-solutions rather than to solutions. The ultimate practical question confronting the rulers of India was not Industrialization versus Non-industrialization but how much could be spared out of India's scarce resources for industrialization after providing for proper food supplies or a proper basis. The superficiality had been made the worse by the intellectual arrogance which marked his first (and most powerful) decade as Prime Minister. He ridiculed criticism of the Plans; for instance when Sucheta Kripalani criticized his vague scheme for Co-operative Farming in 1958. And so he swung from one enthusiasm to another, such as Big Hydro-electric Dams, Land Ceilings, Grow More Food Campaigns, Co-operative Farming, Steel Plants, the 30,000 acre farm at Suratgarh ('the biggest farm in Asia'), and from one magician to another who promised to produce quick answers. Nehru was superficial mostly because he was in too much of a hurry; in a tempestuous hurry to set India irrevocably on the road to industrialization and socialism before he left the scene.

But if all the facts were known a major responsibility for the failures in the Plans would, after the population explosion, lie on the sycophants who surrounded him. The Planning Commission, or certain influential Members (for there were others who were both disinterested and able), took up his ideas, or enthusiasms, or prejudices, with the servility of lackeys. Throughout the 'fifties neither the Congress Party nor Parliament nor Cabinet had the courage to controvert Nehru, not even on his enthusiasm (short-lived) for Co-operative Farming, which, if it meant anything, meant Russian-type Collective Farms. Such was the sycophancy that a senior Departmental official of my acquaintance, whose Minister had announced again and again that India was about to become self-sufficient in food, but who himself believed that it would take 15 years at the earliest for the Plans to achieve this self-sufficiency, when chided about his Minister's misleading optimism, replied, 'How can I tell my Minister that we will

[1] Quoted by Rajagopalachari in *Swarajya*. August 1961.

not be self-sufficient next year? It is politically impossible.' A long series of eminent or allegedly expert foreign visitors, most of them in India at the cost of the Indian or other taxpayers, added to Nehru's myopia by assuring him that the Plans were good and realistic. Almost any visitor, with or without any relevant competence, just above the tourist level could be sure to be written up in the Indian press if he praised the Plans; rather in the same way as any visitor to Australia can be written up in the Australian press if he announces that the future of wool is secure. Month after month over the years some foreign visitor would be praising the Plans. I remember after a visit of some international banking magnates, in India for only a few days, the gleeful satisfaction with which Nehru told me that they had praised the Plans and said that they were not at all too ambitious. That was two or three years before his death. As late as December 1963 he told Parliament that the Plans were without parallel anywhere.

Rajagopalachari's attacks on Nehru's economic and social philosophy annoyed Nehru considerably. To a foreign observer valuing both men, and loving India, much of what Rajagopalachari was saying was more than telling. It was the truth. Yet, such is the intractability of Indian poverty and over-population that Rajagopalachari failed to establish convincing solutions for the problem as a whole. And for how long could India withdraw into Indian-ness? Whatever his mistakes it can be said for Nehru that he did try to find solutions in terms of the modern world.

Parliamentary Democracy

After planning for industrialization and socialism Nehru's next great concern was to set India off securely on the road to Parliamentary Democracy.

Is India after Nehru's disappearance likely to retain such degree of Parliamentary Democracy as she achieved under him? It is enough to say here that although India is the only Parliamentary Democracy functioning in the whole area lying between the Far East and Western Europe, its future is not assured. There might be a Hindu *raj*, fascist in shape; as would be the case if the Hindu revivalist movement triumphed, a prospect which haunted Nehru like a recurrent nightmare. There might be a Communist type of dictatorship. There might be a military dictatorship. There might be a characteristically Indian amalgam of all three. India's genius for survival would make it possible for her to combine what we would regard as incompatibles. This amalgam could prevail over India as a whole; or there could be a confederation with a Fascist-type of dictatorship in some regions, Communist-type dictatorships in other regions, and military dictatorships in others, and perhaps even parliamentary democracy in others. Much variety is possible among 500 to 1,000 million Indians. All one can be certain of is unsettlement—the unsettlement caused by the millions of children now at school and college who when they leave will see themselves as too good for the work and station of their illiterate parents and whose vision of the life they want will be coloured by the cinema, but who will be unable to get jobs. Here is the ready-made market for mass-circulation papers or for subversive tracts; politicians buying votes with the promise of plenty and a good time; essentials out-stripped by ever-rising population; millions of unemployed; continual inflation; the popular press buying circulation through playing on hatreds and irrationality; and the outcastes and the low castes—the majority—discovering their power in the secret ballot box.

Two factors working for dictatorship, and for the discipline which goes with dictatorship, be it Fascist, or Communist, or military, have to be borne in mind. They have a bearing on the shortfalls in Nehru's Plans, too. One is the slap-dash inefficiency universal in India: engine drivers and railway employees who incur serious accidents by not bothering to carry out the elementary precautions, doctors and nurses who don't bother with elementary hygiene or the right medicines, and so on endlessly. The other is the corruption, equally universal in India; as endemic as dysentery or malaria. The British *raj* held it in hand but could never eradicate it. It has swollen to vast proportions since Independence, and especially, as has been said, since the Plans introduced a network of licences, permits, and protectionism.

And what hurts the average man more than the corruption, which in any case is most Asian countries accepted as unavoidable, like bad weather, is the law and order situation. Banditry, crime, and personal violence are, to say the least, not on the decrease.

But there is another side to the picture—and this is the case for optimism—devoted officials; much ability; a temperamental preference for what is moderate and sane; and that remarkable capacity for surviving already noted. Those who know India well mostly feel that somehow, and in the end, and despite all the signs to the contrary, and all the strains on stability, she will come through and will remain more or less what she is now, namely the Parliamentary Democracy which Nehru left behind him. The Indians share with the British a long-term preference for the middle of the road.

An incidental point is worth touching on here, and that is that friends as well as enemies used to complain that government in India was bad or deteriorating because, amongst other reasons, Nehru was no administrator. Only a senior official inside the Cabinet secretariat or the External Affairs Ministry could speak with authority on this. What is true is that Nehru did not husband his time well, being too generous with it, for instance in receiving foreign visitors who would not be received by their Mayor, let alone their Prime Minister, in their own countries;[1] and perhaps, too, in making too many speeches and too many public appearances, though this seems to be an unavoidable part of the process of leadership in a parliamentary democracy. But there is no Cabinet Minister known to me in any country I have served in who was more orderly, and more insistent on seeing a process through from the talking stage to the practical stage, than Nehru. The leader of the Socialist Party once commended to his Party the example set by Nehru in dealing with correspondence promptly. 'You will always get a reply from him within 48 hours.'[2] This was common knowledge in Delhi. Nehru was not one of those Ministers who have a safe full of awkward 'pending papers'.

On the other hand, his administrative work did suffer from defective judgement of men, and sometimes of things; and also from a failure to delegate work and responsibility. He was, of course, far from being the only Prime Minister of whom these things, especially the former, could be said. He undoubtedly had too much to do, as well as wasting too much time in seeing too many people and in attending too many merely formal ceremonies. As a result, especially in his later years, he could not read essential papers, or master essential details, or get time for reflection.[3] This increased his superficiality and also his predisposition to be taken in by plausible talkers. But he was genuinely a practitioner as well as a believer in efficient administration no less than in Democracy.

Democracy is a tender plant in the Indian soil and though the smooth change-over from Nehru to his successor was a good omen there should be no illusions about its fragility. He cherished Democracy and nurtured it; yet he did one great disservice to it. This was

---

[1] Like most Ambassadors in Delhi, anxious to save Nehru from touring nationals who could have no claim on his time, such as minor politicians and academics and even teenagers winning some commercial travel raffle or other, I have declined their request to ask Nehru for an interview for them only to discover later that they had gone to his office or house and had somehow got in to see him. His senior officials, waiting for hours, or even days, to see him, complained bitterly of this practice of his.

[2] Press, January 22, 1961.

[3] Cf. his statement of August 27, 1961, on 'the overwhelming number of engagements' he had to fulfil, leaving him hardly any time for solid work. 'My work, many people seem to think, should be full of laying foundation-stones, opening buildings, attending celebrations and so on. VIPs who come here take a lot of time. I have to attend banquets and lunches and civic receptions. All this hardly leaves any time for solid work.' He added that he was becoming reluctant to accept any engagements. This reluctance did not triumph!

that he held so many offices, and, especially, that he held on to the office of Prime Minister for so long.

There is a great deal of ability available in India, some courage, and a widespread desire amongst politically-minded Indians, that is to say largely the literate and largely the English-speaking minority, to carry on with the present parliamentary régime. India is no Indonesia. It is therefore strange that Nehru, who was given his chance by Gandhi while he was still in his thirties, and whose mistakes were covered up again and again by his elders—he 'began at a high level on the ladder', as he told one of his biographers[1]—did not consciously gather around him a band of younger men, including from that *corps d'élite*, the ICS, men already adopt in the techniques of modern government, who could be counted on for carrying on the torch after he went. It was much more than a matter of his selecting or foreshadowing his successor; there was much (but not everything) to be said in excuse of his reluctance to have a Dauphin. The case of Smuts is not irrelevant. For forty years Smuts was a name to reckon with outside South Africa as well as in it. But Smuts had trained up no band of assured potential successors of the quality required. Today most of the things Smuts stood for are in ruins. It is no less strange that Nehru clung to office for so long. It would have been of help to the cause of Parliamentary Democracy in India if he had stood down and let the confusion inevitable on his withdrawal from the scene take place in his own life-time, and while he was still in good health, so that he was at hand to steady the ship of state if the weather became too rough. This is what Kemal Ataturk did. Further, his very domination had so many elements of dictatorship, unintended, or even disliked, by Nehru though they were, that it militated against the Parliamentary Democracy sending down as deep roots as it could have under his protection. He would never have truck with ideas of dictatorship in any form, but he did have a strong strain of the authoritarian in him. For one thing his long domination sapped the Opposition; the Opposition is an essential part of Parliamentary Democracy. For another, he kept too much power in his own hands, and so in effect he encouraged bad habits of dependence. Cabinet responsibility might have been collective in principle but in practice there was much more *primus* than *primus inter pares;* the position being made the worse by the circumambient mixture of sycophancy and flattery. And here is the main cause of Nehru's domination—the gaping inequality in ability and character between himself and his Ministers or his Party or his fellow politicians. What one of his Ministers once said is near the truth: Nehru was like the Banyan tree, so big and so overshadowing that nothing could grow under it.

[1] Michael Brecher, *Nehru: A Political Biography*, 1959, p. 615.

Foreign Affairs

We will now look at Nehru's performance in foreign affairs. This was a subject in which he had always taken a lively interest. His special contribution to the Nationalist Movement had been his unflagging demand, firstly, that the Nationalists think about the kind of India they wanted after they got independence, and, secondly, that they think about a foreign policy. He antagonized not a few on the first account; and bored most on the second. Nehru's enthusiasm for discussing the international situation became a subject of joking. As Prime Minister he showed an interest in it not second even to his interest in the economic and social reconstruction of India. He was criticized for giving too much time to it.

He insisted on keeping the portfolio of External Affairs for himself. It was a disadvantage to him that he did so, because, as Head of the whole government of India, he had to deal with a range of internal problems already too much for one mind. And it was a disadvantage to the Indian Foreign Office and the Indian Diplomatic Service. In effect he did damage to both, and at a formative and impressionable stage of their growth. Notwithstanding some able men in it, such as N. R. Pillai, M. J. Desai, and the Dayals, it was not a good Service—nothing like good enough for a country of India's importance. There was not enough training or professional competence, not enough *esprit de corps*, and too much eagerness to please the boss. It had been made the worse by an excessive habit of propaganda.[1] Nehru was too busy and too preoccupied to get to know the necessary detail, or to get to know the officers except for a handful of very senior ones or a few favourites. This encouraged sycophancy, personal *ad hoc* approaches, and a mixture of amateurishness and subjectivity. Indian Embassies were too often sending back to Delhi the kind of reports which they thought would be congenial to their master. It was scarcely improved by the ambiguous position allowed to Krishna Menon, who in some fields was virtually second Foreign Minister for five years or so prior to his fall in 1962; whence resulted liveliness and initiative but also subjectivity and extra-office approaches and manoeuvres, not to mention short shrift to 'American stooges' 'British dupes' or 'Fascists'. Another effect of Nehru's monopolizing foreign affairs was that members

---

[1] Again and again in Parliament and in the press in India it was complained that India's case was not sufficiently explained abroad and that more emphasis on 'public relations' should be given. The truth is that there has been far too much 'public relations' paper being sent out from Indian Embassies. Few recipients took it seriously. The *India News* brought out by the Indian High Commission in London, ten or so pages of loaded news, was an example. India, of course, was not alone in this erroneous approach; it is common today.

of his Party were excluded from a training in the subtleties of the subject, or from a basic knowledge of international relations.

As for Nehru's own concern for foreign affairs, for years little of moment happened anywhere without his making a public statement on it, often lecturing some Government or other; often, in the first half of his term, a Western if not the British Government itself; and often in a lofty way. His speeches and statements on foreign affairs must run into hundreds of thousands of words; perhaps millions.[1] In the early days of his Government, while the speeches were apt to be scolding they consisted at the same time too much of vague generalities. They gave a good deal of offence in Washington, and sometimes in London. On the other hand the Cold War, the armaments race, and the looming menace of a thermo-nuclear holocaust, were of interest to every human being; India had a concern no less than America or Russia; and reasons were certainly not lacking for pointing the finger at the fomentors of the Cold War. When the documents become available they will probably establish that on the whole Nehru was a valuable counterpoise to the brinkmanship of the most dangerous of the Dulles years.

Non-Alignment and Real-Politik

The starting-point of Nehru's foreign policy was Non-Alignment. This had variations in detail from time to time which led to a good deal of confusion about it for some years. It did not mean, for instance, neutrality (e.g. of the Swiss kind). Nor did it mean that either Nehru or India would ordinarily be neutral in a conflict between Freedom and the opposite, the 1956 Hungary affair notwithstanding. Still less did it mean Non-Violence, though Nehru himself was not without pacifist inclinations. It was essentially a refusal to align India with either one of the two Power blocs around which the world was then polarized; in particular, a refusal to join with the United States or to allow the United States to have bases on Indian soil. Nehru claimed a freedom to judge every issue on its merits.

After the Chinese invasion of Indian territory in 1962 Non-Alignment was much criticized in India, partly as an indirect attack on the Communist Party, on Socialism, and on Nehru himself, but partly, too, for itself. Yet for the preceding fifteen years there were very few Indians who had questioned it; very few who did not praise it. It responded, in fact, to that non-attachment which is deeply rooted in Hindu psychology, as well as in Nehru's own predisposition to avoid all

[1] A selection is available in Jawaharlal Nehru, *India's Foreign Policy Selected Speeches September '54–April '61* and *Nehru's Speeches 1949–53*; Govt. of India, Publications Division.

emotional involvement with others. Nehru once said that he would rather India be reduced to dust than to give up Non-Alignment. It responded, too, surely, to the best interests of India; at least up until the Chinese attack in 1962. Whether one of the claims made repeatedly by Nehru, namely that the extension of armed alliances made the Cold War more likely to become a Hot War, was correct or not, and whether 'international communism' from after Stalin's death was or was not the danger Dulles and his associates said it was, there could be no doubt than an American alliance was not worth the price of Russian enmity to India. Russia is much nearer to India than America; and, further, she, like India, shares a long frontier with China—and the troubles which common frontiers bring. It is true that the policy of Non-Alignment was sometimes conducted in such a way, or with such hectoring words, as to make India disliked unnecessarily. It is true, too, that Indians were inconsistent in 1962–63, in being shocked that their fellow protagonists of, and former pupils in, the doctrine of Non-Alignment, such as Burma, Ceylon, Indonesia or Ghana, refused to align themselves with India against China; and that India while moralizing against the Cold War was up to the eyes in a Cold War of her own with Pakistan. How she was angered by Non-Alignment in others as regards the Indo-Pakistan Cold War was demonstrated again and again. But Non-Alignment paid India. The figures for the Aid she has received from both sides show this. The West has in fact virtually committed itself to India's defence as well as to its Plans; and Russia no less than the West goes on giving both civil and military Aid. Non-Alignment has been found profitable by other new or undeveloped countries too. And did it really do harm to the cause of peace or to the true, as distinct from the imaginary, interests of the West?

India's attitude to Armed Alliances was often confused, even by Indians, perhaps at times by Nehru himself, with the policy of Non-Alignment. Both attitudes were connected with India's and Nehru's genuine concern for peace and to stop the spread of the Cold War, especially in Asia. But a good deal of Nehru's condemnation of Armed Alliances derived from his objection to the United States giving arms to Pakistan and to Pakistan's being a member of SEATO and of CENTO (originally known as the Baghdad Pact). Nehru, like most Indians, feared that Pakistan by virtue of this tie-up would be given a military advantage over India which might be decisive in the event of war breaking out between them. And, of course, it was largely for this reason that Pakistan had, in Dulles' words, been willing to 'stand up and be counted' (against international communism). So many high principles were proclaimed so often on all sides that the basic motivation became lost in the deceiving or rationalizing verbiage.

Nehru

During Nehru's long domination of Indian foreign policy there were changes, naturally. For one thing India's relations with the outside world expanded greatly. In 1950 there were about thirty foreign missions in Delhi; today there are about eighty. In an average year a score or so of international conferences now meet in India. Accompanying this change in the quantity of India's external relations there has been a change in their quality—a change from a sort of pacifist internationalist idealistic approach to a sort of *macht politik*. The Gandhian doctrine of Soul Force came to count for little. Krishna Menon, not Gandhi, became the symbol of Indian foreign policy. The Indian Armed Forces came to take up a sizeable proportion of the Indian budget, even before the Chinese attack in 1962. At the end there were also some second thoughts on the Afro-Asian brotherhood. Without tracing steps in the progress from Soul Force to Power Politics, from Gandhi to Krishna Menon, or without disentangling policies from the three separate levels between which they were apt to oscillate in Nehru's time, namely idealist, emotional, and *real politik*, I will now deal with the subjects which were of main concern.

Relations with Pakistan

First, relations with Pakistan.

Two alternative policies had been possible as regards Jinnah's agitation for Pakistan. First, accept the fact that religion is the great divider; and so, in the interests of that homogeneity without which no State can function, let the Muslims go, let them have Pakistan. Muslims, it can be added, had some reason for distrust about their security in India, at least as far as some Hindus of importance were concerned; and, further, their religion was based on an entirely different, often on an antithetical, world-view, as well as on different social customs and different laws, from that of the Hindus. Or, second, refuse to accept that religion need be a divider, at least for long, and accept the fact that all Muslims in India will not or cannot go to Pakistan. The corollary of this policy would be that India should either have fought a civil war, just as the Americans fought their Civil War, in order to prevent the dismemberment of the sub-continent; or, more wisely, that they should have played along with Jinnah and his successors, leaving the door open, at almost any cost, so that the Pakistanis could make their return, or at least that they could be brought into a confederation. Until as late as the 1937 Congress Cabinets, perhaps even as late as the War years, the proponents of Pakistan probably did not expect, or even want, Pakistan to be created. Gandhi's *Quit India* movement of 1942 had much to do with making Pakistan practical politics for Jinnah, the vain, cold-hearted, clever, impressive demagogue, himself so little Muslim that apparently he had not mastered the prayer ritual. How much Nehru's famous *gaffe* at a press conference decided, or enabled, Jinnah to turn the agitation for Pakistan from a bargaining point into a commitment for a separate sovereign Muslim State can be left to the historians. It is enough to say here that after both Congress and the Muslim League, following on the Attlee Government's decision in July or August 1945 to give India independence as soon as possible and to send Cripps and two other Ministers out to India to arrange the terms, had accepted the British Cabinet Mission's plan of a Centre with control over Defence, Foreign Affairs, and Communications, while other matters were to be left to the control of Muslim Provinces and Non-Muslim Provinces, Nehru, following Azad as President of Congress, suddenly announced, without consulting his party, that the Plan, a precarious compromise in a very difficult situation, was not binding on Congress. He blurted this out because he was hungering for the strongly centralized state dear to all revolutionaries and socialists and was still refusing to see the reality of Muslim fears and hatred and separatism. Jinnah decided to strike. The Congress–Muslim interim Government of 1946 thus never really functioned. When Mountbatten arrived in Delhi in March 1947 he decided that the only way to avoid bloodshed and chaos was to accept Partition and for England to quit that summer instead of in June 1948, the date mentioned by Attlee just before Mountbatten had left London.

From time to time it is said by journalists—who often repeat one another—that the partition of the sub-continent, that is to say the creation of Pakistan, was 'the supreme failure of the British'. The truth, on the contrary, is that the British had no blame for it. The blame was religious hatred. Religious hatred was stirred up to the pitch where the two communities lacked the necessary minimum homogeneity for constituting a single State. This is the reason why Ireland is partitioned, and Korea (for ideological hatreds are the same as religious hatreds); just as it is the reason why some Swiss Cantons or German principalities were entirely Protestant and others entirely Catholic, on the well-established principle of *cuius regio eius religio*. Rajagopalachari, with his usual penetration, saw, and was reconciled to, the case for Partition years before it came. If Mountbatten can be blamed at all, which is questionable, it would be for hastening with so much speed that the boundaries were not decided upon before Pakistan was created, and that the necessary protective measures against communal disturbances had not been worked out.[1]

[1] According to one of the Indian doctors attending Jinnah in the latter part of his fatal illness Jinnah said that the creation of Pakistan was a mistake and

Partitioning Bengal should have been resisted. At least an attempt should have been made to set it up as a third Republic. Here again the blame belongs to the Hindu and Muslim leaders and to religious hatred.

The creation of Pakistan was a disappointment to Nehru; probably a mortifying disappointment as it cut against his conviction that the State must always be secular, and therefore against his sense of the rational. But his own record in the affair was one of exasperation rather than cold statesmanship, and of a hurry to get Independence. He certainly did not agree with those, reportedly Gandhi among them at the end, who thought that it would have been better to delay Independence for a generation or two rather than to pay the price of Partition. About Muslims he was always ambivalent—insisting on protecting them and encouraging them on the ground that they were Indians but at the same time irritated, often angered, with them because they took their religion, which he little valued, so seriously.

Confronted with the existence of Pakistan as a fact, however, Nehru did try his best to coexist with it—to live and let live. Unluckily, after the death of Liaqat Ali Khan he had to deal with Heads of State and Heads of Government in Pakistan, such as Nazimuddin, Ghulam Mohamed, and the two Mohamed Alis, most of whom were incomparably inferior to him in intellect or in integrity and all of whom were incomparably inferior to him in political standing inside their own country. It was not unreasonable that he should be circumspect or distrustful. Ayub was another matter; but Ayub did not arrive until the end of 1958.

On the issues dividing India and Pakistan, with one exception only, Nehru always insisted, often against the advice or wishes of his Ministers or of his senior officials, on the generous view and on giving Pakistan the benefit of the doubt. This was so in the case of the financial disputes, in the Canal Waters affair, in frontier readjustments, and in movement of persons. In India itself he always made it clear that he was the unflinching protector of the Muslim minority; by then a rather frightened demoralized minority. Thus the Muslims were allowed to retain customs which Nehru himself regarded as barbarous, such as polygamy, and which were made illegal for Hindus. He also gave place and promotion to more than one Muslim who was inferior to Hindu candidates just because he was a Muslim. He refused to exchange missions with Israel because he wanted the goodwill of the Arab countries, which are Muslim.

The one exception was Kashmir.

that rather than create it the better course would have been to delay independence.

Kashmir, like other such cases, Schleswig-Holstein or Trieste or Danzig, attained an emotional and political status altogether out of proportion to its intrinsic importance. The emotionally political is always very difficult to deal with rationally. The millions of words uttered on Kashmir by both sides inflamed public opinion and produced rigidities and quasi-commitments which made it almost impossible to negotiate. The Security Council had held no less than 124 meetings on Kashmir up to April 1964. The millions of words also befogged the truth. Thus the weaknesses on Pakistan's side were sometimes overlooked. Thus, too, little men and big scoundrels were given an importance and a respectability they could not have dreamed of otherwise.

Without going into details it is enough to say here that after fighting broke out in Kashmir Nehru, in effect, undertook to have 'a fair and impartial plebiscite' and to abide by its results. That is the first plain truth. The Indian Delegate told the Security Council in 1948—I happened to be there at the time— that the accession to India was not unalterable and that after the emergency Kashmir would be free to ratify the accession to India, or to accede to Pakistan, or to become independent.[1] The second plain truth is that after making that promise India refused to hold the plebiscite. Splitting straws and trailing red herrings, such as about aggression—the Indian claim being that Pakistan had sent the Pathan marauders into Kashmir—or about the validity of the instrument of accession signed by the fugitive Maharaja, or about the validity of its confirmation by the packed Kashmir Assembly, and building up a huge sandhill of legalism, has been on a scale, and with a subtlety, familiar to those who know the workings of lawyers and the Courts in India and Pakistan. The detached student, however, can find little escape from the presumption that Nehru circumvented the plebiscite because, in the Valley at least—and it is the Valley which is wanted—it would have gone against India.

Why did he persist in this circumvention?

The Kashmir Affair is one of the mysteries in Nehru's political life. It remains a mystery even when we allow that the West exaggerated Pakistan's innocence or Pakistan's Westernism; Pakistan, as we have noted, joined SEATO and CENTO as an insurance policy against fire from India. By 1963, when India, under the stress of her fears of China, and of Anglo-American pressures, was offering concessions unimaginable a little earlier, Pakistan refused to compromise. The West on more than one occasion increased the tension between the two countries by well-meaning but ill-formed efforts to mediate

---

[1] *Security Council Off Records, 5th February–2nd March*, p. 30. Also see Shiva Rao's articles on Sir B. Rau.

instead of letting the two countries feel their own way to a solution. But why, in the first instance, did Nehru promise a plebiscite? Was it because he thought at the time that he could win it? If so he made a big mistake in not holding the plebiscite at once. And why did he take the issue to the United Nations? And, not long after promising a plebiscite and taking the issue to the United Nations, why did he do so much, and go so far, to get out of the plebiscite? Had he come to believe that he could not win it? Had he some personal infatuation for Kashmir? His family was Kashmiri Brahman by origin but they left Kashmir seven generations ago. Or was his motivation political?

If the motivation was political what exactly were the considerations? Foreigners in Delhi in my time used to be told by Officials and Ministers what Delegates were told at the UN, namely that Nehru and India must insist on keeping Kashmir because Kashmir, the whole of Kashmir, had legally acceded to India and its accession was irrevocable, so that there was thus no need and no case for a plebiscite; indeed, it was added, the portion of Kashmir occupied by Pakistan was held by aggression and that portion should also rightly be under India. Officials and Ministers would then go on to say that India must have this Muslim community in order to show both Indians and the world that India was really a secular State, unlike Pakistan which was a theocratic State. Further, if India let Kashmir go to Pakistan there would be a terrible Hindu uprising against the Muslims inside India, for instance in the UP and Bihar, and another terrible carnage like that of 1947. Few found this official Indian line convincing. Nor, when foreign observers were assured that India was ready to make concessions to Pakistan, could they get more than vague generalities. And since 1954 most foreign observers, not to put too fine a point on it or to go into details, were curious about Krishna Menon's part in official policy.[1]

Though wavering about Kashmir for a month or so after the Chinese attack in October–November 1962, Nehru soon became adamant again. And, in fairness to him, it must be admitted that Indian public opinion, once it recovered from the shock of the Chinese attack, as expressed in Parliament or the Congress Party or the press, was by then no less adamant than Nehru, and much less restrained. How easy it was to inflame Indian public opinion (by which is meant, as always, the politically-minded groups—a fraction of the total Indian population—and which had always been kept ignorant by the Indian press as to how the UN or the world at large felt about India's case in

[1] A brief statement of Krishna Menon's thesis will be found in his article, 'What is at stake?' in *Seminar*, June 1964. His statements in the UN require several days to read.

Kashmir) was shown in the excited reaction to the request made by Britain in the Security Council when Pakistan once more, in January 1964, brought to it the Kashmir question. The British Delegate was unable to accept the Indian plea that no dispute existed and that therefore there was nothing to negotiate; he requested that both parties hold constructive and sincere talks. This was denounced in India as a betrayal by Britain and there was the familiar clamour for leaving the Commonwealth. Krishna Menon brightened his armour, somewhat tarnished since his fall a year or so earlier, by denouncing, with much applause in Parliament, 'the temerity of Britain' in asking India to negotiate with Pakistan 'after Britain had misruled India for 150 years'. Britain, he went on, was trying to get the Empire back by the side-door.[1] Chou En-lai's choosing to visit Pakistan in that February (1964), and while there to express China's support for Pakistan's case for a plebiscite in Kashmir, did nothing to cool the excitement. Pakistan had been flirting with China for some time in a way which could only irritate when it did not alarm Indians.

As usual in India, however, one could count on some cool and objective heads.[2] But the excitement was enough to ensure the defeat of the proposals put up to India at this time by the United States for an Independent Kashmir guaranteed jointly by India and Pakistan under the UN. These proposals were in fact close to what Sheikh Abdullah, at that time Prime Minister of Kashmir, cautiously but quite unmistakably adumbrated to me twelve years earlier in 1952 when I met him in Kashmir. India's reaction to the American proposals was, once more, that Kashmir is an integral part of India—rather as Portugal had said that Goa was an integral part of Portugal—that the union is irrevocable and so there is nothing to discuss.

After the fever of nationalism fomented by the Sino-India border dispute Nehru would have seen the acutest political difficulties in changing his old stand on the plebiscite, or to make significant concessions to Pakistan. Yet after the massacres in Bihar and Orissa in 1964 he came to believe that the change must be made; that communal feeling was rising so dangerously that it risked war with Pakistan as well as massacres inside India on a scale which might end the secular State. So he had Sheikh Abdullah released in April, after eleven years of jail. This was a very courageous step.

According to one of the members of the first UN Commission sent out to Kashmir (1949–51), Nehru was adamant already by 1950.

---

[1] February 15, 1964.
[2] Cf. the writings of the veteran correspondent and ex-M.P., Shiva Rao, e.g. in *The Hindu* May 29, 1963, as well as various statements by Rajagopalachari and J. P. Narayan.

This Commission consisted of five members,[1] and one of the members happened thirteen years later to be a fellow Ambassador of mine in a certain European capital and used to talk about his experiences on the Commission. He said that the Commission had come to the conclusion privately that the plebiscite ought to be held; that a plebiscite would result in a majority for Pakistan; and that Nehru, knowing this, was determined to get out of a plebiscite. He recounted how he and two other members had a meeting with Nehru in Delhi and, on a personal basis, made the suggestion that the only solution was to hold the plebiscite. This apparently provoked Nehru into one of his tempers. The outburst impressed my informant deeply. 'We saw all at once,' he said, 'that inside this fine man was a gorilla.' Nehru was no gorilla; but for years he always bared his fangs at the mention of a plebiscite or of any real UN intervention in Kashmir.

The damage done by Kashmir to Nehru's enviable moral prestige throughout the world was great. His prestige in Pakistan itself, which was second only to his prestige in India, was also thereby sullied and largely squandered. For Kashmir he threw away the one chance since Partition, presented to him by Ayub, of moving towards reasonable relations with Pakistan through an able and honourable ruler of Pakistan. And when Nehru was forced to make the offers he did in 1963 Ayub was no longer strong enough inside Pakistan to accept them, though they would have been a sensation five years earlier. Nehru lost a big chance when he visited Ayub in Pakistan in 1962; just as Ayub has lost a big chance by failing to attend Nehru's funeral. The long years of Nehru's rule thus left the Kashmir question exactly where it was in 1947, even to returning Sheikh Abdullah, that experienced and not unattractive but diffuse politician, to the scene.

But having said this we must be clear the Kashmir was not the basic divider between India and Pakistan. It was the symbol of the basic division between them: a testimony of the fear and the hate which had yet to be exorcized. Will the historians, even when allowing for the extreme difficulties of Nehru's dilemma, conclude that he had become too static, too legalistic, too weary in dealing with Pakistan? There was little or no growth in his Pakistan policy over seventeen years until a few weeks before his death. There was none of the dynamism which could have worked for at least some confederal arrangement. Even the Pakistan proposals for a *No War Declaration* had received little courtesy and no attention. Suggestions for looking into common defence arrangements between the two countries met with the same reception. A boldly imaginative stroke like offering to see whether

[1] One member, Dr Korbel, wrote a book on it. A fair-minded book on the origins of the Kashmir question is Lord Birdwood's.

Bengal could be reunited occurred to no one, not even to Nehru, in that world of fear and hate. Kashmir did most to keep alive the fear and hate.

Is there any escape from the conclusion that the price paid by Nehru for Kashmir was out of balance?

What value, strategic or economic, did Kashmir have for India? For years India was pouring money into the coffers of a satellite government which was as corrupt, as repressive, as inefficient, and as unreliable to India, as it was unrespected by its subjects. Far from being a Parliamentary Democracy it was a One-Party régime and virtually a dictatorship. The rule was as bad as that of the bad Princely governments which Nehru used to condemn so passionately. Bakshi, though not without likeable traits, after supplanting, some say betraying, his old master, Sheikh Abdullah, and keeping him in jail for eleven years, turned his family of cab-men and stable-boys into magnates. Pilfering and exploitation went so far that Ministers interfered with school and University examiners to see that their relatives or protégés were given passes. There is no doubt that there were some Ministers of quality in Kashmir who preferred their country to be part of India; but the indications, which could be proved or disproved only by a plebiscite, were that they did not represent the majority.

How much Nehru distrusted, and perhaps feared, Pakistan was illustrated by his violent outbursts against United States military aid to it in 1953–54, and by his attitude to Pakistan's membership of SEATO and CENTO. The High Commissioners sent by Pakistan to India would, with one or two exceptions, not have predisposed him to different feelings. Such was the mental climate that the emergence of China as an enemy did little to soften or to re-orientate his own feelings, or Indian feelings in general. So Nehru's lack of directness with Ayub in 1960–62; his pouring ridicule on efforts and notions for an Indo-Pakistan military agreement; and his acquiescing in Krishna Menon's line that the real enemy was Pakistan. This line allowed Krishna Menon, from his world-wide coverage at the UN and his bellicose speeches in India, to build up a picture of himself invaluable to a man who was mostly unknown to the Indian public before then, but damaging to Indo-Pakistan coexistence.

During the ten years I was watching India relations between India and Pakistan got worse, not better, and by 1961 I was prepared for a war between the two. It was only China's rout of Indian troops at the end of 1962 which mitigated this risk. But it did not obliterate it. War could be precipitated by Pakistan in some or other onrush of resentment over a massacre of Muslims in India, for these have been happening every year; or by an accident on the frontier, where the bulk of the armed forces of both countries have been facing each other, and where shooting incidents have been common; or by a nationalistic or a leftist group in India, for instance the Jan Sangh on the one hand or some demagogic leftist group on the other, seeking votes or popularity by operating on the familiar principle that nationalism is the last refuge of the scoundrel. The documentary film on Kashmir brought out in 1961 by the Government, apparently under the direct supervision of a Minister, and seen by millions of Indians in the moviehouses, was not a reassuring precedent. For the essence of the predicament, which is tragic and beyond any moralizing on our part, or denials by Indians themselves, is that for the average Hindu in North India the enemy of the heart is the Muslim. This is true to a surprising degree even of normally balanced persons, even of sophisticated rationalists, and not merely of the people. Nehru, who never got over his experiences with Jinnah, but alarmed by the massacres in March 1964, saw that nothing less than a drastic reversal was called for. He alone could hope to force through the reversal. No one else had the authority to try to do it. He arranged to meet Ayub in June. But it was too late. He was dead by May.

Relations with China

The second subject of main concern in Nehru's foreign policy was China.

India's relations with Communist China seemed, until the end of 1959, at least to the outside world, and to nearly all Indians, to be very friendly. Pakistan and the European Colonialists were the only enemies; China was not often thought of but when it was it was only as a friend and sterling Asian. When it was urged that a common defence arrangement for the sub-Continent should be made with Pakistan Nehru crushed the suggestion with the sarcastic retort, 'Defence against whom?'.

Nehru had had amicable personal relations with Chiang Kai-shek, but this did not prevent India from being among the first to recognize the Communist régime. Sardar Panikkar, that brilliant quicksilver Indian intellectual, after being Ambassador to the K.M.T. Government stayed on as Ambassador to the Communist Government. India showed an equal speed in recognizing China's 'liberation of the Tibet Region of China', as the Chinese styled the invasion and occupation of Tibet in October 1950. When the Dalai Lama put out feelers in 1950 for fleeing to India the Indian Government discouraged him. When in November, a month after the Chinese invasion, the Dalai Lama appealed to the UN against Chinese aggression, adding that Tibet did not recognize China's claim, that it had been exercising independence since 1914, and that in any case China's claims did not justify the use of force, India obstructed the appeal and got consideration of it adjourned *sine die*. The British delegation supported India, apparently at the request of the Indian Government; and the United States announced that she too would accept India's plea. So the UN heard nothing more of Tibet until nine years later when the Dalai Lama, having fled to India, appealed to the UN once again. It was being said in Delhi in 1952–53 that Nehru, in private and semi-private, justified the Chinese invasion of Tibet; but I did not hear him do this.[1]

In 1952 and 1953 cultural delegations were exchanged between India and China, and there were many speeches by Indian political leaders, and many articles in the Indian press, on the theme that 'for thousands of years' there had been undisturbed peace and brotherhood between the two great Asian friends and neighbours. It was implied, and sometimes said explicitly, that only Europeans could be Imperialists; Asians never. This was a familiar theme of one of Nehru's kinsmen, a senior member of the Indian Foreign Office. The wife of the Indian Ambassador in Peking claimed a little later to be running enthusiastic classes in Hindi for the wives of highly placed Chinese Communist dignitaries, including Mrs Chou En-lai; these Chinese ladies so loved India that they wanted to learn 'the national language'. But the theme of India–China brotherhood was common not only in the circle around Nehru but throughout India in these years, including in the newspapers which were attacking Nehru most strongly in 1962–63 for his China policy.

In 1954 Chou En-lai came to India as a State Guest and was accorded receptions and banquets, at some of which I happened to be present. He was given a warm welcome by the public. The famous declaration of *Panch Shil*, the Five Principles of Coexistence, sealed the visit. In 1955, largely through the efforts of Nehru, Chou En-lai, with a sizeable entourage, came to the Afro-Asian Conference at Bandung and, as I could see during that memorable week, he had a similar success there. His intelligence and drive were manifest; he had not a little charm; but whether his voice had the same depreciatory effect or not on those who understood Chinese it came as a shock to others to hear someone so good looking and with such deportment speaking

[1] On the background cf. H. L. Richardson, *Tibet and its History*; the author, a former member of the Indian Political Service, served in Tibet. A complication as regards Tibet, since 1956 at least, which will not be discussed but should be noted, is that the Dalai Lama himself had come to regard his régime, or much of it, as an anachronism. He no longer believed in his own theocracy. Cf. Lois Lang-Sims, *The Presence of Tibet* 1963. I met the Dalai Lama on several occasions.

in so high-pitched a tenor—rather like the shock of hearing big burly men like Chesterton or Belloc piping in their trebles. Bismarck seems to have had a similar effect; and Chou En-lai might well have had more of Bismarck about him than the voice.

India, step by step, renounced the hard-won special position in Tibet which Britain had bequeathed to her, and she accepted Chinese suzerainty in principle and Chinese sovereignty in fact. Nehru dismissed the notion of Tibet as a buffer state—'A buffer between whom ?' —and described India's previous special position there as an outmoded relic of imperialism. India's renunciation was sealed in a series of Sino-Indian Agreements, the most important being the *Agreement on Trade and Intercourse between the Tibet Region of China and India* signed in 1954. From 1952 onwards, India gave up all her old rights. Thus the Indian Mission at Lhasa was reduced to a Consulate-General and the Trade Agencies, at Gyantse, Gartok, and Yalung, were brought under it; and a Chinese Consulate-General was opened at Bombay and Trade Agencies at Kalimpong (notorious as a spy centre), New Delhi, and Calcutta (where China already had a Consulate-General). India, moreover, agreed to withdraw her military escorts and to hand over her rights and equipment for posts, telegraphs and telephones; and the twelve Indian Rest Houses or Compounds and the land she owned were also handed over.

In the UN India pleaded year after year for seating Communist China.

In 1956 Chou En-lai was back in Delhi as a State Guest. The Dalai Lama happened to be in India at the same time; he asked Nehru secretly if he could stay on in India. Nehru advised him to go back. The Dalai Lama dragged on his stay so much that it was March 1957 by the time he got back to Tibet.

Two years later, in March 1959, the Dalai Lama fled to India as a refugee. This was a world sensation for the next three months or so.

Then followed in India, for the ensuing year, and with increasing heat, a series of statements in Parliament, a series of press articles, and a series of public meetings, which were new to Nehru's India. I had returned to India for a second term a few months before the Dalai Lama made his flight; the criticisms of Nehru voiced in Parliament and in the press from then onwards were unthinkable to anyone who had seen Nehru dealing with foreign affairs and his critics three years earlier. Much confidence had manifestly been lost in Nehru's conduct of foreign policy; his monopoly was cracked. By 1960 his monopoly was broken. He now had to explain, and to defend, his foreign policy moves instead of just announcing them or, as at times in the past, saying nothing about them.

In September 1959 the first of the White Papers on Sino-Indian relations was published.[1] It covered the period 1954–59 and came as one more sensation, revealing that India and China had been having border disputes, unknown to the public, indeed unknown to all but a handful of officials and political leaders, as far back as five years. Three more *White Books* followed, bringing the story up to the end of 1960. In 1961 this was capped by the lengthy Report, published as a White Book, of the discussions on the Boundary Question carried out between the officials of the Government of India and of China.[2]

The result of these revelations was an upsurge of nationalism in India of a bitter, at times of a frenzied, kind. It equalled the nationalism against Britain at its most fervid a couple of decades earlier, and that against Pakistan after Partition. In China, on the other hand, there was some, but apparently less, or at least a less vocal, upsurge of nationalistic feeling against India. The exchanges between the two Governments, however, became rancorous; so much so that, possibly at the instance of the Communist Party of India, the Chinese Government early in 1960 made conciliatory gestures. Chou En-lai offered to come to India to discuss the border. He came in April 1960. It was rumoured, and it is probable, that he offered to accept India's claims to NEFA in return for a recognition of China's claims to Aksai Chin; for it was through Aksai Chin that the Chinese had built the important strategic road linking Tibet and Sinkiang. There were no results. In view of the political compulsions there scarcely could have been any. Such was the nationalistic excitement in India that Nehru could have negotiated a settlement with Chou En-lai only at the risk of his own Party unseating him. The press clamoured that not an inch of India's sacred soil must be lost.

I will touch on some of the main points in the question of Sino-Indian relations briefly, only at enough length to show, in so far as is now known, what Nehru did, why he did it, and what he was up against.

The border between India and China is about 2,500 miles long, and runs through wild, largely mountainous, largely unsettled, and largely

[1] *Notes, Memoranda and Letters Exchanged Between the Governments of India and China*, Vols. I, II, III, IV.

[2] *Report of officials of the Governments of India and the People's Republic of China on the Boundary Question*, February 1961. The Chinese produced 245 items of evidence; the Indians 630; a mine of information but not the last word. Cf. Alastair Lamb, *The China–India Border*, 1964 as regards the MacDonald Line of 1899 but also for some of the essential historical and geographical *milieu* to the Boundary Question. See *Times Literary Supplement* from January 2, 1964, and subsequent numbers for discussion, including letters of Dr Gopal (head of the Historical Section of the Indian External Affairs Ministry). Also cf. G. J. Alder, *British India's Northern Frontier 1865–1895*, London 1964.

unproductive land. The disputed areas can be divided into three sections, of which only two have importance, namely the North Eastern border (the so-called NEFA area), which involves the complexities of the McMahon Line, and, second, the Ladakh (West Tibet) border, which involves the greater complexities of the MacDonald Line and much other vagueness. India is more interested in the former; China is more interested in the latter. A *quid pro quo* settlement would have been practicable, and sensible, if Indian public opinion, or Chinese patience or goodwill, would have allowed it.

Since the Boundary dispute became important, and especially since the Chinese attack of 1962, claims are commonly made in India that the boundary—to quote from a recent Indian book—is 'definitively settled by history . . . determined by geography, confirmed by tradition and custom, sanctified by treaties, and reinforced by continuous exercise, through the centuries, of administrative jurisdiction'. The truth is much more amorphous. There has been little that has been definitive. And, whatever the truth, it is hard to dig it out from the vast sandheap of legalistic and propaganda verbiage which has been piled up on both sides. As the boundary question is technical it will be enough for our purposes merely to say that there is no such definitiveness as that claimed by the Indian author cited, just because no one cared very much about the boundary, certainly not until China became a neighbour of India through occupying Tibet. Both sides, India and China, put up cases which were weaker in law, and in history, than either allowed. It is not excluded that the Chinese believed that Aksai Chin did not belong to India, though they, no less than India, subsequently overstated their case. This wild and virtually uninhabited land had not been brought under Indian control. The fact that the Chinese could have built the Sinkiang–Tibet road through it without the Indians knowing for some years is significant. As for the North Eastern Frontier area, where India had a stronger case than China, though whether or not a 'definitive' case can be left to the experts, that area is peopled by Mongolian tribes who have little or no affinities, in blood or languages or culture or past history, with the Indians. Temperamentally they are unlike Indians. The rebellion of the Nagas is connected with this fact. In British times most of the area was left unoccupied and un-administered; subsidies—a species of Danegeld—were given to dissuade the Mongolian tribesmen from raiding into India proper; and in Nehru's time it was not until from 1954 that the Indians occupied much of it, apparently in order to anticipate possible Chinese occupation.

That troubles over the Indo-Tibetan border were to be expected, and that it was not fixed incontrovertibly, was shown before the

Chinese Communists took over. Thus when the Indian Government informed the Dalai Lama's Government at Lhasa that India had become independent and that Lhasa could count on relations being not less friendly than they were in the days of the British *raj*, the Tibetan authorities replied, in effect, 'Thank you. This is all very fine; but what about the border?' The Lhasa authorities then proceeded to enumerate, as points at issue, just about every point which came up for dispute between India and China after 1955.[1] I have been told by some officials concerned that Nehru himself from the early 'fifties expected trouble over the border, and his policy was to play for time and let sleeping dogs lie. But other officials have told me that he was indifferent or complacent about the problem. Historians will certainly want to look into Bajpai's minute written at the time of the Chinese occupation,[2] allegedly warning the Government, and opposing Panikkar's reasoning; and into what Nehru's reactions were. (They will also want to know Nehru's real thinking on the Korea War.) It was said in my day by some retired senior officers, both from the External Affairs Ministry and from the General Staff, that when Nehru had been advised against losing Tibet as a buffer state, or losing the privileged Indian position in Tibet, he refused to listen, and in some cases was scornful of the advisers concerned and virtually reprimanded them. Did he, as used to be said in high places in Delhi, refuse to discuss with U Nu of Burma, or, later, Ayub of Pakistan or the King of Nepal, not to mention the Prime Minister of Japan, relations with China in general or the border question in particular when these dignitaries visited Delhi and sought to discuss them?

It must be remembered, on the other hand, that at the time when the Chinese invaded Tibet, in 1949–50, India was preoccupied with her millions of refugees and with strained relations with Pakistan, including the Kashmir affair. A war with China over Tibet, for instance, would at that date have been impossible for India. The External Affairs Ministry, too, was small, amateurish, and overstretched, while the Cabinet Ministers were mostly new to Government itself, over and above their ignorance of foreign and military affairs. The Indian Embassy in China, notably Panikkar, appears to have recommended to Nehru to give in to Chinese claims because the gratitude and good-will of the Chinese Communists thereby resulting would provide the best guarantee for the Sino-Indian border. The Indian Embassy also explained how Chinese plans for internal developments would keep them busy for years and make expansionism both impracticable as well as unwanted. Nehru certainly made this last point about Com-

[1] It is not time for revealing the source of this information yet.
[2] Sir G. Bajpai was Secretary General, External Affairs Ministry, until 1952.

munist China to various Ambassadors and foreign visitors as well as
to his Party. What the historians will want to know is not whether
Nehru should have fought a war with China in 1950 but what were the
motivations of his policy and his estimates of the India–China situation.
These are not fully known yet.

A great deal of material on the Sino–Indian border affair has already
been published. Exchanges between India and China, and Government
speeches in the Indian Parliament and to the Indian public, run into
thousands of pages; and Indian newspaper comment at the time,
and Indian books since then, run into hundreds of thousands of words.
But some essential facts are still unrevealed. Indians in high places
showed themselves, not for the first time, to have a capacity for secretiveness which is remarkable. Did any diplomat in Delhi in 1955–58,
not to go back further, guess at the state of Sino–Indian relations
which was revealed in the *White Books*? The same secretiveness had
been practised over Kashmir. Was it due to orders from Nehru?
Again and again serious diplomats known to be well disposed to India
tried to find out from the Indian External Affairs Ministry what was
happening on the Border; they were invariably put off with banalities.

Nehru's fundamental approach to China seems to have been com-
pounded of beliefs that Asians would in this Asian century be brotherly,
expecially the polite and now socially-minded Chinese; that China
would be busy for years with her internal socialist revolution; and that
the only conceivable subject of dispute was Tibet, and Tibet had been
liquidated through India's renouncing all rights and claims there.
In the absence of documented facts one can only guess, and my guess,
for what it is worth, is that until about 1959 Nehru did not see the
Border as a subject of much importance to either country, let alone as a
likely cause of bitter disputation. The *Panch Shil* declaration, proposed
by the Chinese in the first instance, had been approved in draft form
in February–March 1954. Chou En-lai visited India and signed the
Declaration in June of that year. In the following month, July, (it was
revealed some years later,) the first Border incident took place, at
Bara Hoti. Nehru, however, attached, as far as one can see, no significance to it; he felt secure in the *Panch Shil* declaration. For the same
reason he continued to feel secure as the other Border incidents took
place, in 1955, 1956, 1957, 1958, and perhaps into 1959. When Chinese
maps showing as Chinese territory what the Indians regarded as theirs
had come to the notice of the Indians and they pointed it out, the
Chinese would reply, in effect, 'Don't worry. These are old KMT maps
and we're too busy now to bring out our own maps.' It is probable that
by 1957 or 1958 Nehru would have felt uneasy at times over the
Border incidents, but if so he could well have judged it wiser to keep the

matter from the public, and to avoid any excitement, against the day when the whole Border question could be taken up and settled sensibly. Perhaps he had in mind a deal with the Chinese, such as Aksai Chin to China in return for India's incontrovertible title to NEFA. This would have suited China and it would have betrayed no real interest of India. As for the *Panch Shil* declaration, this was a better move from the viewpoint of India's interests than Indian critics were allowing in the next decade. It was tantamount to a No-War declaration.

It must be remembered that in these years, on the whole the most satisfying and the most confident in his Prime Ministership, Nehru was concentrating on internal Indian matters, like the Plans, and on standing up against much of the foreign policy associated with Dulles. He almost certainly had more distrust for Dulles than he had for Chou En-lai.

Was China trying to trick India all along, as is now commonly thought? Or were there genuine misunderstandings?

There are several puzzles still to be solved, as regards India's as well as regards China's part.

Why did Nehru publish the *White Books*? They were bound to unleash nationalist passion in India, probably to a degree which could deprive him of any leeway for negotiating. Pique? Nationalist passion in himself? or Calculation, for instance to exert pressure on China as well as to anticipate criticisms of his border policy in India? Perhaps all three were part of the motivation; but probably the biggest factor was that after the leak of information about the road in Aksai Chin, and still more after the exposures made in Parliament in 1959, the safest course was to make a clean breast of it.

But why did India set up the forty new check posts in the disputed area in 1962? Could China accept this *Forward Policy* without reaction? This must surely have risked a military confrontation.

And if India was going to play this provocative game why did she still have most of her armed forces facing Pakistan and not China? Further, if the Border dispute was serious should not India have tried to work out a common border policy with India's fellow-neighbours of China, notably Nepal, Burma, and Thailand, if not Pakistan itself?

What seems certain is that the Chinese had lost trust in the Government of India and had become as convinced that they were being tricked by it as the Indians had become convinced that they were being tricked by the Chinese Government.

It would throw some light on motivations if we knew whether the Dalai Lama, when he escaped from Tibet in 1959, slipped through the fingers of the Chinese to get into India, or whether the Chinese intentionally let him, and perhaps in essence encouraged him, to go. One of the men best informed on the subject, a former head of the

Nepal Foreign Office, expressed to me the latter view. The ruler of one of the border States, a Protectorate of India, and also well informed, expressed to me the former view, which also accords with the Dalai Lama's account in his autobiography.[1] The Chinese, it seems, already knew of the Dalai Lama's wishes to fly to India in 1950, and again in 1956. In 1954 they took him to China. (It was on that occasion that the Indian Secretary General of External Affairs on meeting the Dalai Lama at Peking and asking him politely, through a Chinese interpreter, how he was doing, received the answer, through the interpreter, equally politely, that he was doing well and was 'most happy to be in the capital of the Motherland'.) Moreover, the Dalai Lama had been infiltrating some treasure into Sikkim; which the Chinese knew of or suspected. Did the Chinese decide in 1956 or thereabouts that they would not succeed in getting the Dalai Lama to collaborate in, or to refuse to oppose, their policies, and therefore fell back on the traditional enemy of the Dalai Lama, the Panchen Lama, using him until they were ready to destroy him? For this reason, and for some others, they would have had an advantage in getting the Dalai Lama out of Tibet and into India. His going would be a sensation at the moment, but would be no more than a nine-day wonder. They could assume that nothing concrete would come out of his presence in India; in a few months, or years, he would be forgotten. Whatever the background to the Dalai Lama's flight, the train which accompanied the Dalai Lama to India consisted of about 80 mules, and a retinue of 95 Tibetans. As this conspicuous group followed well-known paths it is possible, but it seems hardly probable, that the Chinese were unaware; the less so as by that time they knew the geography of the Tibetan border country well besides having a fairly efficient control of the totalitarian kind. The Chinese seem, too, to have had knowledge, presumably by interception, of wireless telegraphy messages passing between the Dalai Lama and India. As far as Sino–Indian relations are concerned, the Dalai Lama's flight would in any case have sharpened Chinese suspicions of India, which were already sharp by then.[2]

---

[1] *My Land and People*, 1962.

[2] The behaviour of the press, not only in India but especially in the United States, the United Kingdom and other Western countries, during the various Sino-Indian conflicts and especially during and just after the Dalai Lama's flight, was an eye-opener even to Diplomats familiar with the unreliability of much, and the unscrupulousness of some, newspaper reporting. The reporting in certain mass circulation newspapers in the United Kingdom and the United States was worse than inaccurate: it was often grossly fabricated. One newspaper chartered an aeroplane and poured out money without let. Some of the correspondents concerned purported to have gone to places, and to have had interviews, which were imaginary. They reported not the facts but what their

Virtually nothing is known about why the Chinese took this or that step in Sino–Indian relations. Did Chou En-lai in 1954 think that he was outwitting Nehru? Or did the two men fail in directness, or even in communication, with each other? There are signs that the barrier of language did exist, and that there was genuine misunderstanding on both sides. That the barrier continued to exist was suggested in the condolences which Chou En-lai telegraphed to Nehru's daughter in 1964. He then described her father's death as 'unfortunate'. At all events, by 1956–57 the Chinese were highly suspicious of India. By the time the Indian *Forward Policy* was launched they were convinced of trickery and bad faith.

There is evidence that after his talks with Nehru in 1954 and in 1955, increasingly in 1956, and again in 1960, Chou En-lai came to feel that he had got little understanding with Nehru, and that Nehru was not straight. Nehru's manner and indirectness had over the years caused more than one interlocutor to feel like that. Nehru, on the other hand, came to feel the same about Chou En-lai. There is evidence in fact for an oddly personal factor on the side of both men, difficult though this might be to credit in a world of power politics. According to a Foreign Minister of a certain Asian country, Chou En-lai, speaking about the Sino–Indian boundary dispute, told him that Nehru was impossible to negotiate with, being both unreliable and impenetrable. This is not the only suggestion that a personal disenchantment grew up, and developed into personal dislike, between the two Prime Ministers. In 1963 I found, in the course of a talk with Nehru when I returned to Delhi on a visit, for all his guardedness, an unusual personal note in his remarks. He was puzzled over China because the points at issue—this or that piece of land—were not important in themselves; but, still more, he was disappointed and aggrieved. He spoke of the strain of arrogance in the Chinese character, and about the stage through which the Communist Revolution there was going, and he wondered about their deeper purposes. In talks with India they had been both rigid and calculating. From other sources one heard in 1963 that Nehru had become rigid himself and did not want to negotiate though he must have known that Aksai Chin was beyond recovery. A member of Nehru's family circle made it still more personal: Chou En-lai from Bandung onwards had shown himself jealous of Nehru, and the

editors or proprietors wanted to foist on the public, or something to glamorize themselves. The reporting by some Diplomatic Missions in Delhi was not much better. Diplomats come to know of at least some of the reports sent in by their colleagues. Too many of these reports copied the untruthful newspapers, or sent back to their Governments what they knew their Governments would like to believe.

jealousy was increased because of India's getting Aid from Russia which China coveted as hers of right.

The important point about the Sino–Indian Border dispute is not what areas belong to India or China but that China, at the risk of making enemies of a neighbouring State numbering 500 millions, hitherto well disposed to her, and speaking up repeatedly for her full acceptance in the comity of nations, should go to the lengths of treating India as an enemy. Was any real interest of China involved which justified so high a cost? Did it not matter if India should be provoked into giving up non-alignment and into making an alliance with the West? Did it not matter that the Communist movement in India should have the ground cut from under its feet? Did it not matter that the *Panch Shil* declaration should be seen as a mere piece of paper?

The explanations favoured in the West, or in India, at the time need not be examined here. There were many, and some seem over-sophisticated.

As for the fundamental factors in the relations between China and India, China, under population pressure, or under fear of attacks from enemy bases in weak neighbouring States, could conceivably spill over into the rice bowl of South-East Asia, but what motive could she have for coming down into poverty-stricken over-populated India? Nehru was surely right in thinking that China and India can live and let live; and surely he was not surprising in feeling that his goodwill had been recompensed with guile and brutality. But China is bound to be more powerful than India; and the two peoples, moreover, are antithetical in temperament. The theme-song in 1950–58 of three thousand years of unbroken peace between the two Asian brothers had been a manifestation of Indian nationalism in its racial or anti-European form as well as nonsense.

Anti-Colonialism

A third specific concern of Nehru's foreign policy was anti-colonialism.

This cannot be understood without account being taken of the deeply formative effect of his long years as a fighter against the British Empire, and of feelings born of his resentments of European domination. His suspiciousness about European policies got near at times to being racialist; though it must be admitted that there were at times reason for his suspiciousness.

Nehru had scarcely become Head of the Congress–Muslim Coalition Government in 1946, which, as we have seen, was formed before the Muslim League broke away in the following year to set up Pakistan, and he therefore had more than enough to occupy him with in India, when he took in hand the calling of the *Asian Relations Conference.* It met in March–April 1947, while the rumblings of hatred between Hindu and Muslim were already sounding ominously. He addressed it enthusiastically on Asia-ism. This looked to some like anti-Europe-ism but was nothing much more than anti-European-colonialism. A few weeks later the die was cast for the division of the Indian sub-continent into India and Pakistan; and a few months later the great Hindu–Muslim massacres began.

In January 1949, not many months after the massacres, though sporadic killings were still taking place, Nehru called a *Second Asian Relations Conference* in New Delhi, this time as a move against the Dutch in Indonesia. Amongst the 19 Powers invited were Australia and New Zealand. Australia, then under a Labour Government, attended but China, Nepal, New Zealand and Thailand sent only observers, while Turkey declined the invitation. Australia and New Zealand were the only non-Asian countries invited. Nehru had already decided that anything like a line-up of 'coloured' peoples would be deplorable and could be disastrous. It was for the same reason that he put out feelers in 1954 for inviting Australia to the Bandung Afro-Asia Conference of 1955; a significant gesture on his part which has not been sufficiently noted.

Year after year the anti-colonial passion of India manifested itself in one episode or over one place after another—South-East Asia, Tunisia, Algeria, Negro Africa, South Africa. At times there was good reason for Indian passion, as what went on in Algeria for example was of a horrifying bestiality; but at times it was ill-informed and un-constructive, and occasionally unreasonable. India did all she could to break up the European Empires, with little thought as to what might follow their break-up, and with little done to save Indians in Ceylon from treatment which was worse than the treatment meted out to Africans in European colonies in Africa. Not a few Africans, who to the astonishment of India disliked the Indians in their midst sometimes more than they disliked the Europeans, soon showed signs that they would mete out similar treatment to Indians as the Ceylonese were meting out once they had got the independence which Nehru was demanding for them. Nehru himself was often in high indignation at some manifestation or other of what he saw as colonialism or Europe-ism, but feelings ran even higher amongst the Indian intelligentsia, which was anti-colonialist to a man.

The driving force behind Indian, and more particularly Nehru's, anti-colonialism was disapproval of foreign overlordship—'good government is no substitute for self-government'. But there was also in it, as there had been in the old anti-British Nationalist movement in

India, a strong undercurrent of racial feeling born of sensitiveness about colour. That is why Maharajas and Brahmans even more than the low castes hated colonialism, or South Africa, or Immigration laws excluding people on the basis of colour. What caused particular resentment was the lumping of all non-European peoples, and independently of cultures, into a single category.[1]

It is questionable whether the best interests of the colonial peoples themselves were always served by the manner or the speed with which independence came to them. In more than one case the new State consisted of a congeries of tribes which India officially insisted on treating as a nation. At Bandung in 1955 Nehru said, 'I think there is nothing more terrible than the infinite tragedy of Africa in the past few hundred years.' Such was his emotion that he did feel that Europeans were largely responsible for the fact that Africa was not 'developed'—like France or Denmark. Most politically-minded Indians shared these feelings to the full. They also concurred, as the politically-minded majority in most countries concur, in double standards—in insisting on one code of behaviour for India and another for others, one as regards the Nagas in NEFA but another as regards Africans in French Guinea.

The affairs of the Congo and Indian reactions thereto provided a characteristic example of India's, and of Nehru's, emotional involvement in anti-colonialism. Only a few points need be mentioned here though the Congo story is complex. After the breakdown of Belgian rule in 1960 Indian passions became quickly engaged. As a result, the bulk of the military force first sent to the Congo to carry out UN policy, which expressed the wishes of the majority of the Afro-Asian bloc in association with the United States, was Indian. Indian troops and aircraft were sent to the Congo at the personal request of Hammarskjold, the Secretary-General of the UN.[2] At the same time he arranged personally with his own Government, that of Sweden, to send a Swedish contingent. Various African troops were brought in later. But Indian forces were the spearhead; and they remained the decisive force for a long time. Some of the Indians concerned in the enterprise saw it as a crusade.

In December 1961 India, dedicated to breaking the Katanga secession, tried to force the hands of the British Government to send 24 half-ton bombs from Britain for Indian planes to drop on Katanga.

[1] My inaugural address to the Australian National University, *The Racial Factor in International Relations*, published in 1956, bears on this and connected points.

[2] According to Conor Cruise O'Brien, his representative in Katanga, Hammarskjold had in effect falsified reports; *To Katanga and back*, p. 67. Hammarskjold's diaries are revealing of the man.

(This was the moment when the Goa attack was being worked out.) It was hoped that in this way the ground lost in the unsuccessful effort to crush Tshombe's Katanga régime in September could be recovered. This Indian initiative came only two months or so after Hammarskjold's plane had crashed, which caused excitement and indignation in India. Some newspapers described it as 'a British murder', and 'a crime engineered by the British Secret Service'. The *Indian Express*, for instance, wrote, 'Never have British hands been so blood-stained....' Nehru himself, who had recently taken part in the memorial celebrations for Lumumba, made some dark hints.

The UN forces did not pull out of the Congo until the summer of 1964. By then the anarchy was similar to that in 1960–61; Tshombe had returned, with American blessings this time; and the UN had spent over £150 million on its intervention.

By colonialism most Indians meant both more and less than colonies. Relatively few Indian anti-colonialists would be worried about their country's subjugation of the Mongolian peoples of Nagaland,[1] or about Indonesia's subjugation of Papuans. What most Indians had in mind about colonialism was any superior place or advantage in the world for the Europeans. It was largely social. Indians, sober and sane as they are on most relations of life, can sometimes lose their balance on race relations as quickly as they can on Muslims or Pakistan. It is the more confusing because it is confused in their own minds. In private they have an infatuation with fair complexions, and, conversely, a distaste for the African's complexion. African students in India have sensed this and have voiced their resentment of what they regard as Indians' race prejudices against Africans just as in Communist China African students have sensed and protested against Chinese race prejudices. Yet no African or Asian people become so passionate about race relations as do Indians. This fact stands though the Indian authorities are now doing their best for African students, and though all race, like all caste, discrimination is illegal in India.

The fall of the European empires was ardently worked for by Nehru's India. Towards the end Indians lost some of their ardour, disenchanted by the discriminatory treatment meted out to Indians in some of the new African States, or by the warrings between Indians and Negroes in British Guiana, and by the decline in the prestige and popularity of

---

[1] Nehru did his best to conciliate the Nagas, and to see that the policies—sound British Colonial Service policies—recommended by Verrier Elwin, to whom he showed great kindness, were carried out. Elwin, son of a Bishop of Sierra Leone, and himself once Chaplain of Oriel College, Oxford, came to India as a Christian missionary in the 'twenties and after a period with Gandhi ended up as a rationalist. He became an Indian citizen, and did valuable anthropological work on the tribal peoples.

India itself throughout Africa. In general, and increasingly in latter years, Nehru's own part was moderating. What was humanist and universalist in him revolted against racialism, including the vestiges of racialism remaining in himself. He knew after the Nazi and other European behaviour that Africans and Asians had nothing to teach Europeans in the way of atrocities; but he also knew, and felt strongly, that what was bad was not just European racial cruelties or prejudices but all racial cruelties and prejudices. Thus at the Afro-Asian Conference in Bandung in his closing speech, reacting against Sukarno's environment, and against the self-pity of some of the delegates, he urged them to move from merely thinking about the faults of their erstwhile masters on to reconstructing their countries; and he urged them to remember that people who had been under colonial régimes had normally fallen under them because of defects of their own. This advice was not popular at Bandung. Remembering racial fears amongst certain peoples of European origin he went on:

'We mean no ill to anybody. We send our greetings to Europe and America. We send our greetings to Australia and New Zealand. And indeed Australia and New Zealand are almost in our region. They certainly do not belong to Europe, much less to America. They are next to us and I should like Australia and New Zealand to come nearer to Asia.'

And reacting against Sukarno once more, this time at the Conference of Non-Aligned Powers held in Belgrade in 1961, Nehru, with typical courage, opposed the Indonesian President's attempt to turn the conference from a move against the Atomic Armaments race into merely one more occasion for anti-colonialist slogans.

If Smuts and Nehru could have been thrown together and cut off from everyone else in some mountain hut for a week or two they would have astonished each other by discovering how much they had in common, including their doubts.

The Commonwealth
Nehru insisted on India's remaining in the Commonwealth. It is true that India got a good deal out of it while she was required to give little or nothing in return. It is true, too, that the first country India turned on in any mood of ill-temper was usually the United Kingdom, as the Suez affair, the Congo, Hammarskjold's death, African affairs in general, the Common Market, Kashmir, or the British Immigration restrictions, bear witness. No claims or distortions could be too extravagant in these attacks; and the refrain was often accompanied with a threat about leaving the Commonwealth. It is true, again, that

as regards relations with other Commonwealth Members, the country India regarded as her worst enemy, Pakistan, was a fellow member, and the country she hated most next after Pakistan, namely South Africa, was until latterly another fellow member.

The attitude of India to the Commonwealth in Nehru's day was thus one of wanting the best of both worlds—to be treated as part of England, and a part of the West, and to be given aid and comfort from it, and yet to be free to damn it when feeling so disposed. But it was also tempered with a strain of goodwill, even of sentimentality, especially as regards England. Indians' attitude to England has been a tangle of love–hate. Krishna Menon, as an actue English diplomat once said, has been at once the worst enemy and the best friend of Britain in India. The Indian regard for Britain might be eroded away as the generations trained by Englishmen die off, but the British have been wise enough to be forebearing and, usually, silent under irritable Indian press attacks, like those noted above. Indian ill-temper rarely endures for long. In view of the historical connections—a large proportion of British families have had some connection with it at some time or other—England owes something to India.

An example of both the destructive and the constructive side of Nehru was provided by the question of South Africa's place in the Commonwealth. He had something to do with South Africa's leaving the Commonwealth. South Africa is a hard case; but keeping her out of the Commonwealth had not a little in common with keeping China out of the UN. Nehru, however, was convinced that the Commonwealth could have no reality unless it was multi-racial, and sincerely multi-racial. It was on that ground that he was using his influence to keep the new African States in the Commonwealth. Nehru, in short, had a good deal to do with making the Commonwealth the multi-racial group it is today.

The Cold War

Nehru's attitudes to the West and to the East respectively came in for much criticism in the West.

His power and his sense of achievement and fulfilment were at their highest in the years 1952 to 1958. These were also the years during which McCarthy flourished, symbolizing the hysteria and conformism which gripped many Americans; the years when Dulles dominated the foreign policy of the United States and, as Nehru thought, the foreign policy of the West as a whole. Nehru saw Dulles's policy as misconceived and as encouraging the arms race and thereby involving grave risk of war, and so nothing less than the survival of humanity.

As late as 1956, Dulles, who distrusted Nehru as much as Nehru distrusted him—as was not concealed when Dulles visited India in 1954—said that 'the conception of neutrality is obsolete, immoral, and short-sighted'. For Dulles neutrality in all forms, including non-alignment, was a refusal to choose between evil and good; that is to say, between Communism and anti-Communism. Nehru, who did not much bother about some of Dulles's men describing him as a crypto-Communist, felt that this was too uncomplicated a definition of good and evil. Nor did he miss the irony that, as regards the sanctity of the Free World and the Free Life proclaimed by Dulles, he, damned by Dulles, was carrying India through a gargantuan effort towards Parliamentary Democracy, the rule of law, freedom and equality for all religions, and social and economic reforms, while among the countries which Dulles praised and subsidized because they were 'willing to stand up and be counted' as anti-Communist were effete or persecuting tyrannies, oligarchies and theocracies, sometimes corrupt as well as retrograde. Dulles was as disinterested and as brave as Nehru himself, as rock-like in character, and he had no difficulty in showing up the discreditable part played by many Communist intellectuals and Communist Parties over the years, and the results of their doctrine that the ends justify the means or that the interests of a certain foreign Power always take precedence. But he never changed the conviction of most educated Indians that foreign policy, including American foreign policy, dealt mostly, and inevitably, if regrettably, with the world as it is, which is to say with power. It dealt with the interests and the security of States rather than with morality. Still less were most educated Indians convinced that American-type Capitalism was the only moral or, in every case, the most utilitarian, way to run an economic system.

Some of the conditioning factors in Nehru's outlook have already been touched on. Thus all along he refused to see the Communist States as a monolith. He was early aware of the frictions and rivalries among them. He was aware, too, already in the early 'fifties, on the one hand of developments inside Russia, which would mean a richer and different Russia from the war-wrecked Russia of Stalin, and, on the other hand, of certain basic similarities and affinities between Russians and Americans. I recall his talking on these matters with great force, as also on relations between Russia and China, as far back as 1954. For some years before others sensed the position, Nehru was convinced of tensions between China and Russia, and that the tensions would grow. Later he came to see in Russia a counterpoise to China. Perhaps he felt that in the long run China would inevitably be more powerful than Russia.

On the other hand Dulles was correct in feeling that Nehru's neutralism was not always strictly neutral between East and West; that Nehru was apt to show an indulgence towards the Communist States which he did not show towards the United States. The Socialist in Nehru, and the enthusiast for the kind of planning and constructiveness and hopefulness which he credited to Russia ever since his visit there in 1927, did predispose him that way. His obituary speech on Stalin delivered in the Indian Parliament in 1953 carried the praise rather further than these obituary occasions require and so confirmed some Americans in their worst fears about Nehru. The rein he gave to Krishna Menon in certain fields of foreign relations reinforced their fears. Year after year he sent him to the UN where he became a byword for a certain line of action as well as for occasional eccentric exhibitionism; in an environment which stimulated exhibitionism to a peculiar degree, over and beyond the fact that men in public gatherings tend to vanity and a lower level of behaviour than in private life. It is true, too, that Nehru's indignant outburst on the Suez affair was not matched by any outburst on Russia's suppression of the Hungary uprising; though, from the books coming out on the Suez affair, it is not manifest why it should have been. Over the years Nehru's foreign policy was not pro-Communist nor pro-East. It was punctilious about Non-Alignment, and for the rest it exerted itself on the side of good sense and peace. Nehru undoubtedly had a deep abiding uneasiness about America's fitness for her primacy in the world but his opposition to American talk of military intervention in South-East Asia in 1954 after Dien Bien Phu, or to the activities of the CIA, or to the threats of brinkmanship and massive retaliation voiced by American admirals and generals before President Kennedy restored normal Service discipline, was approved of by many people in the West, and indeed by some people in the United States. Nor did Nehru's conviction that some kind of neutralization was the least dangerous policy for Laos in particular and for South-East Asia in general have anything to do with the pro-East prejudices which were alleged against him. Nehru found the Communist's only-one-way absolutist account of life, and grounds for policy, as unacceptable as Dulles's categories of good and evil. Both were far too simple for him.

To sum up, Nehru's attitude to the Cold War between West and East was based not on any Communist sympathies but on a concern to safeguard peace in the world, qualified by a concern to safeguard India's interests. He did contribute to peace, notably in Korea. There is reason to believe that he refused certain Russian overtures about the Congo. Whether this non-alignment was a luxury which India could permit herself only because she could always come in under the American umbrella in case of need is a question which can be answered only when we have more documentary and other knowledge than we have now. The answer will depend on whether Soviet Russia really had expansionist and revolutionary designs, or could be reasonably assumed from the information then available to Dulles and other leaders in the West to have any, and really was a threat to the peace, especially after Stalin's death.

The question remains, however, whether, given the potentiality and the mood of Communist China, India might now have a case for giving up Nehru's policy and of aligning itself with the West. Rajagopalachari, for instance, has argued that, given the facts of the world as they are, there is no sense in India's bankrupting itself by trying to go it alone, and that India's independence sought through second-class armaments, purchased on credit, is liable to be apparent not real independence. The answer to this question must depend on the degree to which China is a danger to India or to world peace. In any case it would still seem to serve no interest of India to align herself with the West at the cost of Russia's enmity. Rajagopalachari meets this point by looking forward to the day when Russia will also be aligned with the West, indirectly if not directly. At all events Indians will probably come to see what Nehru declined to admit, namely that in the world of Power Politics as it exists some countries, owing to their geographical or to other circumstances, have good reason for entering into a defensive alliance. Nehru was too absolutist in his condemnation of SEATO, NATO and CENTO.

Other Foreign Policy Matters

Little need be said about the other subjects in foreign relations with which Nehru was concerned. As regards the *Arms Race*, he was sincere in wanting to stop it, but any role he could have played was defeated partly by his failure to offer anything constructive and partly because, thanks largely to Kashmir and Goa, his own *bona fides* were suspect in some quarters. He refused to allow India to have any part in the making of thermonuclear weapons. The pressure to make them is likely to grow significantly now that he has gone.

As regards *the UN*, he valued it as a potential peace-maker and as a step towards the world-government which he believed inevitable in the long run if mankind was not to destroy itself. But he valued it no less as an institution which gave India, and other Afro-Asian or non-aligned nations, almost powerless in the world from the military point of view, a forum where their voice could not be ignored. The UN gave a majority to the Afro-Asian countries. They could pass resolutions which were treated as of a quasi-legislative validity (for instance on the Congo), and which continuously needled the developed countries into giving money for Aid programmes, while towards the huge costs of running this institution (including its dozen Specialized Agencies) India and her Afro-Asian allies, though calling so much of the tune, paid a mere trifle. It was the West, and mainly half a dozen countries, which bore the financial burden as well as the political burden of the UN. Why Nehru did not press for India's being a permanent member of the Security Council is not clear. India's claim is already nearly as strong as that of Britain or France. It will no doubt be pressed in the future; and then a similar claim will come from Pakistan and others.

As for *Aid*, India under Nehru sought to get as much of it as she could out of the West though for some time Nehru had been opposed to accepting it, fearing its effects on non-alignment or independence. His passion to push on with his Plans, which could not survive without Aid, ended his opposition. India, like Indonesia, soon learnt that she need do little in order to get the Aid in huge volume, and that its flow would be neither diminished nor interrupted by policies of hers disliked by the West, because the West had so great fear of Communism that it would spare no effort which it reckoned on as keeping India away from Communism. India became confident that even Belgium and Holland, two countries she had denounced unsparingly over colonialism, would in the end join the *Aid India Club*; as in fact they did by 1963.

As regards *the essential international problem*, namely how to replace the law of the jungle with the rule of civilized law, Nehru, like many Indians, was keenly aware of the need. In Indians in general there remains, as has been noted earlier, in spite of so many signs and so much activity to the contrary, not only an instinct for tolerance, for live and let live, but also another heritage left by the Buddhists, a dislike of force or violence. Gandhi's doctrine of Soul Force was not an accident. Nehru himself, a Brahman, traditionally a caste which had nothing to do with arms, had yearnings after Pacificism. So long as he lived those Indians who wanted to embark on a programme of thermonuclear weapons would not have their way. But Indians, like most of mankind, also want things the getting of which means resorting to the law of the jungle. Their nationalism, more emotional than they usually allow, or we usually believe, predisposes them to courses which would ordinarily end in violence. Their tendency, too, to hold at the same time mutually incompatible propositions (for instance Nehru's speeches on peace just before and just after the Goa affair) undermined, inevitably if unjustly, confidence in their sincerity.

Nehru spoke much and often about the need for world peace,

sometimes censoriously. Men of goodwill in all countries listened to him for years with respect and with hope. They knew he had negligeable military power but they saw him as a representative of light, of moral authority, of Soul Force. Some of the more naif saw him through the roseate hues of notions about 'the spirituality of India'—notions well advertised by *swamis*, commercially or otherwise, and by a few Indian diplomats. That was not Nehru's fault. He did render practical service to the cause of peace. Thus he played a personal mediatory role between Russia and the West; a valuable service in the Dulles days and prior to the time Macmillan broke the ice by his visit to Moscow; he kept world attention on the thermonuclear armaments race; he was a steadying influence in the Afro-Asian group at a time when it much needed steadying; he was a steadying influence on nationalist passion inside India; and, in particular, he insisted on a level of restraint and patience in dealing with small neighbours often acting unjustly to India, such as Burma, Ceylon, and Nepal, which is rare in foreign relations. Where he was mainly at fault was that in passing judgement on the international situation he often failed to offer any concrete plan for achieving world peace; and that was so because he had in fact mastered no basic intellectual analysis of this very difficult problem, and had no solution. Who has? Furthermore, as regards certain interests of India Nehru's policy, whether unavoidably or otherwise, was founded on force; nor was it invariably innocent of double talk.

Nehru's unresting concern with international relations, damned by certain Indians as much as by Dulles, came not from eccentricity or vanity or any desire to shine on the world stage. It came from his interest in the total human situation, and from the fact that he had vision enough to distinguish the bigger things from the smaller things— for instance to see that if a thermonuclear or poison-gas or bacterial war could befall us all other human endeavour is futile. This truth is not altered by any failure in himself to resolve the conflict between national interests and the international order. The dilemma faced by men of goodwill who acquire power and responsibility is remorseless. Speaking of Nehru's imprisonment of Sheikh Abdullah, Toynbee has said, 'It is more blessed to be imprisoned for the sake of one's ideals than to imprison other people, incongruously, in the name of the same ideals. Nehru lived to have both experiences.'[1] This was the nemesis of his taking on the responsibility of governing India. What passed between Nehru and Sheikh Abdullah during their talks a few days before Nehru died, and just after the Sheikh had been released from his eleven years in jail is not yet known. It is a theme for great drama; and, if men will ever recover the art of poetry again, a theme for great

[1] *Encounter*, August 1964, p. 5.

verse. If only we could know what passed in Nehru's mind, that strong yet emotional mind, during those hours!

Anti-Climax

Nehru began his fifteenth year as Prime Minister with the Goa Affair, in November and December 1961. He began his sixteenth year with the Chinese rout of Indian forces and the Chinese occupation of some thousands of square miles of territory hitherto occupied by India, in October and November 1962. Both events shook India's standing in the world; the Chinese attack shook Nehru's standing in India as well. His long Prime Ministership was thus brought to an anti-climax. By the time 1963 dawned there remained to him only a fraction of his former authority. His old inner self-assurance had been undermined.

Goa

Towards midnight on Sunday December 17, 1961, Indian forces invaded Goa. Three columns of infantry, led by parachutists and supported by tanks and artillery, crossed the Indo-Portuguese border at three points, while the Indian Air Force bombed the one Portuguese airport and the Indian Navy, marshalled in strength along the Goa coast, shelled the only Portuguese craft in Goa, an old-fashioned frigate. Armed Services Attachés in the various Embassies in Delhi later, after study, believed that there was no cause for either air or naval bombarding except to allow the Air Force and the Navy to share in the glory of the conquest. At the same time as the attack on Goa was launched the two other, and much less important, Portuguese territories, Damao and Diu, were occupied.

On the following day, Monday, December 18th, the Security Council of the United Nations was seized of a Portuguese complaint of Indian aggression. Soviet Russia vetoed discussion of the subject.

Nehru had been back only a few weeks from a peace tour which had taken him to Belgrade, Moscow, Washington, Mexico and the UN. At the UN he had proposed a year devoted to peaceful co-operation.

Goa, with an area of about 1,500 square miles, and lying about 200 miles south of Bombay, had been under Portuguese sovereignty for four and a half centuries. Nearly half the population of Goa were Catholics of long standing; a large proportion of the non-Catholics were of immigrant stock from India. The standard of living was higher, and taxes were lower, than in India; for which reason Indians liked to migrate there. Life was easygoing and relaxed in the Portuguese way; there was no self-government of the British kind but Government was paternalistic as well as more efficient than in India, and, except for a handful of malcontents, most of whom had migrated to Bombay, and, in spite of Indian money or other support given to the agitators among this handful of malcontents, there was no appreciable discontent and no appreciable demand for absorption into India. The Portuguese Governor-General was respected, and by all accounts deserved to be. Portugal's retention of Goa might have been an anachronism but it was not resented by most Goans. India's claim to Goa was never stronger than that she had a right to the whole Peninsula (saving Pakistan); by which logic Spain has a right to Portugal or the Irish Republic has a right to Ulster. This is simply the claim of *I want it*.

The Indians had worked for a *coup d'etat* in 1954; but their plans had failed. Indian propaganda about an uprising inside Goa for joining India had been exposed at the time. The reports of *The Times* correspondent exemplify the position. As is usual in Portuguese colonies, race and personal relations were good. Nehru appears to have had little or no part in the 1954 affair, but he did break off diplomatic relations with Portugal. Since 1954 considerable effort had been made from time to time to whip up a pro-India movement. Among the people in Goa the movement met with indifference when not with hostility; just as throughout India as a whole there was no interest in Goa. The only success was in Bombay amongst the Goanese migrants, mostly professional people; and it was difficult to know how sincere their agitation was. One of these people, a medical man, for instance, gained Nehru's attention in the 'fifties and got a good medical appointment, though he was not well regarded by leaders of the medical profession in Delhi. Agitating inside India and amongst Indians against Portugal gave such Goanese a certain standing which they would not otherwise have had; an escape from anonymity. Now that Goa has been taken over they have relapsed into a few hundred or thousand amongst 500 million Indians and count for nothing.

In the last week of November 1961 the Indian press, on information supplied by Government, reported an incident of what was officially described in headlines as 'Portuguese firing on an Indian passenger ship'. (It later turned out, though this was reported in only a few papers, that 'the passenger ship' was a 'country craft' sailing-boat of yawl size, and that it was in Portuguese territorial waters apparently flouting warning signals.) This was followed by what was played up, on Government prodding, as 'another Portuguese firing incident', this time an Indian fishing boat. This incident was blown up enough to awaken the ever acute nationalistic sensibilities in India. It was not revealed that the boat was poaching in Portuguese waters. Some missions at Delhi believed (but as far as I know produced no evidence for their belief) that the boat had been sent there by the Indian authorities as an *agent provocateur*. Next came a series of reports, blown up more and more, about what were described, again in headlines, as 'Portuguese attacks on Indian villages'. The information was highly coloured, but also highly vague; as were the accompanying allgations about 'Portuguese troops massed on the Indian border'. Some of the Indian newspapers, presumably not by accident, published articles on the Inquisition in the Goa of the sixteenth–seventeenth centuries at the same time as they published the reports alleging Portuguese aggression. By the beginning of December troop movements from all over India towards the Portuguese territories, more particuarly towards Goa, were on such a scale that they could not be concealed. Passenger and ordinary freight services were cancelled by the Railways for some days on end. Around Delhi itself we could see the trains moving troops and material to the south, day after day.

Nehru made many statements from late November. As was not unknown with him, the statements could mean several things; the blankets of verbiage wrapped up his meanings so thickly that they were hard to unravel. But two points were repeated. First, there is a crisis. The crisis was indicated only vaguely. Second, and more boldly, if Portugal does not renounce sovereignty over Goa in favour of India, and do so forthwith, there can be no peace. The time for negotiation has passed.

Foreign Governments, receiving reports from their missions in Delhi, began to sense that something untoward might be afoot. Diplomatic efforts were therefore initiated from several quarters to forestall violence. Several Latin-American Governments, notably Brazil, offered help and suggested mediatory courses. The British Government also offered its services, asked Nehru to give an assurance that India would not resort to force (which he refused), and pressed for a diplomatic solution. U Thant on behalf of the UN, like the United States, also asked India not to resort to force, but with more perfunctoriness than the British or the Latin-Americans. U Thant did offer to send UN observers to the Indo-Portuguese border; Nehru rejected the offer.

Nehru announced to the Indian public, with more frequency and in increasingly bellicose tones, that India's patience was coming to an end. With diplomats, however, he was indirect. Although shifting his ground with them more than once, certain points did recur. These were:

(*a*) Goa was a threat to India's security. There was 'a tremendous military build-up' there; it had become 'an armed camp'; 'aggressive manoeuvres' were going on which India could not ignore. (After, but, so far as I could find out, not before, the Indian invasion, Nehru spoke darkly of 'NATO weapons'—which the Indian public took to mean nuclear weapons—in Goa, and of a 'tie-up with Pakistan which made the problem more urgent than the border dispute with China'.)

(*b*) Inside Goa law and order had broken down because of a nationalist uprising of the people against the Portuguese. The 'white Portuguese'—another significant phrase—after trying to crush the uprising with 'a reign of terror', 'mass imprisonment', 'torture atrocities' and 'massacres', which Nehru characterized as 'gruesome', were fleeing the country to escape from their overwrought subjects. At one stage the Governor-General was announced to have fled; untruthfully. Further, at Belgaun, near the border, there were said to be between 15,000 and 20,000 volunteers and 'Goa commandos' waiting to rush in to relieve their martyred compatriots. The Indian Army could not hold back these volunteers much longer. When the invasion was at last announced the Order of the Day to the Indian troops said that they were going in to liberate the people in Goa and to restore law and order, which 'the colonialists can no longer maintain'. On the following day, the 18th, Heads of Mission in Delhi were given a Note on the invasion in which it was stated, *inter alia*, that the Indian Army was taking over Goa 'to end the holocaust and massacres', as well as to end the threat to Indian security.

(*c*) The pressures on the Indian Government to take over Goa were 'irresistible', 'unbelievable'; all the Parties in India, Ambassadors and foreign pressmen were told, wanted India to take over; if Nehru did not acquiesce he would have to resign as Prime Minister.

(*d*) India had exhausted all her efforts for peaceful settlement and now had no alternative than to use force. (Some months before that he had said that India would never use force to solve the Goa problem.) India would not negotiate except over matters to be settled after Portugal had handed over Goa to India. But Portugal must quit, and at once.

Certain foreign newspapers of standing, like the *New York Times*, the *Baltimore Sun*, the *Daily Telegraph*, and *The Times*, happened to have had their correspondents, responsible and trained observers, in Goa at this time; two of them there for a fortnight before the invasion as well as during it. What struck them all were the lies—'fantastic lies' was the term used to me by two of them—about the internal situation in Goa being poured out over the Indian radio and in the Indian press prior to and during the invasion. Some of the correspondents doubted if there were any volunteers at Belgaun at all. One thought that there might have been a handful there, mostly clerks and minor political types brought down from Bombay and dressed up for the occasion, for photographic propaganda purposes. As for 'the tremendous military build-up', a senior General concerned with the operation told me months later, by which time Volunteers and 'the Goa Commandos' had been forgotten (and were never heard of again), that it would have been criminal on the part of the Portuguese authorities to have resisted the Indian invasion as they had only about 2,500 troops; and they were poorly trained and without proper equipment, and they had no armour or artillery worth speaking of, no air support, and only one naval vessel, the old-fashioned frigate already mentioned.

The Times representative, some weeks after the invasion, and after collecting and collating the facts, wrote a long objective article; but his editor, in the interests of good Anglo-Indian relations, decided not to publish it. The plain facts were not agreeable.

For against the exiguous Portuguese forces the Indians sent in an invading force estimated at between 30,000 and 50,000 troops, trained, highly equipped, and with support weapons. Most of the Indian newspapers did their best to glorify the invasion, including spreading misinformation about the Portuguese, such as that they had carried out 'a scorched earth policy'. Indian journalists in fact were not allowed into Goa for nearly a week after the invasion. The truth became available only because some foreign journalists happened to be there when the invasion took place.

Not that the Portuguese authorities were above criticism. There is little or nothing to be charged against those on the spot but the Government in Portugal persisted right to the end in an unrealistic attitude, as well as in the legalism about Goa being no colony but an integral part of Portugal, years after warning had been given. Confronted with the claims of the Indian Government, and with the position in the UN, Portugal should have offered to hold a plebiscite in Goa, under UN supervision if possible, otherwise under any *ad hoc* international supervisory group, for or against the *status quo*. It is doubtful if India would have won the plebiscite.

The reaction in India to the Goa affair surprised most foreign diplomats. Some it astounded, as did the whole affair. They had not expected, on the one hand, such a conformist acceptance of what was so manifestly a put-up job, or, on the other, such an outburst of nationalism of the crude tribal sort. Very few Indians at any level protested against it. J. P. Narayan was one of the leaders who did. Rajagopalachari, great and greatly courageous once more, after so many great occasions, denounced it squarely for what it was. This was only a few weeks before the General elections; he knew that it would cost votes to the party he was leading, but he did not hesitate.[1] Various other people of importance, including at least two Cabinet Ministers, deplored it, but only in private. Krishna Menon, not Gandhi, was now the guide for policy. For whether, as was thought, Krishna Menon conceived and launched this aggression or not it was surely in his

[1] Cf. *Swarajya*, December 15, 1961, January 6, 1962.

spirit. Prior to the invasion he, in his role of Minister of Defence, proclaimed to the Indian forces that they were 'going to help the people of Goa following on the collapse of colonial administration due to the liberation movement of the local people'.

After the aggression not a few speeches were made. Nehru spoke several times. Then on December 28th he spoke for two hours. Evading the real issues, he argued that the action was not against, but in conformity with, UN principles; that it was virtually non-violent; and that Gandhi would have justified it (a claim disputed by several of the few genuine Gandhians left in Indian public life). Then came dark hints about the racial division of the world; it was only the whites who had criticized India, and how terrible this racial division could become ('for the whites'—this was not added in words but was clearly intended). On January 13th he made a speech at Banares praising the Army—he would have known nothing of the black marketing or the assaults alleged on Goan women—for its 'brilliant manner' in 'restoring Goa to the Motherland' and 'ending Portuguese colonialism'. Krishna Menon also spoke on several occasions but without Nehur's cat-like delicacy in leaping from one hot brick to another. Krishna Menon just dropped the bricks. For instance, he ridiculed the idea that there was anything in the affair contrary to the UN; India on the contrary was carrying out the UN resolution on ending colonialism. Once Nehru, commenting on a suggestion in the *New York Times* that India, in remorse for her unilateral violence, should now return Goa to Portugal, said that if any effort were made to get India out of Goa there would be thermo-nuclear war (presumably launched by Russia, who was praised handsomely for showing that she was a true friend to India because she had vetoed the Portuguese complaint in the Security Council. That Russia was also one of the Whites seems to have been overlooked).

The Indian press throughout the Goa affair had disappointed most foreign observers, especially those not long in India. Nehru's part in it had outraged them. More than one who hitherto had been admirers and lauders of Nehru now turned on him and denounced him as a cynical imposter. Nehru sensed his loss of status. When, three weeks or so after the invasion, a Head of Government arrived at Delhi airport and the Ambassadors were there to take part in the usual welcoming ceremonies, Nehru, for the first time in my experience, did not greet the assembled Ambassadors and he avoided looking at them. A member of his family at this time told me that he was 'crucifying himself over Goa'. Letters regretting what he had done written to him by men whom he respected were said to have cut him to the quick. When reproached by an old fellow-Gandhian of my acquaintance he justified himself, with some sadness, and urged that his conscience was 'absolutely clear'; but my Gandhian friend was convinced that his conscience was not clear.

Why, how, and when, it was decided to take Goa are questions which cannot yet be answered. On these questions the habitual secrecy of the Indian ruling group remains unpierced. Few of those in the ruling group, too, were in the know. The secret was as restricted and as well kept as was the secret of Eden's Suez adventure five years earlier. At the time various Indians in politics said that there had been no discussion in Cabinet. This has since been denied, but it is likely enough that there was no real discussion. The part played by certain individuals, such as the police officer Handoo, and General Kaul (who later retired from the Army after an unenviable performance during the Chinese attack a year later), would be of interest. Probably the part played by Krishna Menon was crucial. Even the factors leading to the aggression are not yet certain though among those cited at one time or another the following probably counted:

1. *The Elections*. They were due to be held in the following month, January. The Government had an interest in taking voters' eyes off the Sino-Indian border where incidents had been disturbing public opinion which was inclined to be critical of Krishna Menon's part in Army and Border policy. Further, in Bombay itself, the only place where there was any sustained interest in Goa, Krishna Menon was fighting a key election against Kripalani, a former President of the Congress Party and the only man left in Parliament who could speak to Nehru with some semblance of equality. Nehru regarded this election as of exceptional importance, as his subsequent, and angry, campaigning there on behalf of Krishna Menon showed.

2. Goa has the *best deep-sea harbour* in the Indian sub-continent.

3. Goa has *great mineral wealth*, especially iron ore.

4. If India was to strike she must strike now as *efforts to provoke much interest*, let alone an uprising in Goa itself, had failed, while inside India interest would not last long so that if there was to be action delay would diminish its political value.

5. It would please the *Afro-Asian bloc* who would thus see that India is no Uncle Tom.

No one could be surprised that Nehru or India had wanted to end colonialism, or was sensitive about European rulers in Asia, or disliked Salazar. But India had no legal right to Goa; and it is not easy to see where, or how, she had any moral right to it. In any case she used force, she used it unilaterally, and she used it after being given an opportunity for negotiation and mediation. This was aggression. And the aggression was without provocation. Moreover, it was aggression on a virtually unarmed neighbour. This, too, was the India of Nehru where hundreds of thousands of words had been uttered on peace and in condemning both force and unilateral action, particularly when gone in for by the West.[1] Indeed not long before the aggression Nehru had made an eloquent plea to the World Council of Churches, then meeting in Delhi, against war. His plea made such an impression that I recall a visiting clergyman saying to me after Nehru's address that Nehru was teaching them to be better Christians. At the moment he made that speech the troop trains were already moving relentlessly towards Goa. Finally, the aggression was preceded by a campaign about Goa which was as impudent as anything Mussolini had said about Albania, or Hitler about Sudetenland, before they gorged those countries.

It was not for nothing that Nehru did not set foot in Goa until eighteen months after the invasion. By then the prosperity of Portuguese times had gone and the people of Goa, more particularly the Catholic and educated half, were more resentful than ever. The elections were not held until two years after the invasion. Nehru's party, Congress, then lost in every one of the 28 seats they contested. The United Goan Party, which wanted a separate Goa State, won half the seats; illustrating the clear division between the Catholic Portuguese-speaking Goans and the Hindus, illiterate low-castes predominating among the latter. Goa was still ruled directly from Delhi.

Nehru's biographers, if they care for the high moral reputation which he had enjoyed for so long, and for its decline, will have to seek for the

[1] Cf. some of the examples from speeches made by Nehru collected by the *Daily Express* at this time, e.g.

'Peaceful co-existence has been the Indian way of life and is as old as India's thought and culture.'—Speech during Bulganin–Khrushchev visit, December 1955.

'India has given a symbol to its people—the symbol of the Asoka Wheel, which represents peace, morality, and the ancient culture and peaceful ways of this country.'—Speech in Delhi, July 1951.

'To seek to impose a settlement by force is to disregard the rights of nations.' —On Suez, September 1956.

'It is the attitude of regarding one's own conception as righteous and everything else wrong that leads to conflicts.'—At Red Cross Conference, Delhi, October 1957.

'A very small conflict has the shadow of a big conflict behind it, and a big conflict has the shadow of a world war behind it.'—On Syrian crisis, September 1957.

'The only approach we can make is an approach of tolerance, of avoidance of violence and hatred.'—About cold war danger, Delhi, October 1957.

'We do not show the clenched fist to anyone. We extend our hand in friendship towards everyone.'—On Kashmir, August 19, 1956.

'War today solves no problems but leaves behind only brutalized humanity and a trail of bitterness and hatred which forms the basis of another war.'— Speech on Gandhi's teachings, January 1953.

reasons which led him to Goa, no less than for the reasons which led to his stand on Kashmir. Until then Nehru remains charged with machiavellianism. We who watched him for so long are sure that he was not as machiavellian as this, and that he did not knowingly utter so much untruth. Nehru, in spite of Goa, was no hypocrite and no imposter. We do not yet know what were the compulsions he was under. But whatever the reasons, while he lost a great deal for something as small as Kashmir he lost still more for something still smaller, Goa. And whether, as is probable, he allowed himself to be edged, bit by bit, and especially because he was ill at the time as well as old and tired (he had to have teeth extracted because of a toxic condition a few days after the aggression, and a few weeks later a serious kidney disease was diagnosed), into a situation from which escape was very difficult, he can be acquitted of hypocrisy. But he can not be acquitted of a failure.

The Chinese Attack

The second anti-climax of his Prime Ministership took place a year later, in November 1962, when Chinese troops suddenly crossed the disputed border and virtually destroyed the Indian troops opposing them—troops of that Indian Army which he had praised for their brilliant performance in Goa.

As a result Nehru was forced, within the space of a few weeks, to dismiss Krishna Menon from the Government; to witness an explosion of nationalism inside India exceeding even that of 1959–60; and to undertake to increase the Armed Forces to almost double and to give Army leaders, whom he had always distrusted, a standing which could make the Army, hitherto without political importance, a force no longer to be ignored in Indian political life, and, finally, to accept the principle of military aid from the West, notably from USA and Britain, which could jeopardize his cherished policy of non-alignment. For a week or so towards the end of 1962 it looked as though he himself might be swept from office. The agitation against him was fomented to the utmost by those groups which wanted to get rid of him because of his Socialism and by those politicians who had old personal scores to pay off, but most of it came from disillusionment with Nehru's foreign policy and from fear that China would launch an invasion deep into India. Indians felt that they had been misled by their leader, rather as the British felt about Baldwin in 1939–40.

Such was the mood that there were even attacks on his patriotism; demands were made for giving up non-alignment; and some Indian jingoes, including overweight Members of Parliament who were too unfit to waddle half a mile, cried out for an Indian invasion of Tibet and for full-scale war with China.

I 127

For a while Nehru almost lost his *sang froid*. His own mood was even more disillusioned and more bitter than that of the people; because he was wounded by the Indian people as well as by the Chinese Government. He was completely taken aback by the Chinese proceeding to the lengths of such a scale of attack, by the scale of the defeat of the Indian troops, and by the scale of the reactions in Indian public opinion. He sent letters to President Kennedy, Prime Minister Macmillan and to other leaders, written under the impression that the Chinese might push right into India and not merely into the semi No-man's-land in NEFA; he appealed urgently for help. There are claims, not wholly without evidence, that he asked the Americans about, and apparently for, American air intervention or protection.

Two days after he sent his appeals the Chinese made their own cease-fire and offered to withdraw to the positions they had been occupying before the attack. This saved Nehru. He might well not have survived a continuation of the Chinese thrust, or even the Chinese presence in the territory they had won, given the panic and the resentments against him in India at the time. It also saved him from the kind of military aid from the West which could have ended non-alignment. Such was Nehru's resilience, and his adroitness, that he weathered the storm and within a few weeks was regarded once more by the majority of Indians as indispensable. The malcontents had to be content with lesser scapegoats, such as General Kaul, the nominee of Krishna Menon who was commanding the Indian Army in NEFA, not gloriously, Thapar, the Army Chief of Staff, and, at length, Krishna Menon himself, the Defence Minister. By then Nehru was probably regretting his appeals to the United States and the United Kingdom and was probably turning his mind to ways of getting such help as they would give without allowing the West either bases or forces in India, just filling in some gaps in India's armed strength, such as supersonic fighters. He refused to break off diplomatic relations with China.

One thing he could not cancel was the speech he made on not letting Chinese have an inch of Indian territory. This might have been politially expedient but he went on repeating it to the extent that it made it difficult for him later to come to a settlement with China.

The Indian press and politicians at the time spoke much about 'the Chinese hordes' near the Indian border; and some spoke of the invincibility of the numbers involved, or of Chinese plans to get control over India's oil in Assam, or even over the port of Calcutta. This is to be taken as a sign of the fright which the Chinese attack made on Indians. The truth is that there were only two or three Chinese Divisions involved, and that the Indian Army suffered a limited defeat. As the official Indian report on the affair a year later pointed out,[1] and as anyone familiar with the Indian Army at the time could have guessed, the Chinese were tougher, better trained, better equipped, and better led. The Indian Army, which has troops with a fighting potential as good as any in the world, especially from what in British days were called (and correctly called, though Indian nationalists had repudiated the term) the martial races, had been giving too much time to ceremonial parades. The report referred to the inferior training in mountain warfare, the inferior quality in officers, especially at the senior level, where there was incompetence and negligence, and the inferior information about the Chinese. The orientation of the Army had been directed against Pakistan; war had been thought of as the kind of war which would take place along and across the Punjab frontier; that is where the bulk of the Indian striking force was kept. It should be added that no politican of rank or standing in India, and perhaps a dozen at the most at any level in political life, had had any experience of soldiering. It is doubtful if there were half a dozen M.P.s at Delhi who had any personal knowledge of, or who took any interest in, or had any instinct for, Army or defence matters.

Nehru had had to bend to the storm. But he escaped surrender. He took various steps to appease public opinion, such as setting up the Defence Council and putting some of the critics of himself on it; but he gave it no real power; it enabled him to hamstring the discontented retired Generals. He circumvented the pressures for giving up non-alignment and for accepting the proffered Western umbrella. He circumvented the pressures for giving up the Plans or for turning the Indian economy into a war economy; or for concentrating the Armed Services on the hypothesis of China as the enemy; or for breaking off relations with China. At the same time he managed to get more aid out of the West—the Pakistanis feared that it would be enough to tip the balance against them still more—though he failed to get the supersonic jet fighters. What he got, as someone said at the time, was military reliance without military alliance; which was not little. He bowed to some pressures from the United States and England, notably to hold talks with Pakistan; but, helped by Pakistan's over-playing its hand, he let the talks drag on for a few months until they petered out. He got the United States, apparently with the help of an American Ambassador who was new to these matters and to Diplomacy, to recognize the McMahon Line. Hitherto the Department of State had refused to recognize it, a fact not without significance; the White House now overruled the Department of State. And inside India itself he put the Emergency to good use by getting more power for the

[1] Henderson–Brook's report; some of the contents were released to Parliament by the Defence Minister in September 1963. No names were mentioned.

Central Government. It was a virtuoso's performance; and the more remarkable as Nehru, not long recovered from the first serious illness in his life, was old and tired. But he could not recover what mattered most: his former standing as leader in his Party and in Parliament or with the educated classes.

And the picture of India which emerged then was not one to give comfort to his drooping spirit. He could not have been happy about a good deal in the nationalism which had come over India. Indians, until recently soporific from the years of speeches about the India–China brotherhood, felt black betrayal by China. Under the first shock Indian mobs fell on harmless Chinese who had been living in India for many years—Japanese diplomats, who looked like Chinese to the Indian mob, felt obliged to put signs on their cars to the effect that they were not Chinese. This reaction against the Chinese, understandably heated at the beginning, settled in a few quarters into a 'nationalism which was narrow-minded, self-centred, legalistic, and moralising.[1] Just as India had insisted that there was nothing to discuss with Portugal over Goa or with Pakistan over Kashmir she now took the line that there was nothing to discuss with China. China must accept the so-called Colombo Power proposals *in toto*, though in fact those Powers had had their doubts about at least some of India's case just as few if any Afro-Asian countries were convinced that there was no case for discussion. When in October 1963, a year after the attack, Chou En-lai offered to visit Delhi to discuss a settlement this was dismissed as 'a mere propaganda trick'. Nehru, in short, was left with little if any leeway for negotiating what was negotiable.

Evening Light

As 1963 opened Nehru looked on a prospect littered with ruins—the ruins of his hopes, and the ruins of a prestige seemingly so impregnable for a dozen years or more. Kashmir; Goa; the Chinese border; Indian standing in Africa and South-East Asia; in India itself the Naga uprising; Indian nationalism getting out of hand; Hindu revivalism gaining ground; Communal violence worse than ever; more and more money on armaments; the Plans awry; hunger; more inefficiency in Government at all levels; corruption at all levels, including amongst his own Ministers; gloom about what would happen on a scene which he must soon leave. Indians were even impugning his patriotism. Nehru probably took little comfort from the fact that whatever the truth about his failures the biggest truth of all was the immense scale of the problems the first Prime Minister of India had had to wrestle with, and how successful he had been with some of the problems and

[1] Some Indians recognized this. Cf. Amlan Dutt, *Seminar*, No. 51.

how near to succeeding with others. By 1962 and 1963 anyone knowing him over the preceding ten years was struck with the marks of sadness. His voice had lost some of its timbre; his silences had become longer and more enigmatic.

The Chinese invasion was the blow of havoc. The existence of Pakistan, like the connected massacring of Muslims by Hindus and of Hindus by Muslims, outraged his sense of reason, his belief that the world is, or can be made, a rational place. Goa had undermined his confidence in himself. The Chinese invasion had undermined his confidence in men, in Indian men as well as in Chinese men; it had repeated the outrage on his sense of reason, but it had done more: it had betrayed a trust; a trust given generously, and for great ends. Trust is the foothold of life itself. Betrayal, the basest wrong, shatters the very ground on which we walk and have our being; that oaths are straw, that men's faiths are wafer cakes . . . Nehru walked in a dazed way after Goa. After the Chinese invasion he never walked firmly again.

Did this lover of poetry know Browning's lines on Aeschylus soliloquizing in his last years?

> I am an old and solitary man,
> Mine eyes feel dimly out the setting sun,
> Which drops its great red fruit of bitterness,
> Today as other days as every day,
> Within the patient waters.

Chapter 5

THE MAN

During my years in India I kept a collection of photographs of Nehru taken from the Indian press. The day was infrequent when some newspaper or other did not publish one. The photographs are a revelation of his many sides and many moods. They leave no doubt that in any discussion on him the first question to be disposed of is: Which Nehru are you talking about? Is it the internationalist with hankerings after pacificism? or Nehru the planner of the Goa takeover? or the Nehru who made the moving speech on Gandhi's assassination? or the Nehru who risked his life when the Hindu mob fell on the Muslims in 1948? or the agnostic Nehru who was drawn to Buddhism? or the revolutionary in a hurry? or Nehru the wily politician? or Nehru the connoisseur of poetry and roses? His variousness was also reflected in the variety of people he was happy to give his time to—scientists, writers, artists, actors, social workers, and certain men of religion, as well as the administrators, politicians and soldiers native to a political leader's world. There were two men in Dr Jekyll and Mr Hyde; there were more like twenty in Nehru.

Of at least one thing, then, can we be certain: Nehru was complicated—even more than the average man, who is complicated enough. He was divided within himself as few men could be who at the same time retain overriding purpose and essential balance. It is because of this complexity that one cannot be sure of having penetrated to the core of his motivation in any particular action or policy, let alone to the core of the man himself. There is more than one passage in his life which is still to be explained.

And we can be certain of another thing. Politics was far from being the whole world of Nehru; which it is of many, if not of most, ruling men.

Aesthetic

The dominant impression left on a person meeting Nehru for the first time would be aesthetic—his elegance. He was always well dressed,

132

not foppishly but in good material, cut well, worn well, and usually adorned with a rosebud in his button hole; the whole matching his good looks and the grace with which he bore himself. Up until the last year or two, when his health was failing, there was little of the old man about him. He never got slovenly. The elegance was more than just clothes; more even than the good breeding which was an inseparable part of him. At times his face took on an expression which got near to beauty; the kind of expression sometimes seen on the face of Yahudi Menuhin (for whom Nehru had regard) or in portraits of Cardinal Newman or the young Dickens. The clothes were an expression of an internal elegance—an absence of all coarseness. It was not for nothing that one of his severest animadversions was 'vulgar'.

Nehru arrived at Bandung for the first Afro-Asian Conference in 1955, after a long tiring motor journey under an equatorial sun. His entourage arrived dishevelled and weary, as did most of the delegates. Nehru arrived looking as though he had just had a bath after a refreshing sleep. It was the same after his journeyings in hot dusty India. His comeliness stayed with him, whatever his surroundings.

His body was slight but well-shaped and athletic; his features were clear-cut and handsome; his skin, light brown in colouring, was perfect in texture and healthiness; and his eyes, even more than Indian eyes in general, were large and striking. Grace was as natural to him as it is to a leopard.

His manners were punctilious and his courtesy fine. He was scrupulous in such things as not keeping people waiting, or seeing them to the door. There was, doubtless, some acting; there usually is some acting in civilized living, and, still more, in political leadership. Nehru certainly did some acting on public occasions and before the TV cameras; but never much. The acting was never worse than the pose of *Cha Cha* (Uncle) Nehru with the children. This was at its worst on his birthday for a few years when sycophants organized groups of children, with flowers and copious photographing, to parade with him. It was out of character; his interest in children was slender. But his acting was on the periphery of his personality. He did not fake. His readiness to grant TV or newspaper interviews sprang in part from the fact that he enjoyed doing what he did so well, but also in part from the fact that he was reluctant to disappoint people who had come to India to see him. Most of the TV and radio interviewers got a rich haul for their pains. And whatever little acting he might have gone in for, it never made him self-conscious. Normally, too, if he was angry he did not conceal it. If not pleased he was apt to project his lower lip. Those familiar with him at once recognized this for what it was, a storm signal.

His grace was heightened by his aliveness, his mobility of face, his taking in and responding to everything around him, which gave him, to a degree seen in few men, a flame-like quality. At times, such as when confronting the Opposition, there was, for all his sensitiveness, in later years his tormented sensitiveness, something eagle-like about him. And for all his sensitiveness he was never touchy. His charm lost nothing from a whiff of natural hauteur.

He spoke quietly as a rule. He was not talkative; at times he was taciturn. His speech was in a voice which rose and fell engagingly and was clearly articulated. It was well suited to his conversation, which was usually reasoning as well as reasonable. In later years his voice had an undertone of pathos. He was never loud or trivial or gossipy.

It was due to his fastidiousness that Nehru found a certain type of American, and certain American ways, uncongenial, though he had an admiration for some Americans and for some aspects of America. After his death his family found amongst his papers some verses he had recently copied in his own handwriting from the American poet Frost. Nor were some Australian characteristics, or figures, to his taste though he had a regard for others. He saw a good deal of Lord Casey.

A mixture of distinction and charm was the keynote to Nehru's presence, be it in Parliamentary debate, or around his dining table, or on such banal occasions as presenting prizes or laying foundation-stones. He was a master of the art of saying nothing of substance to his interlocutors if need be and yet of leaving them feeling unoffended or even flattered. On occasions he heightened his charm by flashes of wit unexpected in a man often serious to the point of greyness, and on occasions even by funny stories. Once I heard him ask a foreign visitor, who was a little dashed by the Indian practice of eating with one's fingers, whether he knew what a Shah of Persia had said: the Shah found eating with a fork like making love through an interpreter. (Nehru himself always ate with a knife and fork.) Most people found Nehru captivating. I certainly did. When in his presence I usually found it necessary to keep jolting myself back into detachment.

Body

Nehru would have been an exceptional man if he were judged by his physical endowment alone. In the words of an Indian who worked closely with him during the first twelve years of Independence, he was a 'miracle of health'. His outpouring could have had few parallels in this or in any age.

During the years I knew him, in his sixties and early seventies, Nehru worked seven days a week. He rose at dawn, or even earlier, took exercise, including Yogic *asanas*, and including for some years the dubious exercise of standing on his head. He sometimes went horse-back riding. He used to be fond of swimming in earlier years. It was only after seventy that the Yogic exercises were given up or curtailed. For a time he followed the régime of a Kashmiri master of Yoga who came to the house. (Yogic exercises are normally aimed not at muscle development but at harmoniousness and lack of tension.) For a time, too, he had a herbalist attached to his household. But no man was less hypochondriacal than Nehru. Sukarno's addiction to medicine bottles was foreign to him.

After bathing he used to prepare his own breakfast, which was frugal, though latterly it was being prepared for him. For years any one could come to his garden at about 8.30 in the morning and bring grievances, or just talk to, or look at, him for half an hour or so. From then onwards he worked through the day without let except for lunch and dinner—state papers, staff, political and other conferences and committees, interviews, visitors of every conceivable variety, sitting in and running Parliament or Cabinet, giving decisions, writing minutes and letters, and, several times a week, not unoften several times a day, making speeches. The background to this outpouring of energy was never-ending crisis, and therefore never-ending stress. In addition to being Prime Minister he was Foreign Minister, Chairman of the Planning Commission (which meant Minister in charge of the National Economy), Minister for Atomic Energy, at times Minister for Defence, as well as leader of the Congress Party with its Governments in sixteen or seventeen States to watch over. Lunch and dinner, especially until the last five or six years, were used as occasions for talking to, or receiving, or showing attention to, people. At 10.00 or 10.30 at night, when he parted from his dinner guests, he would go the office in his house and work until about midnight or 1.00 in the morning. The minutes memoranda and letters he then wrote, tersely and with effect, must add up to hundreds of thousands of words over the years. He usually read for ten to thirty minutes in bed until he dropped off to sleep.

He slept about five to six hours a night. In his seventies he took to having a half-hour nap occasionally on Sunday afternoons and in the hottest weather; and for some years he had been dropping off to sleep in aeroplanes. Though using up relatively few hours of the twenty-four in sleep he had a life-saving capacity for putting himself to sleep whenever he wanted to—he either worked out a problem or he put it out of his mind. He had never known insomnia, just as he had never known headaches. In his seventies he sometimes dropped off to sleep for a while at meetings.

On an average he used to receive in the latter years about 500 letters and 100 telegrams each day; callers from outside (i.e. not his officials), chosen out of 50 or 60 applicants, averaged about seven each day; he made about 25 speeches a month; and he was away from Delhi on official tours about sixty days, or two months, each year. He kept up this pace until his first illness, in 1962; and he had got back to most of it before his stroke hit him early in 1964.

Anyone associated for some years with government in Delhi became so familiar with Nehru's capacity for sustained effort that he took it for granted. And Nehru's example somehow affected his Departments of State. You could always tell whether he was in Delhi or not, without asking. There was a spring about the senior officials when Nehru was in town.

Of the many examples of his capacity for work which could be cited here are two.

A Governor of the Reserve Bank, who was once Nehru's Principal Private Secretary, recounted one of his experiences.[1] In August 1947, during the Partition troubles, Nehru and his party set out at six one morning. They flew for an hour and then travelled by car and jeep through the scenes of the massacres in the Punjab, where, in addition to the physical strain was the nervous strain of experiencing 'his hopes, his dreams, his faith in human nature . . . crashing down'. It was 9 at night when they got back to base. Then, after a meal, Nehru held discussions with the Pakistan Prime Minister until midnight. He then worked on papers, writing or dictating minutes and instructions, until 2. He was up again at 5.30. 'Something like it,' his Principal Private Secretary wrote, 'some sixteen to seventeen hours out of twenty-four, has been the practice with him day after day, week after week, month after month, all these thirteen years. The members of his staff, who are all much younger than himself, have never been able to keep pace with him . . . this extraordinary vitality.'

Another Indian official who worked closely with him for several years as head of the External Affairs Ministry told me how after a gruelling four-day official tour of Nepal Nehru slept a little on the plane on the way back to Delhi but as soon as he got to his house he set to work on urgent papers and continued working until 4 in the morning. After a couple of hours of sleep he was at work again until midday. He then went to the airport to keep an appointment with the Gliding Club to try a new glider. He spent an hour in the air, though it was a day of dust and with the thermometer standing at 110. This informant had already been astonished by Nehru's performance in Bhutan in 1958 when he trekked on foot tirelessly and out-paced men some twenty years younger than himself.

[1] H. V. R. Iengar, Rafiq Zakaria, *op. cit.* 117 *et seq.*

For years he took no holiday.

It is said by those who have lived with him, for instance in prison, that Nehru while not fussy, and never hypochondriacal, always took care of his health. He did not drink alcohol and though he smoked he rationed himself (ten cigarettes a day in latter years), he took exercise regularly, and he ate moderately though well. This care, or prudence, however, was the mere fringe to a physical endowment which, like Churchill's, amounted to genius. During the years I knew him I can recall only two occasions when he had to take to his bed other than for the kidney ailment in 1962. Both occasions were for a cold and they lasted only a day or two. His physical capacity was paralleled by a will to live every minute of his life—his zest was as great as his vitality. And both zest and vitality were at the command of an unusual will power.

Mind

Nehru's intellectual endowment was also exceptional. It was not better than that of Rajagopalachari, the sharpest mind in Indian public life for many years; and it did not have the originality of Gandhi, for Gandhi had a power of mind to match his power of spirit. And, in general, Nehru was probably clever and wide-ranging and lively rather than profound. But few indeed have been Heads of Government in our time with such a force, or such a range, of mind. In history he is to be compared in this, as also in his capacity for the written word, and for his sustained physical effort, with Napoleon. Napoleon in office, however, was nearly thirty years younger than Nehru, he ruled for a shorter time, and he suffered little from the lashings of conscience. Once when I took a scientist to Nehru, a biologist and Nobel Prizeman, the latter made a careless statement about some work. Nehru pounced on it, politely, and demolished it. This was typical. Few errors in reasoning escaped him. I have seen and heard a dozen or more Prime Ministers at Nehru's table: all but two or three were yokels beside him. If his knowledge lacked solidity, this was normally because he lacked time, though there are those knowing him who insist that it was his nature to skim the surface. For many years his reading had to be done in odd minutes snatched from public cares.

Nehru began with the advantage of the best formal education possible; and just as he improved on his physical capital so too throughout his life he improved on his intellectual capital, by the study of books and of men. In particular his years in jail were put to use for a rigorous and systematic course of reading and writing; in particular he used them for developing his sense of History.

An Indian official who for some years was permanent head of a

Department of which Nehru was the Minister used to say that he never ceased to be astonished at how Nehru managed to do real thinking—probing analytical thinking. Nehru's mind, he would add, was extremely quick. He was struck, too, with Nehru's power of concentration, with his memory, and with his natural orderliness. As a result his mind could be brought into instant and effective play, like a gun always loaded.

Nehru's range of interests extended over Science (especially Physics and Biology), and Literature as well as over History and Statecraft. He had a fair knowledge of French. He kept up a lively, emphatic, though not always well-informed, interest in Natural History and especially in animals; an example of which will be found in his introduction to Gee's book, *The Wild Life of India*, which he wrote less than three months before he died. The mainspring of his political thinking came from the nineteenth century English socialists, but it was not fossilized at that point in time. He remained sensitive to the currents of thought throughout his lifetime. The bold pioneering side of his outlook is illustrated by the fact that he made his first aeroplane flight as far back as 1912. When only fifteen he was fired by the achievements of the Wright brothers; in 1909 he went and saw Zeppelin's airship in Berlin; in 1927 he saw Lindbergh arrive in Paris; and in 1960 I saw him welcoming Gagarin, the Russian astronaut, in Delhi, with a boyish enthusiasm. His mind was avidly curious, and his most lively interest pertained to anything bearing on man's quest to subdue Nature. That is why he caused the National Laboratories—a score or so—to be set up. He had not the time to check their working and was let down by their staffs again and again. Probably of all the research groups he set up only the Atomic Energy Commission, under Bhabha, completely justified itself. It was his intellectual curiosity which saved his speeches from boredom, however unprepared and rambling they might be; and which made him interesting as a companion; for unless preoccupied or exhausted with public cares he was ready to talk about any subject, and what he talked was never banal.

Nehru's mind, moreover, was on most subjects an open mind as well as a full mind. He had his prejudices—Maharajas, Portugal, Moneylenders, certain American ways, Hinduism, the whites in Africa—and he used to get some illusions, such as about Co-operative Farming or about the progress in Community Development, or about certain persons; and he could be emphatic on a basis of insufficient knowledge; but in most things he was without dogmatism. Only occasionally did his cocksureness take on rigidity. This quality was probably connected with his being a Brahman, the caste to which belongs the custody of truth. His attack on the Prime Minister of Australia at the UN in 1961 was an example, though there were other factors behind that attack. By nature he was intolerant of opposition; so much so that more than one of his senior collaborators considered him unteachable. At times he seemed the exemplar of Swift's dictum that the most positive men are the most credulous, for he could be taken in to a strange degree by people which men of far less perception would have seen through. But rigidity or obstinancy or credulousness ordinarily did not last long.

Nehru's outbursts of temper were due mostly to impatience, especially to the intellectual impatience natural to a quick mind, though sometimes they were due to strain or to emotion. On the emotional factor a revealing statement was made by him in his speech to the Commonwealth Press Union in Delhi in November 1961 on the conditioning factors in national psychologies and how these result in Indians thinking at two levels—intellectual and emotional. (He made this speech without any preparation, coming to the hall straight from the airport and a flight from Calcutta and preceded by twenty-four gruelling hours there.) This mixture of the emotional and the intellectual explains why one of the driving forces in Nehru's life was socialism, why his attitude to Europeans could become ambivalent, why he gave himself to India but in some important respects was out of sympathy with Indian ways, and why on occasions he made absurd statements. Some, but by no means all, of those who worked close to Nehru used to say that he did not want yes-men, and that he was prepared to listen to adverse comment even though he might fly into a temper about it. Whether this point be established or not will depend on evidence still to come. In my own experience nearly all political leaders want yes-men in the last resort; they vary as to how they like the *Yes* to be said. As for his temper, Nehru's bark was worse than his bite. But it could be an intimidating bark.

Though at bottom he remained, as do most Socialists, optimistic, though he was committed to certain viewpoints, and though he allowed himself outbursts of impulsiveness, on occasions a headlong impetuosity, Nehru had detachment. In most things he had it to an unusual degree—including about himself. Here again he was not a Brahman for nothing. Normally he was not involved emotionally in a deep way, or for long. This applied even to the death of those who had been near to him. Some of the officials who had worked closely with him for some years were surprised and hurt to discover on their leaving him that they had meant little to him personally. As one complained to me, they were like discarded coats for which there was no longer a need. Some women also discovered to their surprise that Nehru was not to be impressed. The romantic outlook was, as he himself wrote, foreign to him—though probably not quite as foreign as he believed. He had been apt to see revolutionaries through romantic eyes. His detachment, which grew with the years, was the more remarkable as he was not a cold man. He could weep as well as laugh. Perhaps it began as a defence against his own sensitiveness and his own individualism. With his detachment went an uncommon capacity for abstracting himself from his immediate environment; for instance at a banquet or a concert or a parade, and giving himself to thought. On these occasions, which people sitting next to him did not find flattering, you could almost see his mind working, and the very speed of it.

The detachment was due in part to his balance. He could lose his balance; but usually he recovered it quickly. As a rule he was not only a man of liberal mind but he was 'the sensible man' *par excellence*; a quality of Nehru's which Samuel Johnson would have known how to value. The way he, aided by Radhakrishnan, dealt with the novel *Lolita*, quietly and without censorship, was typical of this side of him. So was his attitude to the press. He believed in the freedom of the press, but he knew that the phrase meant for more than one press proprietor merely the freedom to make profits, without regard to truth or decency.

And the detachment was due in part to his aloneness. He wrote once, 'One must journey through life alone; to rely on others is to invite heartbreak.' What de Gaulle has said, more than once, *la solitude est la misère des hommes supérieurs*, has particular relevance to Nehru. Hence his reserve, which few, if any, managed to penetrate; and hence his having no real confidants. In his last five years or so he was utterly alone; so alone as to be friendless. His aloneness was, to some extent at least, also Brahmanical and rooted in his self-assurance. He felt, for all his Hamlet-like hesitations, that he knew best. A few persons, notably his daughter, and perhaps in some things Lady Mountbatten, had more of his confidence than usual. In latter years Krishna Menon got closest to him in policy for a while, but the relationship with Krishna Menon was *de haut en bas* and was scarcely a personal relationship. It is possible that one reason why he worked so hard was to escape from loneliness. With the progress of time his aloneness got nearer and nearer to isolation; and towards the end it got near to the isolation which is insulation; encasement in the thick wool covered over him by sycophantic politicians or servile officials, and the drugging plaudits of vast anonymous myth-worshipping crowds. Nehru became insulated from some of the realities of India and Indians and from some of the things going on.

The insulation was the worse because Nehru could be strangely at fault in judging people. More than one mountebank and not a few crooks did well out of his aberrations of judgement. How could Nehru have made a Minister of one of the two women he put in his Cabinet? How could he have kept in high office the man to whom he once entrusted

Parliamentary Affairs? Did news of a certain Minister's passing on Cabinet secrets to one of the Mawari magnates escape him? Did he not sense the cynical calculations of a certain buccaneering Chief Minister he took up for a time? And he lacked the succours of a strong sense of humour, or of hobbies. It is impossible to think of him taking up Krishna Menon's hobby of playing with toy trains.

Balance could not have come easily for Nehru, given the ardour of his temperament and the intricate responsiveness of his mind and the resulting bouts of indecision—those painful oscillations back and forth between the case for Yes and the case for No, those contradictions and self-contradictions, and the ineradicable ironies of his position. The dualism was illustrated by his attitude to Gandhi—angry contempt for Gandhi's anti-Science and anti-Rationalist outlook, yet awe for his moral quality. It was this frequently un-Indian Nationalist who wrote of himself in his *Autobiography*: '. . . a queer mixture of the East and the West, out of place everywhere, at home nowhere. . . . Perhaps my thoughts and approach to life are more akin to what is called Western than Eastern, but India clings to me, as she does to all her children, in innumerable ways; and behind me lie somewhere in the subconscious, racial memories of a hundred, or whatever the number may be, generations of Brahmans. I cannot get rid of either that past inheritance or my recent acquisitions. They are both part of me and though they help me in both the East and the West, they also create in me a feeling of spiritual loneliness not only in public activities but in life itself. I am a stranger and alien in the West. I cannot be of it. But, in my own country also, sometimes, I have an exile's feeling.' To have completed this self-judgement he should have added that he did achieve a synthesis between India and Europe and that in himself he demonstrated the realities of coexistence. Some of the lack of precision which certain critics of his complained of were due to his synthesizing; for precision can be the child of rigidity and the foe of coexistence or catholicity. One observer, Tibor Mende, thought that Nehru's *dualité le troublait et le stimulait à la fois*; that he was enlarged by it greatly.[1] What is to be added is that, for all his oscillations, deep down he was stable; the centre was still and fixed.

Some of his associates, more particularly some of his old companions, complained that he had lost the capacity for affection, that he had become impersonal, even that he did not appreciate what was done for him. There may be something in this though on examination the complaint often turned out to be that Nehru had not had as much regard for the complainant as the latter thought he should have had, or had not given him this or that job. From questioning old associates it

[1] In *Le Monde*, Mai 27, 1964. Also see his *Conversations with Nehru*.

seems unlikely that Nehru ever had much capacity for personal affection or for intimacy. With the years he ceased to have emotional involvement with persons at all, only with causes. He seems to have developed something like a horror of intimacy. This aloofness is one reason why, unlike Gandhi, he evoked respect rather than love in those working with him. His father and Gandhi would be amongst the few for whom he got closest to having personal affection; but, like Ravel the composer, or William Morris—the regrets recorded in Wilfred Scawen Blunt's Diaries show how William Morris's indifference struck one gifted observer—Nehru let his life become absorbed so much in other things that personal relations, no less than the small change of existence, meant little to him. So great was his detachment that we can believe him to a large degree when he wrote that even political life touched him only on the surface.

We can be certain that complaints about 'loss of idealism' and being 'spoilt by power' are to be treated with scepticism. Too much power for too long did have an effect on Nehru, though not as great as his having too many exhausting responsibilities for too long. He was concerned to stay in office not because he wanted material goods or to boss others, as do most men who seek power, but became without the power of the Prime Ministership he could not shape India in the form to which he had given his life, or prevent those developments which he reckoned evil for India. There are not many men who have been so little corrupted by power as Nehru. The game of politics no doubt fascinated him; for no game is more fascinating, and it happened to be a game for which Nehru had a flair; but it often disgusted him too, and with the years it sickened him. All along he refused to have anything to do with bickering or intrigue. He fought like a knight.

Like many egalitarians, Nehru himself was authoritarian in temperament. And, like any other ruler, he had to be concerned with harnessing men's wills, and so with manipulating feelings in order to carry out his purposes. He therefore had to be concerned with men in groups, and so with the impression he was creating on them. He could not afford to wear his heart on his sleeve. He had no doubt made compromises, such as winking at the corruption in the Punjab or in certain of his Ministers, believing them necessary for reasons of political expediency. One got the feeling at times that he accepted the thinking common to men concerned with power, and especially in India, that the victors and the rulers are entitled to some booty. But it is certain that he did not take booty himself, or find these booty-taking associates congenial. The fact that a number of his relations, and, still more, Kashmiri Brahmans, were given high office might be due in part to some ineradicable deposit of Indian feeling about family and caste lingering on in Nehru, but it would be due mostly to his belief that they had superior ability. As Head of Government, Nehru, for so long the agitator, learnt as late as his late fifties what running a government is really like as well as learning what average men are really like. Creighton, the saintly historian, who was also an Anglican Bishop, learnt so much about his priests in running his diocese that he came to defend the Renaissance Popes. Nehru in his later years became gentler and with a touch of melancholy. What were his later thoughts on men? on Indians? on trust and trustworthiness?

Having quicker wits than most men, Nehru the politician was no doubt subtler, and therefore a more wily politician, than most of his colleagues. His management, and for years, his domination, of the Congress Party showed this side of him again and again. The evidence for his wiliness—some would use a harsher word—is not lacking. The so-called Kamaraj Plan of 1963, and his thwarting President Prasad's intrigues in 1959, are examples. Towards the end he got near on occasions to guile, and his state-craft got near to craftiness. Yet how untainted he was, and how much more there was to him than to most Prime Ministers!

In 1961, he was persuaded to open the premises of the Ramakrishna Mission Institute in Calcutta and inaugurate a conference on spiritual life. On reaching the place and seeing how grandiose the premises were, he burst, with Nehruesque headstrong reaction, into the following speech:

'I have always avoided using the word spirituality because of the existence of much bogus spirituality. India is a hungry nation. To talk of spirituality to hungry men does not mean anything. . . . It is no good running away from the daily problems of life in the name of spirituality. I am out of place in this gathering—I am supposed to open this building and inaugurate the conference. I do so.'

He then stalked off.[1]

This brings us to his attitude towards religion. The communal—i.e. Hindu versus Muslim and Muslim versus Hindu—frenzy in the 'twenties and 'thirties turned the passive rationalism he had inherited from his father into an active dislike for religion. 'Not only,' he wrote in 1924 to a religious Muslim friend, Syed Mahmud,[2] 'has it broken our backs but it has stultified and almost killed all originality of thought and mind . . . this terrible burden . . . this poison. . . .' After seeing Hindu–Muslim murderings he had come to feel about religion what

---

[1] *Statesman*, November 12, 1961, 'Depth of Poverty'.
[2] R. Zakaria ed., *op. cit.*, p. 14.

many intelligent people in the eighteenth century, after the torturings, burings and Wars of Religion in the seventeenth century, had come to feel about it. Thirty-five years later, under questioning from a Marxist-minded Parsee, Nehru spoke of 'ethical and spiritual solutions'. 'What you say,' interjected the questioner, a little disdainfully, 'raises visions of Mr Nehru in search of God in the evening of his life.' 'Yes,' said Nehru, 'I have changed. The emphasis on ethical and spiritual solutions is not unconscious . . . the human mind is hungry for something deeper in terms of moral and spiritual development, without which all the material advance may not be worthwhile. . . . The old Hindu idea that there is a divine essence in the world, that every individual possesses something of it and can develop it appeals to me.'[1] For some time Nehru had been showing an appreciation for Buddhism. The last occasion I had a talk with him, in 1963, he remarked, 'I am not irreligious.' Two days before he died he wrote in a foreword, 'We must not forget that the essential objective to be aimed at is the quality of the individual and the concept of *Dharma* underlying it.'[2] His agnosticism was not only always uncompromisingly honest and stern—fairy tales were banned from his daughter's reading when she was a child—but it belonged to the religious spirit. Hedonism was repulsive to him. Gandhi, whom Nehru never quite got to the bottom of, knew his Nehru: he refused to regard him as a materialist. It may have been more than old age, too, which made Nehru from his late sixties feel more drawn to Gandhi than he did during most of the days when they were alive together, just as he felt drawn to Buddha. 'Buddha,' he said, 'is in us all.' Whether, seeing how little the Buddha element finds expression in men's actions, he got more consolation or more sadness from the observation is not known.

The Good Man

Nehru's physical and intellectual endowment were, like his aesthetic appeal, extraordinary; but what in the final account impressed me most was his goodness.

> *If only the good were clever!*
> *If only the clever were good!*

Nehru was that rare man who is both clever and good. It is hard to be clever. But it is harder still to be good. He was that very rare person, the clever man wielding power who remained good. No wonder Nehru wrote somewhere of the tempests raging around him being nothing to 'the storms within' him!

[1] Karanjia: *The Mind of Mr Nehru*, p. 48.
[2] Quoted *Swarajya*, June 20, 1964.

Syed Mahmud, one of the leaders of the anti-Jinnah Muslims and of Congress, who had known and lived with the Nehru family for years, who had been with Nehru at Cambridge and then with him in prison off and on, and who in recent years disliked some of Nehru's policies as Prime Minister, always ended any talk on Nehru with some such phrase as 'But Jawaharlal is a good man, a pure man. I am still in love with him.' Syed Mahmud himself, then in his seventies, was also a man of goodness, and his testimony on goodness was worth something.

Another Indian, this one a South Indian Brahman and an intellectual, who also had had some difficulties and disappointments with Nehru, would always finish with some such phrase as 'But Jawaharlal is the truly emancipated man in the sense of your St Paul—he is emancipated from prejudices of caste, religion or money; he is really the man of goodwill'.

An Indian of my acquaintance who had worked with Nehru off and on in the Independence movement but had got separated from him over policy differences, would always praise his quality of 'never making a fetish of his own prestige', and of his always being ready to forgive and as far as possible to forget. Like many others, this person used to touch on another quality in Nehru, namely the life-long dedication to schooling himself, and to hardening his will, though he regretted that this was at the cost of light-heartedness and geniality. But think of nine years in prison without cracking or without deteriorating!

Much schooling indeed must have gone into the process of turning Nehru from the spoilt only son, and the shy, withdrawn, highly-strung and fastidious young man, into the consummate master of crowds, the man living in the public gaze, and the man who, in the interests of politics, suffered an interminable procession of bores and vulgarians and self-seekers. A Muslim Justice of the Supreme Court, now dead, an Allahabad man who knew the Nehru family well, speaking of Jawaharlal as a young man, would end up 'He was impossible'. His growth through self-discipline was therefore the more remarkable.

Great courage had gone into the schooling. Courage in fact was the quality valued above all other qualities by Nehru, as it was by Samuel Johnson; and failure of courage was what he most despised. One of his Ministers told me once just after the death of a terrorist who had been involved in throwing the bomb at Lord Hardinge, the Viceroy, in 1912, that an appeal had been made to Nehru for giving the man a State funeral. He refused angrily; he regarded the man as a coward. The word 'coward', which Ayub of Pakistan once, in an uncharacteristic moment allowed himself to use against Nehru, foolishly as well as unjustly, damaged the prospects of good relations between the two rulers.

His personal kindness, and the trouble to which so over-charged a man gave himself, never failed. Some of his too innocent judgements on individuals, as also his allowing unimportant foreign visitors to encroach upon his time, were due to his kindness as much as to the politician in him. His kindness to people of worth who also had humility was without limit. An old Scotch-Australian scientist had somehow got interested in Nehru and out of this interest he came to India several times at his own expense. He had little money, lived and travelled cheaply, and never thrust himself forward. In due course Nehru came upon him. Savouring his virtue and his mind Nehru arranged tours for him, put transport at his disposal, and spared nothing for the old man and his wife. His interventions in cases of personal hardship were endless. He naturally received a mail too big for him to read all of it but he insisted on knowing about hardship cases. I know of his helping an obscure Indian Christian girl who wanted to marry a Pakistani and was in difficulties; of his intervening in troubles arising over an attempted marriage between a Muslim and a Hindu; of his paying the house rent or education expenses and giving other aid to various people. In Delhi his own house was often the refuge for people in distress. Out of kindness Nehru invited people to stay in his house who could have no conceivable demands on him or be of any conceivable use or of interest to him. It is hardly known, even in India, that though his Government kept Sheikh Abdullah in prison, he arranged payment for the Sheikh's son to do his studies for Medicine in London and that the young man used to spend part of his vacations in Nehru's house. I once asked an Indian politician, of better social class and education than the average, who had been one of Nehru's Parliamentary Private Secretaries for some years, what was the main impression Nehru left on him. He replied: 'Kindness, fatherliness.' Nehru might have avoided emotional engagement as regards most individuals but he remained kind to most, for above all he had compassion for the human lot. Born rich he died poor.

Nehru's temper was a fact. He could be petulant too. He was not always an easy man to work for. His temper was sometimes said to be due to his vanity; rather it was the release required by a highly-strung man who was over-burdened. When one thinks of the wordiness all around him, and the fussiness, and the ineffectuality, and the begging, and the prevarication, and the corruption, the wonder is that the outbursts were not more frequent. Not that he was without any vanity. No man becomes a Tribune of the People without some vanity. And Nehru's vanity sometimes led him into demagogy. Yet few public men were less diverted by vanity than Nehru. He had as little of the typical politician's exhibitionism as he had of his lust for power. He never talked about himself, except inder assiduous prodding, and then little and reluctantly; he never advertised himself; he never held the floor; he never put himself forward. In spite of his occasional lapses, the high-pitched and the ecstatic were distasteful to him, and became more and more so with the years; as did all pomposity and pretence. His was the simplicity which only the good can affect or afford. And as for the temper, when he let fly at someone he later, in expiation, heaped attentions on the victim. A Latin American Ambassador in my time was charged with looking after the interests of a certain country with which India had broken off relations. A foolish man himself, he had received a foolish instruction from his Foreign Minister to see Nehru at once, put up such and such fairly unimportant request, and to remind Nehru that he and the Foreign Minister knew one another. It turned out that Nehru and this Foreign Minister, with dozens of others, had once been at the same international meeting for a day or two. The Ambassador insisted on seeing Nehru, who was busy with serious matters at the time, and on delivering this portentous message. When Nehru, thus interrupted, heard it he flew into a temper. But for weeks afterwards he went out of his way to make up for it to the Ambassador. That is why it used to be said in Delhi that it was an advantage to get Nehru into a temper with you.

But there is no point in lengthening the account of his virtues, such as his innumerable acts of secret benevolence, his loyalty to old friends and to awkward or insignificant persons; his refusal to gossip, or to be petty, or to harbour resentment, or to speak ill of persons except to their face; his generosity, Puritan though he himself was in practice, about human failings; his wholesomeness; his general reliability; and, notwithstanding areas of secretiveness and stratagem, his candour and straightness. When he provoked resentment he usually sought to allay it. Outside of lawful battle he would inflict no wounds. Nehru had less of the common and less of the mean than all but a few men. And he is to be numbered amongst the small band of rulers in history whose power has been matched with pity and mercy. Like Abraham Lincoln, the more Nehru gained in authority the greater his compassion became. I was in India when he was at the height of his popularity and power. I was also there when his popularity sank to its lowest level. He passed both these exacting tests equally well. He wanted power; but he wanted it for a cause, not for himself. The driving force behind most revolutionaries yelping for equality is nothing more than to pull down those above them; they have no objection to being above others. Nehru might have been ignorant or misguided about some matters, and about some persons, but he was always disinterested, always concerned with what he thought would help Indians or mankind. We can be certain that there will be no revelations to make about him of the kind which are often made about celebrities; not even revelations like those of Churchill's disagreeableness. Nehru's private face differed scarcely at all from his public face.

How much a Ruler?

Yet will the historians, looking at his unusual opportunities of person, of position, and of length of office, conclude that Nehru as a ruler of India did as well could be expected?

In his last years, as has been seen, he did little ruling. He largely confined himself to running the machine, to clinging on to certain power points and to concentrating on a few major policy matters. His basis of information became more shallow; often a mere half page or so of potted notes from one of his staff.

It would be out of plumb to judge Nehru on his last few years— years of weariness and disillusionment. His long life must be taken as a whole. Senescence is not to be denied of its toll, even on the strongest frames and nerves. Nehru's lashing out right and left, as at times during the electioneering of 1961–62, the chopped logic, the unfinished or incoherent sentences, the self-righteousness, were mere minutes towards the end of many years of intense activity, and of an epic life. That there was some disintegration is not surprising. What is surprising is that there was so little of it. Usually the nearer rulers get to supreme power the sooner the disintegration sets in. The last years of Napoleon or Stalin or Mussolini as rulers repeat a familiar pattern of nescience and self-delusion. The wonder about Nehru is that he retained so much balance after so long.

The question about Nehru's rule is not how much he disintegrated but how much he was by nature a ruler at all.

Was he in control? Or, to put the point in another way, was too much which mattered out of control? To take a relatively small but revealing example, why did certain things happen right under his eyes while he was exercising quasi-dictator authority?

Thus Delhi itself. That incomparable inheritance for the new Republic, Old Delhi from the Moguls (who had taste) and New Delhi from the British (who put the genius of Lutyens to splendid use), was a capital with no superior for dignity in the world. In Nehru's time it grew from less than a million to over three million inhabitants and, under his own eyes, huge profits year after year were made by exploiting the need for housing the influx. A rash of jerry-built housing estates spread for mile on mile. Prices rose to indefensible heights. One of the Ministers in Delhi, aware of what was happening, and privy to the secret town-planning programme, made a fortune in buying up peasant holdings and then sub-dividing them for urban development. Nehru made speeches thundering against the slums, but year after year the slums grew bigger. Or, to take a trifling but indicative instance, the American-type advertisement hoardings along the ten-mile stretch of road from the airport to the city. Nehru deplored and castigated them more than once. But the hoardings remained. Indeed they multiplied.

Thus, again, to take what was not a trifling matter, the making and selling of spurious drugs. This gross scandal was exposed repeatedly. But nothing was done, although the British had left ample legislative and administrative authority for coping with it. The family of one of Nehru's Ministers was involved in it. Nehru gave much time to the Congo, or other far-away places, or to far-away things like collective farming, but he did little that was effective about more than one largely manageable evil near at hand.

Thus, yet again, the corruption amongst highly placed colleagues in the Party and in the Government. Was it really politically unavoidable for him to connive at these malefactors ? The Prime Minister who could override the politicians to the impressive degree of bringing in an outsider like Radhakrishnan, bearing none of the indispensable tattooings, such as a prison record, not even the Gandhi Cap, a scholar and a philospher and a South Indian Brahman, and imposing him as the first Vice-President and the second President of India, was not afraid of the politicians. Yet in the Punjab, the State which adjoins Delhi, a régime flourished for as long as eight years, the last eight years of Nehru's life, which was vitiated with corruption and abuse of power.[1] The Chief Minister, whose power was based on his majority of kept place-men in the Punjab Legislature, used, or allowed to be used, the apparatus of the State for enriching his family. They specialized in the opportunities which the issue of licences and permits offered but did well out of a wide range of other interests, including deals in real estate and factories and medicines. The Chief Minister, with increasing insolence, interfered with the Civil Service, with the police, and even with the Courts. As far back as 1959 there had been a murder case (the Karnal case) which would have ended his political career in a rooted democracy. The textbooks used in the State schools had eulogies of him; and the mass media at the disposal of the Government were put to singing his praises. The favourite phrase of this saviour of the people was 'the common man'. He held forth about his increasing food production or carrying out development plans in a way which paltered with the truth, to say the least. For some years well-informed persons in North India knew what was going on; but Nehru, apparently convinced that the Chief Minister

[1] The Das Report—Mr Das was formerly Chief Justice of India—was released three weeks after Nehru's death.

was indispensable for maintaining political stability in the Punjab, a State admittedly with serious internal troubles (an influential group of Sikhs were agitating for setting up a Sikh State), and of special military importance because it bordered on Pakistan, resisted demands for an enquiry. What unseated the Chief Minister in the end was his arrogance, not his pillage. And when at length he could no longer live down the revelations and the angry public outcry (though up until a few days before then the press in general had been ambiguous about him) he tried to insist that it would be he who nominated his successor and that his successor must be 'a man of the masses'; by which he intended one of his accomplices. As for himself, he promised to give himself up to religion and, in particular, to 'cleaning up the Sikh temples' (where there is a good deal of wealth).

In another State adjoining Delhi important persons in its Government and in the local Congress Party were involved in large-scale smuggling across the Pakistan–Rajasthan border. The Bakshi régime in Kashmir was another example of misuse of office and it lasted longest of all. There were some other States with Congress Governments which also carried corruption far. And there were some Ministers in Nehru's own Cabinets who could not have survived a proper investigation.

That is to say, Nehru found himself with a degree of power which has rarely been precedented, yet in practice he made relatively little use of it. Why? Subhas Chandra Bose, Nehru's rival in the pre-War Congress, and the founder of the war-time Indian National Army under the protection of the Japanese, thought, according to an intimate of his whom I knew, that Nehru did not have the makings of a ruler.

It is unlikely that a man would have held the place Nehru held for thirty years or more in the Congress Party, which included dozens of men of outstanding ability and ruthless ambition, without having the makings of a ruler. Leaving aside the fact that Bose was in temperament, and perhaps in intention, a Fascist dictator while Nehru was the opposite, Nehru had to an enviable degree some of the qualities of the ruler. He was practical and flexible. He had drive. He had courage. He had a flair for politics. He had a contempt for inefficiency and weakness in governing. In the 'thirties he once wrote and published anonymously a criticism of himself in which he spoke of his 'overwhelming passion to get things done' and that this passion predisposed him against the slowness of democratic processes and therefore towards dictatorship. He had, too, that something which belongs to the born commander of men—the capacity to charm and to enthuse combined with a capacity for keeping men at a distance. This involves amongst other things keeping one's own counsel and keeping men in some way or other in fear of one, even if it is only the fear of verbal lashes.

Yet with all these and other great gifts Nehru does seem to have lacked something required in ruling.

The lack was more than just not delegating authority enough though this did lead to some inefficiency as well as to too little in the way of collective government. It was more, too, than misjudging men. It is hard to believe that in a country producing so much and such varied talent as India does Nehru had no alternative than to people his Cabinets with such a ballast of nonentities as he did; and that he should repeat, and greatly multiply, Smut's mistake in not breeding up a group of young and tested potential successors. There were, too, some strange cases of divulging confidences asked for, for instance about the misconduct of this or that person, and his not seeing that he was letting down the informant.

Was the root of the trouble that Nehru was imperious but not ruthless? He used the iron against himself rather than against colleagues or subordinates or the ruled? Lord Attlee, whose obituary article on Nehru[1] contained a series of penetrating observations on him, said that Nehru 'understood power and he understood poetry but what he didn't see was where one began and the other left off'.

Somebody has said that a man cannot be a good Prime Minister unless he is a good butcher—to slaughter Ministers and others as required. Nehru, on the contrary, dismissed or demoted Ministers and others who were evident failures or liabilities with the utmost reluctance, and only as the last inescapable resort.

But the butcher thesis must not be carried too far in Nehru's case. It is misleading to make out that he was more gentle, or had more of the feminine in him, than was the case. He had a tough side, as was well known to those who worked for or close to him, and as was shown clearly on his face at times. The butcher thesis, too, does insufficient justice to Nehru's deliberate repulsion from anything savouring of dictatorship. Dictatorship was utterly abhorrent to him. I recall Rajkumari Amrit Kaur, for ten years in his Cabinet and one of his few social equals and without fear of him, once going to him to get him to intervene over some matter. He refused. 'What you are asking me,' he said, 'is that I be a dictator. You have come to the wrong person....'

Nehru, for all his intellectual self-confidence, and for all his imperiousness, had a strange reluctance to impose his will on others. He would argue with them, lecture them, ridicule them; but he would rarely command them. For ruling men, for mastering and directing their wills, there is often no alternative to ruthlessness. The ruler rules.

That commanding men went against the grain was due largely, I think, to his tendency to see both sides of a question. He had not the

[1] *Observer*, May 1964.

comfort of the simple-minded who see only what is, or seems to be, just in front of their noses any more than he had the impulses of the bullying power-wielder. It was this awareness of there being two (or more) sides to a question which led to his indecision. He had an indecision over and above the wish to avoid the hard clear-cut decisions which are normally uncongenial to the Hindu temperament. He tried to avoid committing himself; he wobbled on the fence (as at certain points in the Hindi versus English debate); he would make statements which were categorical, even fierce, but were then cancelled out, or which could be interpreted in several ways or which could not be interpreted at all. Again and again he stood hesitating on the brink of a decision until some firmer or coarser or more reckless person edged or pushed him into the plunge. That is to say, the complexity of his mind too often—not always—prevented him from that over-simplifying, that reducing issues to black and white, which is common to the authentic men of action, such as Churchill or even Gandhi.

Probably Nehru's reluctance to command was also connected with the Brahman in him. It is difficult in the climate of our time to make clear what this caste means, this sense of utter race purity, so exalted that wealth or poverty is irrelevant, and this membership in a small ancient unadulterated group to whom the truth has been given, and the hereditary right to expound the truth. It is for those who receive the exposition to carry it out. Brave man though he was Nehru thus had more of the teacher than the ruler in him. How much a teacher he was is shown in amusing things such as his letters to his younger sister.[1] Hence his arrogance of mind coexisting awkwardly with some humility as a commander. He was sure that he could do his own thinking. He did not mind picking up from others a phrase or two, for instance Panikkar's phrase that the Sino-Indian frontier is 'now a live frontier', or the fashionable economic jargon about 'the take-off'; but he felt no need to pick brains. Even critics did not bother him greatly. It was his Kashmiri Brahmanism, too, which had something to do with his habit of not coming to the point directly, of not revealing his mind, of putting up a smoke screen of rambling but purposeful verbiage. The Brahmans have existed as a tight community, biologically, psychologically, and socially, for several thousand years. Shaw, Bertrand Russell and Wells existed only yesterday; and Harrow, Cambridge and the Inner Temple have been in existence for only a few centuries.

His Brahmanism, moreover, might also have predisposed him to certain delusions. He was deluded by certain individuals, but above all he was deluded by the very thing which gave him his strength and his confidence—the crowd and his immense prestige with it. Religion

[1] Krishna Nehru Hutheesing *Nehru's Letters to his Sister*, February 1961.

may or may not be the opiate of the people but the people were the opiate of Nehru. Those adoring applauding millions little understood what Nehru was designing, but, worse, Nehru, more and more insulated, had the illusion that he knew and was in contact with the people of India.

The truth on the contrary was that he was alone—alone on a high bleak peak, largely unsheltered against the ceaseless winds of self-seeking, sycophancy, and tale-bearing.

Human beings in general find living alone with secrets intolerable. They need to share the burden with others. This is particularly true of those with the burden of rule, for an inescapable part of that burden is the carrying and the keeping of secrets. Moreover, those carrying the burden of rule need to check with others the reasoning leading them to this or that decision. Most rulers or leaders have therefore relied on some person or persons. Gladstone and F. D. Roosevelt relied on their wives; some, like Mussolini, on a mistress; some, like Hitler, on an inner gang. Nehru had this need, and all the more so because of his alienation from much that is most characteristic of Mother India; yet—and in this he was like Salazar; a fateful paradigm— he also liked going alone. He could carry the secrets to an unusual degree without going to someone to unburden himself. He had no wife. He had his daughter whom he could and did trust though it is doubtful if he unburdened himself to her entirely on affairs of State, at least before his last years. In the old days he went to his father or to Gandhi when he needed to unburden himself, or to get advice. These two men were never replaced. Up until the mid 'fifties he was going for some political counsel to Kidwai and to Maulana Azad; he had had many years of close political association with these two Congress Muslim leaders. After their death there was no political figure left from the front rank of the Independence struggle except Rajagopalachari. All the rest had died off. Men like Pant were in the second rank; and the rest all owed their position to Nehru. His relations with his Cabinet and with political colleagues in the Party and in the States were purely political and largely routine. Merely from the political point of view Nehru was a solitary by the middle of the 'fifties.

Krishna Menon

It was Nehru's aloneness combined with his reluctance to be ruthless which gave Krishna Menon the special place he came to occupy from the middle of the 'fifties.

Krishna Menon's position puzzled foreigners when it did not appal them. Indians were almost as mystified as Americans, and not less disapproving. The foreigners had seen Krishna Menon in London where he had spent a picturesque quinquennium as High Commissioner, or at the UN in New York, where, with the aid of certain American newspapers, he had made himself the biggest bogey man living outside of Russia, with everything for the role of a Dulles Bad Man except a beard and a fur cap and a Russian accent. At UN meetings even to cool and hardened diplomats and journalists, he seemed eccentric when not needlessly provocative, and at times he seemed mischievous and untruthful; a man born for intrigue and discord.

When Krishna Menon returned to India in 1954 he was less known amongst his compatriots than he was in London or New York. He had been out of India for nearly thirty years. He spoke no Hindi, indeed no Indian language except his maternal Malayalam; gossips said that he had forgotten to speak that properly. In any case Malayalam is spoken in only the extreme south. I remember a lunch party in Nehru's garden in 1954 when two or three elders of the Cabinet snubbed him offensively, and, again, how at a Congress meeting in Central India others tried to put him in his place. For months Maulana Azad stood out against Nehru's wish to get him into the Government.

Krishna Menon began his colourful life in Malabar, in 1897. He belongs to the Nair caste, that gifted South Indian matriarchal community which includes the clans of Pillai, Panikkar and Menon, and which has been associated with government for generations. His father was a lawyer by profession but by tastes a scholar. The family lived according to the usual standards of the professional middle classes; Krishna Menon does not come from the proletariat. He was an only son but there were several—some say eight—daughters in the family. He remained loyal to his family, for all his long absence, just as in his days of power he remained loyal to Londoners who had known him and had dealt with him in his days of obscurity. He has a capacity for giving and evoking affection; amongst highly talented men, like the surgeon Dr Baliga, as well as amongst his nieces. As a boy he was a keen Boy Scout and found his way through the Boy Scout movement to Mrs Annie Besant's Theosophy Centre at Adyar (near Madras). This early enthusiasm and training might have given him some of the flair for the Armed Services which he revealed, rather unexpectedly, as Defence Minister. At Adyar he was noted for his activity and his intelligence but also for his sharpness of tongue and a certain violence in his reactions to persons. Mrs Besant, according to an informant who was there at the time, had to speak to him about these shortcomings. At Adyar, where he trained as a teacher, he became a devotee of J. Krishnamurthi, the young man whom Mrs Besant had selected as the pre-destined New Messiah. It was with help from Mrs Besant that in the mid 'twenties Krishna Menon went to England for further studies. By 1928 he had ceased to be a Theosophist. As a student at the

London School of Economics (where he got a First Class; he was also admitted to the Bar) he had, like so many Indians and other Asians, been influenced by Laski. He also seems to have had contacts with Saklatvala, the Parsee Communist who was a Member of the House of Commons. He soon gave himself to the Indian League, which concentrated on spreading Congress propaganda, and especially amongst Indian students. He remained its secretary and living force from 1927 to 1947. It was during these impoverished days that he formed the habit of living largely on cups of tea—20 or 30 a day—and biscuits. His activity was tireless. He picked up a living in various ways, often by writing. He was the first Editor of the Pelican Books series, a pioneering effort much to his credit, and he was an active member of the Labour Party. As a Labour Party man he was a Borough Councillor for St Pancras from 1934 to 1947; it was he who started the St Pancras Arts Festival. During the War he was noted for his energy as an Air Raid Warden. In 1938–41 he was the selected Labour candidate for Dundee—the seat then held by Dingle Foot as a Liberal—but the selection is said to have been cancelled by Transport House because of Krishna Menon's Communist associations.

Throughout this period in London he was also acting as Nehru's personal representative, including being his literary agent. When Nehru became Prime Minister he chose Krishna Menon, in preference to another whom Gandhi preferred, as High Commissioner to the United Kingdom. When Krishna Menon returned to India in 1954 few foreigners, or Indians, knew that the relationship between Nehru and him was an old one. They soon got to know too much about his faults and too little about his merits to understand why he got so close to Nehru after 1955.

Krishna Menon had some big faults, such as self-assertiveness; rudeness, at times capricious, at times gratuitous; tenseness; a penchant for the mysterious and the conspiratorial; an arbitrary way with the truth; personal likes and dislikes which upset his balance; an incapacity for team work; and what, in public life at least, is worse than wickedness, he had something odd about him, some found it a touch of the fey, some a touch of the twisted, but whatever it was too many found it objectionable.

Yet his virtues were of a kind which put him on a plane reached by few members of Nehru's Cabinet. Most of Nehru's Ministers, like most of the Party caucus, were provincial mediocrities, untravelled, ill-educated, narrow-minded; not a few were lazy; some were cow-worshippers and devotees of ayurvedic medicine and astrology; some were dishonest. Most of them held office because this or that State or language or caste had to be represented in the Government. Few of them believed wholeheartedly in Nehru's policies: some were secretly hostile to them. Nearly all were afraid of him or sycophantic to him. None of these things could be said about Krishna Menon. Moreover, he had a natural appeal for many young people; which other Members of the Cabinet lacked conspicuously. Whatever could be said against him was soon being said in sections of the Indian press as well as in the foreign press. Such became his reputation that as late as 1964 a well-known London financial journal could refer to V. P. Menon—a respected and competent retired senior civil servant: one of several respected and competent retired senior civil servants with the clan name of Menon—as 'the great Mr Menon, not the egregious Mr Menon'. This is when ignorance becomes ludicrous.

The 'egregious Mr Menon' alone in the Cabinet spoke the same political and social language as Nehru though perhaps with some added Marxist inflections. He had a knowledge of the outside world and of foreign relations approached, but scarcely equalled, by only a couple of other Cabinet Ministers, and a wide range of reading; and he could be relied upon to put the case whenever required, usually effectively, and to fight for it. His capacity for work, his drive, his spartanism, and his combative courage, were as great as Nehru's. It was not for nothing that he had spent the war years in London and had made no effort to dodge those front-line dangers. And he had the ruthlessness which Nehru lacked. More than one sculptor and painter was fascinated with his face and gait. Seen against the world of the powerful Mawari plutocrats as exposed in Judge Vivian Bose's report, or against the world of the average politician, and seen against the background of his long past associations with Nehru and against Nehru's aloneness, there is little mystery about Nehru's preference for Krishna Menon as a close political associate.

But a preference that is understandable may not be wise, especially if carried far.

For the five or six years prior to his fall in 1962 Krishna Menon counted. No record of Nehru in those years can leave him out. He got a house opposite Nehru's and, although it became a familiar sight to see him half-whispering to the Prime Minister in some corridor or at some public gathering or other, he developed the habit of slipping over to the Prime Minister's house at night. There was no personal intimacy; there was no equality in the relationship; and Krishna Menon seems to have kept his worse manner well under control when with Nehru. More than once Nehru lost patience with him; especially with the atmosphere of tension he would generate. Whether the dislike for Krishna Menon—no figure in Indian public life aroused so much dislike—was justified or not, it is a fair question to ask if for all his merits he had the equilibrium for the role Nehru allowed to him. Some of his performance at the UN not only did harm to the standing of India. It lacked common sense. He had undoubted gifts yet there was something incomplete about him; and his very merits made the lack the more risky. It is also a fair question to ask if a leader and a ruler of India alienated from certain cherished Indian values to the extent Nehru was could afford as his principal counsellor a man who was alienated from them still further.

Was there another, and perhaps a deeper though possibly not quite conscious, reason for Nehru's relationship with Krishna Menon? Is it too fanciful to wonder if Krishna Menon gave expression from time to time to certain subliminal things in Nehru which he would not allow his conscious self to express, such as on the West or on America or on race? Nehru by nature was an emotional man who had schooled himself into an iron self-control. It is for the psychologists to explain whether Krishna Menon might, over and above the more commonplace connections noted, have served the purpose of expressing Nehru's subconscious mind for him and thus of materializing or getting out of his system certain demonic currents inside him.

Chapter 6

BUILDING AND DESTROYING

How much does a leader lead? How much more can he do than to give expression to the dominant mood of his time and place? Great leaders have no doubt done more than this, such as by slanting, at certain strategic points, the mood this way or that, and by seizing this opportunity or that. But, in general, leaders are less free than we are apt to think. Nehru himself once said in my hearing, when explaining to an Australian physicist why he had not taken a certain measure, that a leader cannot get too far ahead of his public opinion.

Bertrand Russell and Cow Worship

Nehru would have been made acutely aware at times of this limit on him as a leader because his motivations were so different from those of the majority of people in India. The world of Bertrand Russell, Shaw, Wells, and the Fabians, was largely the world of Nehru the political leader. The world of the majority of Indians is a millennium or so away from that world. How far away is recalled to us by what comes out in the Indian police courts; or, if this be thought too special, by what goes on in the villages. Four out of every five Indians live in the villages; the village world is a world of status, with caste as the hard core, of the gods and their sanctions, of the horoscopes, and of the sacred fauna.

That the gap between the world of the British scientific rationalists and socialists on the one hand and the cow-worshippers on the other could be bridged in a score or so of years has been the strange delusion of the Western world as well as of Nehru. But in any case a bridge was required between Nehru and the average Indian, and this would have to be in the form of some man more Indian than himself. His confidant Krishna Menon could not form the bridge. Vinoba Bhave, the leader of the Land Gift movement, one of the few authentic Gandhians left, understood, and was understood by, rural and traditional India. Nehru respected Vinoba Bhave personally but did not seem to take his movement seriously; which can hardly be surprising.

Jaya Prakash Narayan was a different matter. He had as much feeling for the Indian spirit as Vinoba Bhave, but in addition he was internationalist and he understood contemporary economics and sociology. After a courageous period as a revolutionary nationalist he had become a disciple of Gandhi; and in most things he remained a disciple. He had also spent years in the United States and was therefore familiar with the world of machinery and factories and elected rulers; and, as a former Marxist, he was equally familiar with the conceptions of a planned economy. In the early 'fifties Nehru had thought of making him his Dauphin. But Jaya Prakash Narayan, who had already renounced the material world, then renounced the political world. He abdicated his leadership of the Indian Socialists and took to an *ashram*.

He did nor renounce responsibilities as an Indian citizen, however, and, though smitten with diabetes, he travelled, wrote and spoke a good deal, always on the side of intelligence, goodwill and courage. He was never of bigger stature than in the last year of Nehru's life. When so much which was spurious was raising its head he exemplified the India which is mature enough to endure self-criticism and to take the non-conformist line. After the anti-Muslim massacres in Bihar and Orissa he, together with some of his *Sarvodaya* colleagues, visited the scenes and systematically ran down facts. On April 16th he addressed a letter on the subject to the Presiding Officers of both Houses of Parliament and to political leaders. This appears to have impressed Nehru; but on the general public the effect was one of hostility. Undeterred, Jaya Prakash Narayan lost no occasion for pleading for the injection of 'a fresh dose of candour and courage' in place of 'a putrid atmosphere of hatred, hypocrisy, and moral smugness'. This led to bitter attacks on him in India, illustrating, incidentally, how far Nehru's values of an anti-communal India were from a large number of Indians.[1] Early in May his life was threatened. Still undeterred, he turned to India's relations with Pakistan, and notably over Kashmir. He pleaded for a confederal arrangement.[2] Nothing comparable, intellectually or morally, came out of Pakistan. He also turned to the other subject which was inflaming Indian feelings—relations with China. He suggested amongst other things that India should offer to lease Aksai Chin to China.[3]

Because Jaya Prakash Narayan had renounced the political world, one man remained who could have supplied the bridge which Nehru needed, Chakravarti Rajagopalachari.

---

[1] Cf. press, especially vernacular, April 28–29th. There were exceptions, eg. *Maharastra Times*.

[2] Cf. *Hindustan Times*, May 15th; also Indian press August 15–17, 1964.

[3] Cf. Indian press August 24th. Also see his letter to *Statesman* August 9, 1964, urging Indians not to be touchy about Commonwealth matters.

Rajagopalachari

Rajaji, as Rajagopalachari (sometimes written Rajagopalachariya) is usually called in India, would have complemented Nehru. Nehru needed the support of an equal. He needed, too, the criticism of an equal. After the death first of Patel, in 1950, and then of Maulana Azad, in 1954, the only man left who had a political experience, or a record in the Independence Movement, comparable to his own, was Rajaji. Rajaji had joined the Independence Movement as far back as 1907—he was eleven years older than Nehru—and in 1919, at the age of forty, he threw up a highly remunerative law practice to follow Gandhi and austerity. He served five prison sentences. Besides, he was the intellectual and moral equal of Nehru. He could have ended the situation prevailing in which no one could, or would, stand up to the Prime Minister; the situation whereby he was surrounded by men all of whom owed to him their jobs, whether as Cabinet Ministers or as officials.

Endowed with an exceptionally strong and quick mind, Rajaji was in spirit harmonious and without volatility or anything partaking of the theatrical. Vanity was excluded from his nature. Although he had so much affinity for traditional India, he knew the lore of the West, having a good acquaintance with the Bible and Plato and the English classics as well as with Jurisprudence and Economics; and he knew the case for economic development. Although he was religious, and conservative, he was not conformist. He had the true conservative's trait of combining scepticism about what man-made systems can do for human nature with the personal kindliness to individuals which socialists, dealing with human beings as statistical groups and abstractions, sometimes lack. And he had wit, that life-renewing gift.

Rajaji had been one of the first Indians to be Premier of a State, and it would not be easy to show another who was better as Premier. He had stood out as an able administrator as well as a ruler who knew how to command. Like Gandhi, he was though a Brahman, as much a man of action as any soldier. And he knew the game of politics as well as Nehru did. His relations with the DMK during his late eighties showed that his politician's hand lost none of its cunning to the very end. He was thus a practical man. He was a thinker, too. Gandhi leaned on him, for there was no sharper mind in the Independence Movement, which did not lack sharp minds. Gandhi loved Rajaji even when Rajaji refused to accept some of his policies, such as the *Quit India* policy of 1942. Gandhi's son married his daughter. The range and force of Rajaji's mind was illustrated week after week for the post-Gandhi generation in the weekly paper *Swarajya*. His articles were mainly on Indian politics, not always impartial about Nehru, but sometimes on physics, genetics, sociology, or morals. Being as much a citizen of the world as Nehru he gave close attention to the Nuclear Arms race. He was well aware what were the true priorities, and that the invention of the bomb dwarfed other priorities. To this end, at the age of 85, he left India for the first time in his life in order to persuade Kennedy, Macmillan and De Gaulle to give up the tests. Kennedy was delighted with his visitor and gave him his time generously.[1] He was in his eighties when writing his *Swarajya* articles. He was a natural writer. A master of English prose, he is also considered one of the best writers in Tamil, his fables and stories already being classics. His translations from the Sanskrit are also highly regarded.

Rajaji had succeeded Mountbatten as Governor-General; being the first Indian and the last person in that office. He should have been the first President of India. Nehru tried to get him selected; but non-conformist spirits, especially when they join great force of mind to great force of character and to an unbending integrity, may be respected but usually they are too uncomfortable for the majority and so are not liked. The run-of-the-mill Indian politician never felt at home with Rajaji; and for the sufficient reason that Rajaji's was not his home. They preferred Prasad, a respectable man but a natural subordinate, as Head of State.

As the years went by Rajaji became more and more critical of Nehru's policies and practices. In 1959, already over eighty years, he broke away from Congress and founded a new Party, *Swatantra*. It provided the sharpest intellectual opposition to Nehru. He was particularly opposed to all the moves towards turning India into the Leviathan State; and he particularly feared the sort of hypnosis into which he believed Nehru's unique personal standing was lulling both the Indian people and perhaps Nehru himself. He became increasingly sceptical about Non-Alignment; and he had doubts about some of the developments in the Afro–Asian world.[2]

As for the bridge, Rajaji could have been the bridge between South India and North India. South India has counted for too little in the Indian Republic. This is a waste for India as well as an unfairness to South India, because the South has a superiority in certain important things—in its relative lack of violence, its lack of anti-Muslim intolerance, its lack of indiscipline and delinquency in the Universities; in its better educational standards, its better government, and its clean-

---

[1] Information from Shiva Rao, who was present at the Kennedy–Rajaji meeting.

[2] Cf. 'The trend in the mis-governed half-baked democracies in all parts of the world is for elections to disappear and for the military forces to take people by surprise,' he wrote in *Swarajiya* on May 23, 1964.

liness; in its far lesser practice of corruption and its little taste for Hindu revivalism. If the English language is saved to India as a living language it is the South which will save it. But Rajaji could have been a bridge of still greater consequence—a bridge between Nehru and the India of the average Indian; a bridge between the physical and technological needs of contemporary India which fired Nehru and the traditional India of timeless values which Rajaji, like Gandhi, valued.

Rajiji saw himself as standing for the religious view. He believed that, to quote his own words, there is a greater Reality behind the sense reality and that spirit is immortal. He feared that this was being lost sight of under Nehru's Government. He feared, too, the loss of freedom. But Nehru, too, respected the world of spirit; and, as well, he wanted freedom though he thought freedom was meaningless if men were hungry. The synthesis, not unattainable, surely, was never produced between these two freedom-loving and spiritual men. Here was great drama, two figures of Shakespearean scale in contest. And the drama was tragedy, for the contest was needless. Both men were required by India in the two crucial decades following Independence; and both men shared the blame, though perhaps not in equal measure, that there had been fission, not fusion, between them.

Transitoriness of the Nehru Era

Nehru's rule will leave some mark on India, but not as much as is expected. The future is likely to show that the roots did not all strike deep.

In the 'twenties and the 'thirties the British authorities both misunderstood and underrated Nehru. After Independence he was misunderstood once more, but this time the world overrated his régime. What was ephemeral about it was rarely perceived.

Given his long personal dominance, misunderstanding was hardly surprising. His Ministers counted for so little. Could half a dozen of the several scores of them serving in his Cabinets be remembered by the public a couple of years after they left office? Yet the truth is that Nehru's personal dominance masked the continuing existence of the deeper forces in the Hindu world hostile to his viewpoint, such as caste and regionalism. Illusions born of the masking were heightened by the sycophancy and the vested interests of the politicians and the officials who owed their careers to him, and of the journalists who owed their careers to publicising the current dominance.[1] The phrase 'our great

---

[1] As late as November 1963 the *Illustrated Weekly of India* published a profile of this quality though it was a pale reflection of what was common from 1947 to 1960.

leader' became an incantatory ritual. Foreign visitors encouraged the illusion, sincerely if ignorantly. Nehru himself, however, sensed that his policies could be transitory. That is why he was in such a hurry to set India firmly on the road to industrialization and socialism, and why he had such a fear of Hindu revivalism.

Concealment of the truth might well go on for some time after the disappearance of Nehru from the scene. Lip service might well be paid to him years after his policies have been given up, just as lip service was paid to Gandhi years after most of the things Gandhi stood for had been given up. Officially Gandhi remains the Father of the Nation. His policies, however, are, like his famous *ashram* at Sevagram, now far gone in decay.

Not that all the work of Nehru will perish. Even some of the good work, such as the new legal protection for women, might for once not be interred with the bones of the doer. The evil—or if a milder term be preferred, such as the less good—will surely live on. For instance the rousing up of the masses. It was Nehru who, with Gandhi, aroused the mob. In that way he brought new forces into play in Indian life. But they are forces for lower things than Nehru, or Gandhi, had in mind; and they could overwhelm the things he cherished. Then there is the power of unionized labour. Only a fraction of labour is unionized, and India has millions of unemployed, but the blackmailing by certain unionized groups, such as hospital employees or municipal garbage employees, due to the artificial labour scarcity their unions have succeeded in creating in those areas of work, is not reassuring. In addition to mob violence and to restrictive Trade Unionism there is also the related phenomenon of the rise, in all the parties, of a cruder type of leader. It is not merely that the expensively educated gentlemen, like Sir S. Banerjea[1] or the Saprus, have almost disappeared; they belonged to a class which is now disappearing in most countries. It is that the public man is, like the whole world of public life in India, getting on to a different level—less educated, less disinterested, less public-spirited, and more concerned, indeed almost exclusively concerned, with *interests*: local and caste and personal, and in concrete material terms. This earthiness, too, goes with a proneness to narrow nationalism. Examples occur on all sides in India today, and not only examples drawn from the two great vested interests of the Trade Unions and Business. A Bengali writer has shown some examples recently in his study of what he calls the Plebeian Revolution and the resulting change in the leadership of the Communist Party no less than in that of Congress.[2] In South India the revolution takes the form of the campaign against the

[1] Cf. his *Autobiography*, 1925.
[2] Asok Mittra, *Seminar*, November 1963.

Brahmans, who are now rapidly being pushed down to the status of a depressed class.[1]

Nehru the man wanted passionately to destroy the caste system though he remained indestructibly a product of the caste system—through and through a Brahman. When in his youth he came into contact with the English he discovered several things which shook him, as they shook most Indian students coming into contact with England and the English. He discovered that he was an Indian and not merely a Brahman and a Kashmiri from the UP; for that is how the mass of the English, inevitably ignorant of the Indian social system, saw him—as an Indian, not as a member of this or that caste from this or that region. He came to feel, too, a shame-like disapproval for some Indian ways of life; and he discovered what he thought was the means of getting rid of the unworthy things, especially the poverty. The means were the rationalist and socialist ideas which represented the advanced thinking in England at the time.

He was thus in an ironical situation from the beginning. The irony, the inconsistencies, the dilemmas, remained with him throughout life. His long Prime Ministership was stamped with the irony of inescapable inconsistencies. All men exercising power are confronted with dilemmas; all revolutionaries whose revolution has succeeded in unseating the previous rulers, and who are thus called upon to rule, are confronted with special dilemmas; but Nehru was confronted with dilemmas over and above these. His lot was permanent dilemma, and his fate was to be always trying to fight his way out of it.

Thus he needed power to give Indians what are now called human rights as against the status society of Hindus, and to bring to them technological changes for alleviating their hunger and suffering. But to get this power he must have the Congress Party as the ruling Party. That meant conniving at an ever-rising degree of politician boss-ism and corruption, and in some places the reverse of democracy. It also meant keeping, indeed greatly extending, the Preventive Detention—that is to say, imprisonment without trial—which he had damned so passionately in the days of the British *raj*, and which chimed ill with the parliamentary democracy he wanted. So, too, the other inconsistencies, such as insisting on complete independence from foreign commitments yet making the Plans dependent upon foreign aid; hankering after Communist aims but insisting on liberal humanism; or attacking European colonialism in Africa while acquiescing in Indian colonialism in Nagaland. The supreme irony was that most of Nehru's values were nearer to the British, whose *raj* he had been bent on destroying,

[1] Numerous documented examples are available, e.g. 'Caste and Politics in Akola', *Econ. Weekly*, August 24, 1963.

than to the Indians whose subjection to the *raj* he wept over. I have emphasized the Hindu and the Brahman in him. But no less emphasis is required on the European, on the Englishman, in him.

Haunted with dilemmas in this way the strain on the spirit must have been nearly insupportable at times. It says much for his inner strength that he supported the strain. But he found no way out of his dilemmas.

India was finding a way out for him; a way he could not care for. The Indian spirit, good and less good, quietly reasserted itself; those of Nehru's ideas which were too alien to take root in the ancient Indian soil will wither away.

Construction and Reconstruction

Perhaps only another Prime Minister or ruler, knowing the realities of government from the inside and from the top, could pronounce a complete judgement on Nehru's rule. Yet it is probable that when the dust has settled Nehru's achievements as ruler will be scaled down. Scaling down is a common fate for statesmen no less than for writers. It happened with Roosevelt; it will probably happen with Churchill and de Gaulle. The scaling down might be on India as much as on Nehru; or if there is not a scaling down of India there will probably be some de-mystification of it. India without Nehru will lose some of the panache it affected under him. In the words of Alberto Moravia, the Italian novelist (who visited India and was much taken with Nehru), with Nehru's death India enters a prose epoch.

How much is India a better, or indeed a different, place because Nehru lived? It is for the future historians, with more facts at their disposal and with more knowledge of the real currents of the era, to decide. It will be enough here to recapitualte his main achievements.

Indian unity he inherited. He cherished it and fostered it but he did not create it. The apparatus of government—the civil service and administration, the defence services, the law courts, the communications network of roads, railways, telegraph, and wireless—he also inherited. The Constitution adopted in 1951 was itself an adaptation of the British *Government of India Act* of 1935. Inside India Nehru's most important contribution was on atmosphere and attitudes, more particulary against certain old prejudices and superstitions and for social justice and the scientific approach. These took concrete form: firstly in changing the legal status of women and of the outcastes; secondly in the setting up and the maintaining of the secular State; and, thirdly in the planned moves towards an industrialized and partly socialist economy. As regards foreign relations, Nehru's contribution was firstly the policy of Non-Alignment and secondly the acquiring for

India a world presence. As regards peace, he made, though many have contested the point, a contribution, expecially in the Dulles years. He was not free of faults, as over Kashmir or Goa; but as regards India's neighbours, Burma, Ceylon, Nepal, all of them guilty of much provocation, and at times of injustice, to India, Nehru was self-restrained and generous. He contributed to peace, again, by counselling moderation and sanity to the new Afro–Asian States.

These, though seeming to be not a great deal for nearly 18 years of power, were solid achievements of construction and reconstruction.

The Destroyer

Yet there can be little doubt that by 1963 the people of India as a whole were not better fed or clad, or housed, and were worse, and more corruptly, governed, and subject to a worse situation of law and order, with higher taxes, ever rising prices, ever acute foreign exchange difficulties, and more unemployment, than in 1946, the year he became Head of Government. And as regards foreign relations India's borders were menaced, she was embarked on an expensive Armaments race with her two most important neighbours, Pakistan and China, and her popularity was not great amongst other Asian countries or in Africa.

India will almost certainly survive in some way or other. She is too old, too rooted, too enduring, not to survive. But the prospects are years of unsettlement. As I write these lines the press of the world is lauding the stability in India which permitted a smooth succession from Nehru to Lal Bahadur Shastri, and its praise is accompanied with much ignorance and misunderstanding. It is true that in comparison with other Republics recently gaining independence from a colonial régime India is a going concern as a democracy and as a modern state, and she is fairly stable for the time being. It is true, too, that there would have been unsettlement if Nehru had never lived. And allowance must be made for the relativity of stability and instability. But the prospects are for growing unrest. The chances in favour of disintegration, and of tyranny or oligarchy, are connected with, if not directly due to, destroying too hastily the British *raj*, which had created India as a single political entity, and which had given it all its institutions of modern governance, including parliamentary democracy.

Nehru dedicated his life to destroying the British *raj*. So impetuous was his fury to get rid of it that he would accept nothing short of independence at once. For the consequences of this approach, including, if it comes, the disintegration of India, or dictatorship, Nehru must take his share of the blame.

He must take his share of the blame too for a spirit of violence which the Independence movement brought into Indian life. The Independence movement was dedicated to the purpose of breaking the British Government in India by all means possible (though Gandhi would have added, not quite convincingly, 'by all means short of violence', and Nehru, more convincingly, 'by all means short of terrorism'). The Nationalist leaders did have some inhibitions; but in practice they incited violence and anarchy. The students were called away from their classes, efforts were made to subvert the police and the soldiers from their oath of loyalty, various forms of lawlessness were connived at when not encouraged, and, most serious of all, the mob was called in and organized for demonstrations which were almost certainly bound to result in mob violence. It is the less easy to justify this extremism because the British Government though myopic at times was generally humane and generally liberal, and because the Independence struggle involved the nationalists in little suffering of the gross kind, such as was known in Algeria. This is why Indians like Tagore or Sapru were never reconciled to Gandhi's so-called non-violent agitation. The Nationalist agitators called in the mob to sabotage the British Government; but in doing that they risked destroying the principle of government itself, the principle of authority.

Some recovery of authority has been made since Independence; and Nehru himself, who latterly would have had the mob fired on if need be, has much of the credit for the recovery. But the mystical fabric of authority in Indian society has been rent, as it has in more than one country today. Full recovery may no longer be possible without totalitarian coercion. Every now and then, for instance in Calcutta and other big cities, in Jubbalpur, in Assam, and in most of India except the South, the mob takes over for a gruesome day or two or three.

It was on an India so shaken, so unsettled, that Nehru used his years of rule for imposing the Plans for an industrialized and socialized society. The Plans, though big and costly, were not big enough to effect a structural revolution, or even an appreciable rise in the standard of living; but they were big enough to disturb both the economy and the social life of India. They destroyed, for instance, the class of small and medium-sized landowners. Worse, the Plans, and still more the propaganda for them (which followed, moreover, on the Nationalist propaganda about a new heaven as soon as the British had gone), and combined with other modernist propaganda, work towards destroying India's greatest wealth, the contentment of the Indian people. India might have been poor and old-fashioned but its men had a religion which accepted life, the hardest life, uncomplainingly, and which got satisfaction out of simple natural things. It was not to be expected that Nehru would preach the gospel that those who want least are most like the gods, who want nothing. And if there were ever any chance of realizing it there was something to be said for all India becoming a Jamshedpur. But he did preach ideas which the more they succeed the more they would turn India into an atomized cash-nexus *admass* society with the endless pursuit of multiplying wants—TV, radios, cars, mass-produced goods purposely made unfashionable every year, or so, reading fodder of the *Digest* and glossy magazine kind, and cinema films which are having more revolutionary effects in Indian towns than Marxism or any other ideology—and the more would Indians be turned into the envious, self-centred, bored, whining manhood of the Affluent Society and the Welfare State. Nehru, himself with spartan aristocratic standards, did not will this; but he willed things which unavoidably produced this.

Rajaji may have been wrong in this or in that particular attack on Nehru's government, but he was not wrong in his divination that if Nehru succeeded he would destroy something fundamental, and something most valuable, in India. Gandhi, with his opposition to the machine and to centralization, also sensed that the Plans would be along the wrong lines. It is true Gandhi had only fads to offer as regards the greatest problem, population pressure; but his ideas on decentralization, on village democracy, and on what he called basic education, and on the machine, were as relevant to Indian realities as Nehru's industrialization and socialism were only partly relevant. Towards the end Nehru seemed to have doubts at times about whether the direction he had set out on might be as right as he was once sure it was. But it was too late. Nehru destroyed Gandhism as well as the British *raj*.

It is unlikely that there will be a place in India again for a ruler like Nehru—the aristocratic liberal humanist. If India is not run by dictators, Rightist, or Leftist, or Militarist, she will be run by politicians, more and more drawn from, or conditioned by, the outcastes and the low castes. For this is the majority, and, thanks to the ballot-box, it will be the votes of the majority which will set up and pull down governments; votes won through promising more and more to the needy and the many. Some saviour of the people, an individual or a group, could conceivably carry, in due legal form, a plebiscitary election to abolish elections altogether. The convergence of unemployed, or discontented, neo-literates with industrialization is a favourable condition for a mass revolution. Food shortages could precipitate it. In abolishing the British *raj*, and in propagating ideas of equality, so hastily and in the way they did, Nehru and the upper-class Indian nationalists of English education abolished themselves. Nehru destroyed the Nehrus.

Nehru, moreover, was not content with his work of destruction in

India. Through his passionate aid to the anti-colonialist movements in all places he has some responsibility for the destruction of law and order and for the spread of anarchy in Africa and Asia. Self-Government had to come in Africa and Asia; and able and responsible leaders like Kenyatta or Kaunda are not lacking. But, owing to the manner of de-colonialization, there are areas where the prospect is for detribalized slums, and slums which are armed to a dangerous degree or are run by psychopathic bosses whipping up and playing on a manic nationalism. Latin America gained Independence about a century and a half ago but still suffers régimes like Trujillo's in Dominica or the madness of government in Haiti.

Will the capital achievement of Nehru thus turn out to be destruction? Will Nehru the political figure be seen as mainly a destroyer?

Or will the historians judge that there was no escape from his essential predicament, or at least from a large part of it?

Nationalism for instance. He gave the biggest part of his life to fomenting it; yet the great causes he stood for when he was Prime Minister, such as World Government, or the control of the thermo-nuclear arms race, or coexistence both inside and outside India, were damaged or frustrated by nationalism. Nehru however would almost certainly have had no power except for this nationalism. Or, again, industrialization. Everything Gandhi said against it is true; but probably no ruler of India in the climate of this epoch, least of all a Nehru with his passion for technological progress, could ignore the poverty of Indians or this apparent cure for it; and less than ever now that the population was rising explosively. For the greatest destroyer of all in India is population growth; twelve to fifteen million more mouths to feed each year is a bigger revolutionary force than anything brought in by Nehru. Rajaji seems to have had little practical solution to the population problem;[1]

Whether a feeling of the intractability of ruling post-Independent India influenced him at the moment or not, Rajaji said one day of Nehru, 'There is not anyone who would do as well in his place.'[2] And when he learnt of Nerhu's death he wrote:

'Eleven years younger than me, eleven times more important, eleven hundred times more beloved of the nation. . . . I have been fighting Sri Nehru all these ten years over what I consider faults in public policies. But I knew all along that he alone could get them corrected. . . . He is gone leaving me weaker than before in my fight. . . .'[3]

[1] Cf. *Swarajya*, July 4, 1964.
[2] Monica Felton, *I Meet Rajaji*, p. 62.
[3] *Swarajya*, June 6, 1964.

The Crowning Achievement

The tasks Nehru set himself were tasks for a giant; some of them the tasks of Sisyphus. No ruler could carry such a burden without faltering, What is remarkable is not that he experienced failures but that he did not collapse and that he did achieve some success.

And whatever his success or failure, the story of Nehru as ruler will remain of great interest—how a man governed and shaped, or tried to shape, so big and so special a part of the human race in its first two decades of independence. But the man himself is still more interesting than his political history. Nehru might have made misjudgements, even grave misjudgements; he might have been insufficiently in control; he might have destroyed much. But nothing can destroy his distinction. His supreme achievement was to have been Nehru, the fine spirit exercising power, the ruler who remained disinterested and compassionate.

Chapter 7

THE LAST JOURNEY

Nehru was not himself when he got back to India from his overseas tour in November 1961. By Spring, in 1962, he went down with what the doctors diagnosed as a kidney infection; and for the first time in his life he had to take prolonged treatment and to remain in bed. He made a good recovery during the second half of next year. The doctors warned him that he would have to go at a slower pace. He heeded the warning for a while; but throughout most of 1963 he was back at his old pace. What at this time struck those who knew him was not so much the diminution of his physical strength as the diminution of hope.

Early in January 1964 he went to Orissa for a Congress Party meeting. It was to have been an important meeting as Nehru wanted a re-affirmation of his socialist policies; but not long after getting there he collapsed with a stroke. At the end of January it was announced officially that he had recovered 'completely'. He began to make occasional public appearances. On February 10th, for instance, he was present at the opening of Parliament. Most of his mental acuity remained though it was failing towards the end of the day. Everyone could see that he was paralysed on one side. He walked slowly, with a dragging gait; he had to speak sitting; and he articulated with difficulty. In April he began to stand up when speaking. He was coming to his office for a few hours each day. Much of the work of a more or less routine nature was left to Lal Bahadur Shastri but Nehru was making the decisions on major matters. That superb body was broken at last, but not the spirit which it housed. He never accepted defeat. Those who wanted to help him or fuss over him were rebuffed. His sense of the dangers crowding in on the India he had tried to build spurred him on to relentless effort. He became convinced that some new and drastic measures could not be delayed.

Nehru needed no reminding of the transience of human life and the nearness of death to every man. He always claimed to have no time for astrologers: they were now forecasting a year of malignancy. The number of people counting with Nehru who were removed by Death that winter and spring must have sharpened his awareness of how short was time and how much remained to be done. President Kennedy had been struck down in November. In February Rajkumari Amrit Kaur, a member of the Christian branch of the Kapurthala princely family, died suddenly with a heart attack. She had returned to India from her studies in England at the same time as Nehru, over fifty years ago, and she had spent many years near to him, first in Gandhi's *ashrams* and then for ten years as a Minister in his Cabinet. Next V. T. Krishnamachari died. He had headed the Planning Commission during its first ten formative years, and so had been closely associated with some of Nehru's dearest projects. Then followed the deaths of Verrier Elwin, who had been close to Nehru in policies for dealing with the NEFA peoples, and of Harishwar Dayal, the brilliant and reliable Ambassador to Nepal and the leading Indian expert on Tibet and the Himalayan border States. Finally, Dr Baliga dropped dead in London. He was the leading surgeon in India and for years had been a wealthy and disinterested supporter of Krishna Menon as well as a tireless seeker after good relations between India and the Communist States. Nehru respected him and when he heard of his death, a few days before his own, said that a good man had gone, 'a good man devoted to good causes . . . a patriot of great merit and accomplishment'.

A time of troubles. The China border affair was still unresolved; so too was the rebellion of the Nagas, now in its tenth year; so too the reconcilation in Goa, where bomb explosions had just occurred. Outside India overseas Indians, with the ending of British rule in one colony after another, were being threatened with *apartheid* or mass expulsions. Inside India prices were rising, food shortages were so great as to be causing riots, the machinery of government from top to bottom was creaking, and, worst of all, communal passion was rising. Would India remain a secular State? The massacres of Muslims in March had roused little condemnation or revulsion amongst the bulk of Indians. The bad relations with Pakistan, now particularly bad because of the new inflammability in Kashmir, stimulated recklessness amongst the Hindu extremists as well as irritating the Indian public in general. Nehru decided that his former policy on Kashmir would have to be reconsidered. In April, against opposition, he had Sheikh Abdullah released. A little later he decided to see Ayub.

Nor could Nehru, who for years had resisted all pressures either to indicate the Dauphin or to appoint a Deputy Prime Minister, avoid any longer choosing what was in effect his Deputy. His choice fell on

Lal Bahadur Shastri.[1] He had been a member of Nehru's Cabinets since 1952 and before then had played some minor roles in Nehru's home State. He was hardly known to the public and was not much known outside the inner political circle. In recent years Nehru had been using him for confidential work, such as in Kerala at the one end and Kashmir at the other, and was said to value his judgement and his honesty. But as Nehru's Deputy would stand rather more than a fair chance of becoming his successor the choice of Lal Bahadur Shastri caused surprise in some quarters.

> Pitt is to Addington
> What London is to Paddington

the wits were saying a century and a half earlier when the great Pitt gave place to Addington. In some quarters the choice caused concern as well as surprise. Lal Bahadur Shastri in any case would be an anti-climax after Nehru. So small in size and voice, so frail in health, and so withdrawn in manner, was the new Deputy that Nehru himself, according to reports, used to say that you didn't know if he was in the room or not. On the other hand there were others who greeted the appointment with relief because he was a man whose pace and pre-ferences were nearer to the Indian average and who made no one feel uncomfortable. The yearning for mediocrity and parochialism was not unrepresented in this sense of relief. It became clearer when Lal Bahadur Shastri became Prime Minister. One paper then wrote: 'He is much closer to the common man than his predecessor.'[2] Another paper wrote: 'He has not got the Cambridge accent but he is not the poorer for it. . . he is not decked with red roses, restless and impatient, but plain, collected, and sweet-tempered. . . . A child of the soil, he is as far from Cambridge as he is near to the village mud-houses of India.'[3]

A time of troubles. In April Nehru received the Santhaman Report on Corruption. The Das Report on the Kairon régime in the Punjab was not quite ready but he knew the general tenour of its findings. In April, seeking, as always, for better relations with Nepal, a difficult neighbour, he journeyed to the Nepal border to have talks with the

---

[1] His true name is Lal Bahadur, *Shastri* (which can mean a caste name but does not in this case) being tacked on after he got his diploma at an educational institute, the Kashi Vidyapeeth. To call him *Mr Shastri* is thus the same as calling a man Mr B.A. or Mr Dip.Educ. But it is unlikely that the correct usage will now prevail any more than it will in the case of the French word *expertise* now irrevocably established as jargon; the less so as, like most Indians, he has no surname.

[2] *Ananda Bazar*, June 3rd.

[3] *Jugantar*, June 3rd.

King. And in April, having got Abdullah released, he made a speech to Parliament on Indo-Pakistan relations. There was no other way for India and Pakistan to live, he said, except in peace. 'The Pakistanis are a decent folk, but when you excite the people with religious slogans nobody remains decent; they become brutal, be it Hindu or Muslim.' Referring to the massacres in Orissa and Bihar he went on: 'It was scandalous in the extreme that anybody should do what our people have done there. We Indians should not become self-righteous. . . . We Indians think that every evil is being done by Pakistan and China and that we are completely free from wrongdoing.' As for intrusions over the Indo-Pakistan border, 'the big difference is that our intrusions do not give rise to questions in our Parliament whereas the Pakistan intrusions do'. This brave and moving speech provoked interjections but Nehru, maimed in body though he was, insisted on his points.[1]

In May he continued discussions over Kashmir. In mid-May he went to Bombay for a Congress Party meeting and, little to the taste of his audience,[2] he stressed the gravity of anti-Muslim feeling in India and the urgency of the need for a new approach to the great questions of Pakistan, Kashmir, and China. Sheikh Abdullah, now free again, was making statements to the effect that Kashmir's accession to India in 1947 was not irrevocable and that the people of Kashmir had not yet come to a decision. He exasperated Indian public opinion still more by hinting that the best solution would be an independent Kashmir guaranteed jointly by India and Pakistan. On China, Nehru repeated his offer of talks; his offer was couched in reasonable terms.

Back in Delhi from the Bombay meeting he gave some time to the President of Sudan, who was in India on a State visit. He also saw the Dalai Lama. On May 18 he gave a TV interview for America. On May 22 he held a press conference. It was then, in reply to a journalist who asked about his successor, that he said that he had made no arrangements and that his end was some time off yet. During these days he also attended celebrations of the Shakespeare quarter-centenary. On Saturday, May 23rd, he held long talks with Sheikh Abdullah, who had come to Delhi to see him; back in Nehru's house again after the eleven years in jail. Late in the afternoon Nehru flew in a helicopter to Dehra Dun for the week-end. While he was there he worked on papers. He also saw an old family friend and Congress Party colleague, Sri Prakasa, who was also an old and loyal associate of Mrs Annie Besant, and since Independence had spent about 10 years as Governor first of Madras and then of Bombay; a man of elevated and loveable character.

[1] April 13th. On May 13th the *Patriot*, Krishna Menon's paper, wanted Sheikh Abdullah arrested again.
[2] Cf. criticism, e.g. in *Ananda Bazar*, May 19th.

The helicopter brought Nehru back to Delhi on the afternoon of Tuesday, May 26th. He spent a normal evening at home. In the course of it he asked Lal Bahadur Shastri, half jokingly, half seriously, to order some new *achkans* (Indian formal clothing) for the Conference of Commonwealth Prime Ministers. He had decided to take him to London with him and he was looking forward to the conference. He retired to his study in the usual way, finished working on some papers, and went to bed about 11. His own circle was as confident as the public that Nehru's recovery was assured.

Next morning, Wednesday, May 27th, he woke about five. He complained of pains in the abdomen. Considerate as usual, he refused to allow his daughter to call a doctor; he thought the pain would pass and he need not wake up a doctor. But the pain increased, and shortly afterwards he collapsed. Doctors were called; but he never regained consciousness. It was evident that the aorta artery had burst. One of the surgeons wanted to make an emergency operation as the one last chance. Mrs Gandhi consented, but the Cabinet group, like some of the too numerous doctors consulted, fearing to take responsibility, insisted on telephoning to one of the Prime Minister's sisters a thousand miles away. She asked them to wait until she got to Delhi. He was dead by 2 p.m.; she did not get there until a couple of hours after that. Blood transfusions had been tried, though with some difficulty because of Nehru's belonging to a rare blood-group. Mrs Gandhi gave her blood. After his death it was rumoured that he died at about 9 o'clock and that the news had been concealed for political reasons until 2 o'clock; but according to one of the doctors in attendance this rumour is untrue.

He was six months short of 75.

The news of his death soon spread over Delhi; and from Delhi they spread that afternoon and evening throughout India. Shock and sorrow and foreboding accompanied the news. Normal business stopped. Shops were closed immediately, spontaneously. Even the small sophisticated critical minority in Delhi and Bombay were sobered. That a life of a significance above the average had gone out was also felt throughout the world. In most countries Nehru's death took priority over all the other news. Tributes began pouring in from all quarters, from the Pope, from Kings and Presidents and Prime Ministers, and from innumerable individuals. Several important foreign governments decided at once that they would be represented on a level above the normal at the funeral, though it was to take place next day: the Queen of England and Head of the Commonwealth (who was reported to have arranged to offer Nehru at the forthcoming Prime Ministers' Conference the Order of Merit) by Lord Mountbatten, Great Britain by the Prime Minister and the Deputy Leader of the Opposition, the United States by the Secretary of State, Japan by her Foreign Minister, General de Gaulle by a favourite Minister. President Ayub, surprisingly and uncharacteristically, decided not to go to the funeral. Many humble people not important enough to telegraph or publish their tributes, felt, as did millions of Indians, that the world was somehow the darker for Nehru's going and that his life had done honour to humanity.

That Wednesday was overcast, the air heavy and tense with the pre-monsoon storm which burst in the afternoon. This is the hottest time of the year in North India. The crowds took no heed of the weather. They began filing past the body as soon as they were allowed. The body had been brought down to the ground floor in the afternoon and Mrs Gandhi, in the Indian way, sat beside it. A vigil party drawn from high-ranking officers of the Armed Services stood by. Hour after hour the people filed by, many of them weeping. They included both sexes and all ages and from every class and group in Delhi. This went on most of the night, and it continued throughout the next morning, Thursday. The police estimated that half a million had filed by when, in order to make the final preparations for the funeral procession, the gates were shut towards midday on Thursday. People then tried to get over the gates and had to be driven off, which resulted in a stampede: three were trampled to death and others were injured. The funeral was to have taken place at dawn but had been delayed so that Sir Alec Douglas-Home and other foreign dignitaries could get there in time for it.

A little before noon an earthquake shook Delhi.

A little later the pall-bearers, men of high rank, removed the body to a gun-carriage, placing it in a tilted position with the head uncovered and the rest draped with the Indian Flag. Flowers were spread over the gun-carriage. Hindu priests were in attendance, some chanting *mantras*; and some Christians were also there, singing Gandhi's two favourite hymns *Abide with Me* and *Rock of Ages*. About 1.20 the procession set off. For fifty years Nehru had been drawing the biggest crowds in India. Now on his last journey he drew the biggest crowd of all. Some said a million, some said two million, some said three million, watched the passage of his corpse.

The journey lay along the six miles from Nehru's house to the place on the banks of the Jamuna near where Gandhi's body had been cremated some sixteen years before; along the roads and streets where Nehru had driven countless times since then; past the Secretariat where he had worked such long hours, skirting Parliament House where over the years he had dominated Indian politics, up Rajpath (Kingsway) the same route followed by the Republic Day parades which he had so much enjoyed, down Tilak Marg (Hardinge Avenue), and so under the railway bridge and out to the Ring Road, and on to the banks of the Jamuna. There a brick plinth about 5 feet high and 10 feet square had been built, and the pyre of sandalwood was ready for the body.

The funeral procession was headed by a jeep with the General Commanding the Delhi–Rajastan Area, with Servicemen marching in slow time with arms reversed. Men from each of the Services pulled the gun-carriage. This was followed by an open car with Mrs Gandhi and her younger son, Sanjay (the elder boy had not been able to get back in time from Cambridge), and then followed a cavalcade of cars containing the chief mourners, Mrs Pandit, Mrs Hutheesingh and some other members of the Nehru family, the pall-bearers, the President, the Cabinet, the Service Chiefs, and foreign dignitaries.

The immense crowd kept reasonable order until the cortege left Rajpath. They were weeping or chanting or throwing flowers towards the gun-carriage or just looking on; but they kept pushing closer and closer to it. By the time the cortege passed down Hardinge Avenue the crowd did what angered Nehru often in his lifetime: in a herd-like mindless stampede it broke through the police cordon. The police, reinforced by police from the neighbouring States, and at certain points by Army detachments, were overrun. The gun-carriage and the first couple of cars were allowed to proceed on their way but the remaining cars were cut-off. Some of the dignitaries followed on foot and were fortunate not to have been crushed to death. The heat too was suffocating. The crowd was not hostile; in general it was reverent; but it was a crowd, and its behaviour conformed with that quality of the mixed-up, tears and laughter, reverence and inquisitiveness, considerateness and inconsiderateness, which is characteristic of so much in India. Scores of people fainted or were injured. And so on his last journey was Nehru accompanied by the crowdedness, the disorder, the ineffectiveness of the half-finished, the colour, and the peoples' goodwill, which had accompanied him in life for the last twenty years.

It was a little after 4 when the cortege reached the cremation-ground. A helicopter showered rose petals on the gun-carriage as it moved in place. To the sound of muffled drums the body was taken from the gun-carriage and placed on the pyre, among the pall-bearers being Bakshi, the ousted ruler of Kashmir. Hindu and Buddhist priests chanted; the sacred water was sprinkled; and a small group, including the Vice-President (a Muslim), some Cabinet Ministers, and Krishna Menon, filed past the body for the last time, placing little pieces of sandalwood on the pyre. Then the flag was replaced with a white silk scarf and more petals were scattered on it. A little after half past four Sanjay lit the pyre and the flames rose briskly. That part of the ceremony came from India. The next part came from England: a volley of small arms was fired three times and twenty-four buglers sounded *The Last Post*. While the fire was burning the body to ashes thus was symbolized the inextricability of India and England in Nehru's life. Before the fire had died down Sheikh Abdullah leapt on the platform and, weeping unrestrainedly, threw flowers onto the flames; thus was symbolized the inextricability of the Muslim world in Nehru's life and the pathos of the Kashmir affair.

On the following day, Saturday, May 30th, at dawn, in the presence of the President and several Cabinet Ministers as well as of Mrs Gandhi and her two sons (the elder had by this time reached Delhi) and Nehru's two sisters and other members of the family, the ashes were collected. They were sprinkled with water from the sacred Ganges and with milk and were put into copper urns. Early as it was, the crowd standing by numbered several thousands. Many were chanting the *Ram Dhum*.

The urns were taken to Nehru's house and placed under a tree in his garden. During the days they remained there people filed past, hour after hour.

On 2nd June Lal Bahadur Shastri was chosen as Prime Minister.

A week after the death, on June 3rd, passages from Nehru's Will were read out over the All-India Radio by Mrs Pandit. It had been written ten years earlier, in June 1954.[1]

The Will laid down, amongst other things, 'with all earnestness' that no religious ceremonies should be associated with his funeral. 'To submit to them, even as a matter of form, would be hyprocrisy—an attempt to delude ourselves and others'. But he asked that a handful of ashes be thrown over the river Ganges. This, he explained, was not intended to have any religious significance; the Ganges was 'a symbol of India's age-long culture and civilisation, ever changing, ever flowing, and yet ever the same. She reminds me of the snow-covered peaks and deep valleys of the Himalayas which I have loved so much and of the vast plains below where my life and work have been cast.' The remainder of his ashes were to be carried high in an aircraft and 'scattered over the fields where the peasants of India toil so that they might mingle with the dust of the soil of India and become an indistinguishable part of her . . .'. The Will again referred to 'the shackles of religion that bind and constrict her and blind her people. . . .'

[1] Cf. Sir R. Pillai's letter in *The Statesman*, June 5, 1964. He witnessed the Will.

Much of Nehru is in this Will. Here was the man who all his life stood for rationalism; here was the father who had refused to allow Indira when a little girl to hear fairy-tales. But the poetical strain in him was not without religious overtones. For all Indians in any case the Ganges had a religious significance which was beyond words. From beginning to end the long-drawn funeral ceremonies were to the accompaniment of priests and the old priestly cults. And here too was the English strain once more: the Will was written not in Hindi but in English.

On Tuesday June 9th the final ceremony took place. This was to drop the greater portion of the ashes into the river at Sangam, a sacred place near Allahabad, where the Jamuna flows into the Ganges. A train brought the urns from Delhi and reached Nehru's home-town at daybreak. With them were Mrs Gandhi and her two sons and Nehru's two sisters and other members of the family, together with Members of the Central and local State Governments. They also brought Kamala's ashes; Nehru had been keeping them in his room for the 28 years since her death.

Once more there were huge crowds; the authorities estimated them at half a million. Once more there was Sheikh Abdullah, and, also, the Dalai Lama, two unofficial mourners, thus symbolizing the incongruities of the world in which Nehru had played out his life. Once more there were priests, as well as detachments of the Armed Forces, and the old Hindu cults as well as British Army rituals. The procession had 6 miles to go to Sangam. On the way it went into the grounds of the home where Nehru had spent his childhood and much of his adult life; the urns were placed under a long-lived Guhl Mohar tree near the house and flowers were thrown on them. After a pause of about an hour the procession set off again. When it got to Sangam the urns were taken out into the river and the grandsons emptied the ashes into the waters. A helicopter showered petals over the scene, cannons were fired, Vedic *mantras* were chanted, buglers sounded *The Last Post*, and the Jat Regiment band played *Abide with me*.

So ends the long, winding, battle-strewn, course of Samson Agonistes:

> Samson hath quit himself
> Like Samson, and heroically hath
> Finished a life heroic.

INDEX

Index

Johnson, Samuel, 140, 145
Jones, William, 47
Joseph, Pothan, 44, 61
Journalists, 44, 106

Kali, 31
Kamaraj Plan, 73, 143
Karanjia, *The Mind of Mr Nehru*, 144
Kashmir, 34, 92 *et seq.*
Kaul, original name of Nehru, 58
Kaul, General, 128
Kaur, Rajkumar Amrit, 151, 172
Kemal Ataturk, *see* Ataturk
Kennedy, President, 24
Kenyatta, Jomo, 169
Khetri, 59
Khruschev, *see* Kruschev
Kidwai, Rafi Ahmad, 153
Kipling, R., 29
Korea, 91, 103
Kripalani, J. B., 22, 70
Kripalani, Sucheta, 82
Krishnamachari, Sir V. T., 172
Krishna Menon, *see* Menon
Krishnamurti, J., 36, 154
Kruschev, 18, 24

Labour Party, of England, 55
Lal Bahadur Shastri, *see* Shastri
Land-owners, 75
Law and Order, 84
League Against Imperialism, 64
Liaqat Ali Khan, 92
Lingam, 31
Linlithgow, Lord (Viceroy), 47, 65
Linguistic Provinces, *see* Nehru
Lloyd George, Earl, 25
Lolita, 140
Lothian, Lord, 63
Lumumba, 111

Macht Politik, 90
MacDonald Line, 102
MacDonald, J. Ramsay, 21, 55
MacDonald, Malcolm, 29
MacMillan, Harold, 118
Mahabharata, 34
Mahalanobis Committee, 77
Mahmud, Syed, 65
Malan-Menzies axis, 22
Malcolm, Sir J., 47
Marshall, John, 47
Marxism, 34, 168

Matrimonial Advertisements, 50
Maugham, Somerset, 36
Mawari, Businessmen, 76, 82
Mayo, Miss, 37
McMahon Line, 102, 129
Mechanisation, 77
Mende, Tibor, 141
Menon, Krishna, V. K., 22, 49, 61,
    87, 89 94–5, 115, 123, 127, 140,
    153–7
Menzies, Sir R. G., 19, 22, 138–9
Milton, John, 66
Mob, the, 51, 166–7
Mogul, Empire, 39, 58
Mookerjee, S. P., 21
Moon, Sir Penderel, 69
Moraes, Frank, 44
Moravia, Alberto, 165
Morris, William, 142
Mountbatten, Earl, 91
Mountbatten, Lady, 140
Mundhra Affair, *see* Corruption
Muslim, 36, 39, 94
    League, 53
    Massacres, 17
Mussolini, 126
Mutiny, Indian, *see* Indian
Mysore, Maharajah of, 35

Nagas, 110, 172
Naipaul, V. S., 79, 103, 118
Napoleon, 15, 137
Narayan, J. P., 36, 95, 123, 159
Nationalism, 29
    Indian Nationalist Movement, 45
    et seq.
    Gandhi's Non-Violence, 52, 166–7
    Indian cf. Chinese, 51
National Physics Laboratory, *see*
    Institutes
Nature, love, of, 18
Nazis, 17, 65
NEFA, 102
Nepotism, 44
Nehru, Jawaharlal
    Acting, 133
    Adelaide University, 27
    Administrative ability, 84–5
    Africa, 111
    Aloneness, 140, 153
    Anti-colonialism, 169
    Australia, 27, 109, 134
    Authoritarian, 142

183

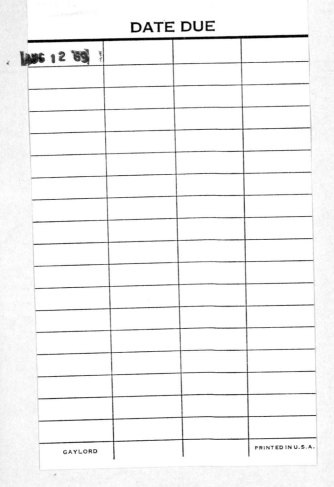

DATE DUE

AUG 12 '69			

GAYLORD